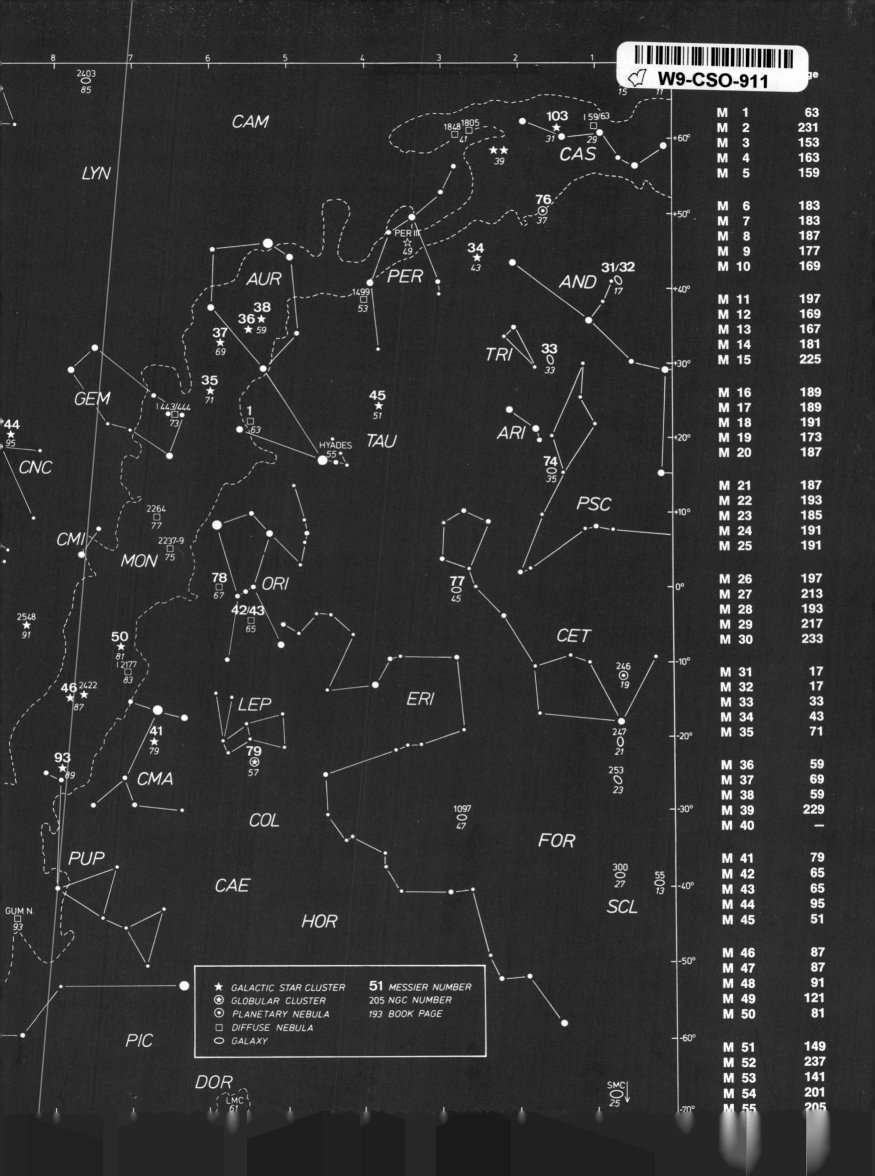

M	1	63
M	2	231
M	3	153
M	4	163
M	5	159
M	6	183
M	7	183
M	8	187
M	9	177
M	10	169
M	11	197
M	12	169
M	13	167
M	14	181
M	15	225
M	16	189
M	17	189
M	18	191
M	19	173
M	20	187
M	21	187
M	22	193
M	23	185
M	24	191
M	25	191
M	26	197
M	27	213
M	28	193
M	29	217
M	30	233
M	31	17
M	32	17
M	33	33
M	34	43
M	35	71
M	36	59
M	37	69
M	38	59
M	39	229
M	40	—
M	41	79
M	42	65
M	43	65
M	44	95
M	45	51
M	46	87
M	47	87
M	48	91
M	49	121
M	50	81
M	51	149
M	52	237
M	53	141
M	54	201
M	55	205

Legend:

★ GALACTIC STAR CLUSTER
⊛ GLOBULAR CLUSTER
⊙ PLANETARY NEBULA
□ DIFFUSE NEBULA
◯ GALAXY

51 MESSIER NUMBER
205 NGC NUMBER
193 BOOK PAGE

Constellation labels: CAM, LYN, CAS, AND, TRI, ARI, PSC, AUR, PER, GEM, CNC, TAU, CMI, MON, ORI, CET, LEP, ERI, FOR, SCL, CMA, COL, PUP, CAE, HOR, PIC, DOR

Object labels:
2403 / 85
103 / 31
I 59/63 / 29
1848 / 41
1805
★★ 39
76 / 37
PER III / 49
34 / 43
31/32 / 17
33 / 33
38
36 / 59
37 / 69
35 / 71
I 443/444 / 73
1 / 63
44 / 95
45 / 51
HYADES / 55
74 / 35
2264 / 77
2237-9 / 75
78 / 67
42/43 / 65
77 / 45
2548 / 91
50 / 81
I 2177 / 83
246 / 19
46 / 87
2422 / 87
41 / 79
79 / 57
247 / 21
93 / 89
253 / 23
1097 / 47
GUM N. / 93
300 / 27
55 / 13
SMC / 25
LMC / 61

Atlas of Deep-Sky Splendors

Fourth edition

Photographic charts and
descriptions of all Messier objects
and more than 300 other celestial wonders.

Hans Vehrenberg

Scientific assistance by U. Güntzel-Lingner,
Astronomisches Rechen-Institut, Heidelberg, and by
the staff of *Sky & Telescope* magazine

Sky Publishing Corporation
Cambridge, Massachusetts

Cambridge University Press
Cambridge   London   New York   New Rochelle   Melbourne   Sydney

Treugesell-Verlag
Düsseldorf

Published by Sky Publishing Corporation
49 Bay State Road, Cambridge, Massachusetts 02238-1290

and by the Press Syndicate of the University of Cambridge
The Pitt Building, Trumpington Street, Cambridge CB2 1RP
32 East 57th Street, New York, New York 10022
296 Beaconsfield Parade, Middle Park, Melbourne 3206, Australia

and by Treugesell-Verlag
Schillerstrasse 17, 4000 Düsseldorf 1, Germany

Fourth Edition

Printed in the United States of America
by Essex Publishing Company, Burlington, Vermont

Library of Congress Cataloging in Publication Data:

Vehrenberg, Hans.
  Atlas of Deep-Sky Splendors.

  Translation of: Mein Messier-Buch.
  Includes index.
  1. Stars — Atlases. 2. Stars — Clusters — Atlases.
  3. Nebulae — Atlases. 4. Galaxies — Atlases. I. Guntzel-
Lingner, Ulrich. II. Sky & Telescope. III. Title.
  QB65.V413   1983   523.8′9   83-7656

ISBN 0-933346-03-4

  Permission to reproduce photographs was given by Eckhard Alt, Ernst Brodkorb, Kurt Rihm, and Jurgen Rusche, pages 38, 50, 102, 188, 190;
Boyden Observatory, page 146; Dennis di Cicco, page 220; R. J. Dufour, page 144; Hamburg-Bergedorf Observatory, page 202; Harvard College
Observatory, page 24; David Healy, page 64; Humanities Research Center, University of Texas at Austin, page 200; Institute for Astronomy, University of Hawaii, pages 36, 224; Kitt Peak National Observatory/Association of Universities for Research in Astronomy, Inc., page 150; Evered
Kreimer, pages 70, 106; Lick Observatory, pages 52, 62, 98, 112, 152, 156, 174, 198, 234; David Malin, page 184; Mt. Wilson and Palomar Observatories (Hale Observatories), pages 16, 22, 24, 34, 44, 72, 76, 84, 96, 100, 104, 108, 116, 120, 126, 130, 136, 138, 142, 154, 166, 188, 216; Meudon Observatory, page 164; Royal Observatory, Edinburgh, pages 66, 186; Karl Schwarzschild Observatory, pages 6, 8, 32, 74, 222; U. S. Naval Observatory,
pages 114, 148, 156, 212, 218.
  All photographs on right-hand pages, and on pages 40, 42, 60, 82, 102, 110, 134, 170, 198, 210, 214, 216, 234, and dust jacket are by the author.
  All rights reserved.

Preface to the fourth edition

Astronomical books that are more or less specialized tend to be long-lived, like the celestial objects they describe, though they are seldom best sellers in the usual sense. This book of mine is no exception to the rule, but it pleases me to know that it has become a standard item on the amateur's bookshelf since the first edition was published in 1965.

It is a fundamental human instinct to collect, whether berries and roots in the prehistoric past or knowledge of the universe today. For several decades, my favorite pastime has been to collect celestial objects on photographs. I will never forget the many thousands of night hours I have spent with my instruments, working peacefully in my telescope shelter as I listened to good music and dreamed about the infinity of the universe.

After first photographing the brighter objects listed by Charles Messier, it was a small step to decide that a collection of all the Messier objects, both well known and obscure, would interest everybody who appreciates the splendors of the heavens. Besides, I found it useful to enlarge the objects to a uniform scale and to show them in an adequately large star field. This enables the interested amateur to gain a realistic impression of their structure, size, and location.

Since the first edition came out, other books with a similar purpose have been published. This stimulated me to expand later editions by adding not only a number of lesser known objects, but also some color photographs: some taken on commercial color film, some prepared by the more difficult three-color composite technique.

Much of the accompanying scientific information was supplied by the late U. Güntzel-Lingner, to whom I am greatly indebted. As astronomical knowledge has improved, revisions have been inevitable. Corrections were supplied by the staff at Sky & Telescope magazine, to whom I wish to express my warmest thanks. It is one thing to write a book from the start; it is another to revise an existing text. I do not doubt that the latter is the harder task.

I hope that this book will be of value for the beginner and for the advanced astronomer, for the visual observer and for the photographer. May they find the same pleasure in seeking out deep-sky splendors as I have!

Hans Vehrenberg

Falkau (Black Forest) W. Germany
February, 1983

Contents

The Cone nebula region in Monoceros, photographed with the world's largest Schmidt camera. Bright and dark nebulae and hot, young stars fill this part of the Milky Way. The Cone nebula is near bottom; the bright star to the lower left of center is S Monocerotis; the small star cluster at top right is NGC 2259. Compare this with the view on page 77.

Fifty minute exposure with the 1.34-meter (clear aperture) Schmidt at Karl Schwarzschild Observatory, Tautenberg, East Germany, on Kodak 103a-E film with an RG1I filter.

Introduction

In 1963 when I started taking exposures for the first edition of this book, my intent was to portray all Messier objects at one uniform scale. It seemed to me that amateurs wish to see what they themselves can find visually and photographically with their telescopes. We all know the excellent photographs that large observatory instruments have taken of the star clusters, galaxies, and nebulae that Messier and his colleague Méchain recorded. But those photographs have large and widely varying scales, and seldom give a realistic impression of the structure, size, and location of the object in an extended star field, as seen by an amateur through a small telescope or photographed with a camera of short focal length.

For example, a comparison of the Andromeda galaxy and the Whirlpool galaxy on the well-known observatory photographs can give the false impression that the two are similar in apparent size. Therefore, it seemed a good idea to portray the relative sizes of heavenly objects for those who wish to observe them, to avoid a common source of frustration and disappointment for the beginner.

As Messier's catalogue was by no means complete even for the brightest objects, in the first edition of this book I added a number of objects which Messier could not detect from Paris, or which are well known through astrophotography. Developments in astrophotography enabled me to include in this fourth revised edition all of the brighter or extended celestial objects, some of which are little known.

The term "celestial object" here means the same as "deep-sky object" in English and American usage — galactic and globular star clusters, planetary and diffuse nebulae, and galaxies; it excludes starlike objects and members of the solar system. German terminology has no synonym for this well-defined phrase, but uses the long-winded description "objects beyond the solar system." For this reason the first German edition was named Mein Messier-Buch (My Messier Book), a title which later produced some misunderstanding. Hence I changed it to Atlas der Schönsten Himmelsobjecte (Atlas of the Finest Celestial Objects).

The chapters listed in the table of contents run continuously on the upper left hand pages as space permits; I must apologize for some interruptions which could not be avoided.

M31, the Andromeda galaxy, with its companions
NGC 205 (upper right) and M32 (below center).
Vast associations of blue supergiant stars are
partly resolved near dust lanes in the spiral arms.
Photographed with the 1.34-meter Tautenberg
Schmidt camera, Karl Schwarzschild Observatory.

On Messier's and Dreyer's catalogues

Before explaining the arrangement of the book, I wish to give a short review of the deep-sky catalogues on which this work is based.

Charles Messier of Paris, "the ferret of comets," as King Louis XV named him, compiled his catalogue in the second half of the 18th century from observations with small telescopes, mainly to help him distinguish nebulous objects from comets. Looking for comets was a major astronomical activity in those days. In its original form, Messier's short, incomplete, and disjointed catalogue has no more than historical interest today. However, its convenient and easily remembered numbers for important sky objects remain in constant use by both amateur and professional astronomers. The amusing story of Messier's catalogue compiling can be read beginning on page 164.

About the same time Messier was cataloguing deep-sky objects, William Herschel began a much more systematic and extensive exploration of the universe beyond the solar system. It was an exciting new undertaking. With his mighty 20-foot telescope, he and later his son John collected several thousand star clusters and nebulae, which eventually formed the core of J. L. E. Dreyer's New General Catalogue (NGC). The NGC is a child of the 19th century, the last and most important catalogue of nonstarlike objects that did not distinguish between various types of objects. The New General Catalogue and its supplementary two-part Index Catalogue (IC) contain 13,226 objects, many found by other astronomers. These catalogue numbers, seen on each page of this book, are by far the most important designations of deep-sky objects even today.

The New General Catalogue consists of three parts: the basic catalogue of 7,840 objects, published in the year 1888, and the two Index Catalogues: the first with 1,529 objects found between 1888 and 1894, and the second containing 3,857 objects found between 1895 and 1907. Practically all the Index Catalogue objects are small or faint.

Continued

NGC 7762 and NGC 7822

Both these objects would have been placed at the end of the book according to their numbers in Dreyer's *New General Catalogue.* But since precession has moved the position of the main object, NGC 7822, across the 0ʰ line of right ascension (1950.0), one of the last NGC objects will begin our list.

The group of emission nebulae of which NGC 7822 is a part consists of a central bright part ¾° in diameter and a weak luminous halo of about 3° diameter, partly broken up into single nebulae. The halo shows filaments and extensive star chains.

NGC 7822 is the large nebulosity at the top of the photograph. More prominent in this photo is the central part of the group, the nebulae Lynds 118.51 and Lynds 118.28. The former is the brightest area, about 20′ in diameter; the latter is the smaller connected patch about 4ᵐ of right ascension to its west. Above the latter is a small galactic cluster of young hot stars. This area is faced by a chain of dark patches, similar to those in the Rosette nebula.

NGC 7762 is a loose and relatively poor galactic star cluster. A striking object is the nameless, small, round nebula at the lower edge of the field. At first glance it might seem to be an emulsion defect, but other exposures confirm its existence.

NGC 7762 NGC 7822

NGC 7762 $23^h47^m5, +67°44'$

NGC 7822 $0^h01^m0, +68°20'$

Cl, 10^m0, 70 ★
$\phi = 10'$, type: d

N + Cl,
$\phi = 220' \times 190'$, type: e

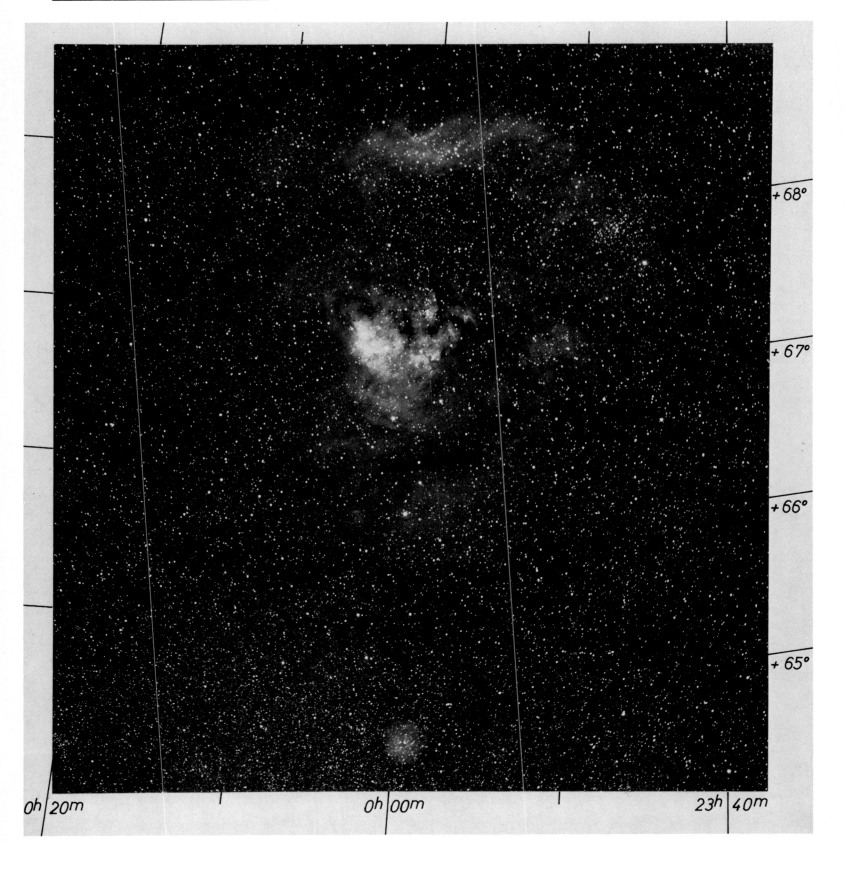

CEPHEUS
NGC 7822
×
×
NGC 7762
L 118.51 L 118.28
× ×

×
CASSIOPEIA

+68°
+67°
+66°
+65°

0ʰ 20ᵐ   0ʰ 00ᵐ   23ʰ 40ᵐ

Interestingly, the first Index Catalogue *contains only a few photographically discovered objects, whereas the second one came mainly from photographs taken by E. E. Barnard and Max Wolf. Sometimes different NGC numbers were given to parts of an object that were later found photographically to be connected. In such a case only the brightest parts can be detected visually, for example, the Veil nebula in Cygnus (page 219).*

Dreyer's catalogue listed objects strictly in order of right ascension, and the objects in this book are similarly arranged. But Dreyer used 1860.0 coordinates. Since then, precession of the coordinates has resulted in occasional catalogue numbers no longer being in strict order of right ascension. For example, in 2000.0 coordinates NGC 7089 is situated at $21^h33^m.5$, whereas NGC 7092 is at $21^h32^m.2$. Both parts of the Index Catalogue *begin with 0^h00^m in right ascension, but the numbers in the second part form a continuation of those in the first part. Previously, astronomers distinguished between IC I and IC II, but nowadays they simply say IC.*

The Messier objects listed in this book can be easily found using the index on the end papers. NGC and IC objects in this book are listed beginning on page 238, together with some minor objects named later on by their discoverers. Today many special catalogues of different objects are in professional use.

Arrangement of this book

The arrangement of this book is easy to understand. The main part contains 113 charts of star fields on the right-hand pages, most of them at the convenient scale of 1 mm = 1 minute of arc. Exceptions are charts from photographs with my 14-inch Schmidt camera, set up in 1975. The scale of these fields varies between 0.75 and 0.85 mm per minute of arc, or 15% to 25% less than the earlier photographs. Since a coordinate grid is given on the edges of each star field, it is easy to determine the angular dimensions of an object.

In a few cases I was forced to halve the scale to 1 mm = 2 minutes of arc in order to accommodate as much as possible of an extended object. These charts, easily recognizable by their circular shape, are used for the two Magellanic Clouds (pages 25 and 61), the Perseus III Association (page 49), the Hyades (page 55), and the Coma star cluster (page 123).

Continued on page 18

NGC 55

NGC 55 is one of the brightest galaxies in the southern sky and resembles the Large Magellanic Cloud (page 61) in its structure. We see this stellar system, which can be partially resolved into single stars, and which is interspersed with dust lanes and emission nebulae, almost edge on. Therefore it is difficult to ascertain its true structural type. G de Vaucouleurs surmises the system to be an old barred galaxy with S-shaped spiral arms attached. Its de Vaucouleurs type is SB(s)m.

NGC 55 is the brightest of six galaxies belonging to a group within 15° of the south galactic pole, known as the Sculptor group. Among this group are found NGC 247 (page 21), NGC 253 (page 23), and NGC 300 (page 27). Apart from our Local Group (which includes the Milky Way and the Andromeda galaxy), the Sculptor group with a distance of 2.5 Mpc is the nearest clustering of galaxies to us in space.

NGC 55

0ʰ12ᵐ5, −39°30′

Ga, 7ᵐ8, 27′.5 × 4′.7
type: SB(s)m(Vau)

SCULPTOR

×
NGC 55

PHOENIX

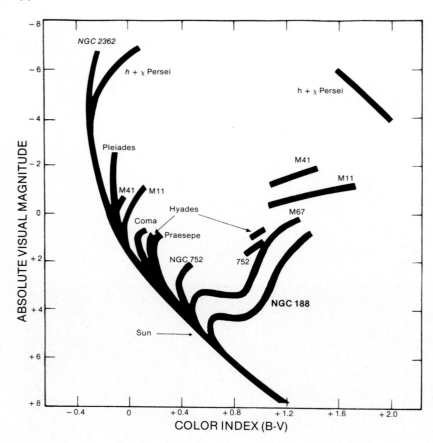

Color-magnitude diagrams of different star clusters, positioned to overlap (according to A. Sandage). See page 30.

NGC 188

The inconspicuous but very rich star cluster NGC 188, which before 1956 seemed to be just another catalogue object, has 2,200 members between magnitudes 10 and 18, according to A. S. Scharov. This object first attracted special interest after K. A. Barchatowa, and later A. Sandage, proved its very old age. They concluded it was 12 to 16 billion years old; a more recent (1981) estimate, based on a variety of studies, is 5 billion years. The stars of NGC 188 lie in the lower part of the Hertzsprung-Russell diagram, with those of M67 (page 97) just above. Barchatowa and M. B. Sinina established an apparent diameter for the cluster of 34′ and a distance of 1200 parsecs.

C. Hoffmeister found four short-period variable stars in NGC 188, which probably have very short periods (three of 6 to 7 hours, and one of 18 hours).

About 1° north of NGC 188 and only 4° from the north pole we see the star 2 Ursae Minoris (4^{m}5), which can be used as a reference star to find the cluster with a medium-sized telescope.

NGC 188
0ʰ39ᵐ4, +85°03'

CI, 9ᵐ3, 2200★
φ = 34', type: c

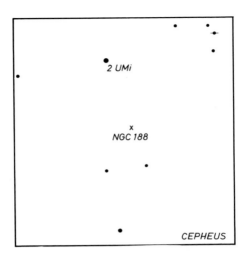

M31 (Andromeda galaxy), M32, M110

The Andromeda galaxy (M31) is the brightest in the sky and can be seen with the naked eye. In size and structure it resembles our own Milky Way, and together with about a score of other galaxies it forms the Local Group, to which the two Magellanic Clouds (page 25 and 61) also belong. A medium-sized telescope will aid in observing its two companion galaxies M32 and M110 (NGC 205).

According to K. G. Jones, M31 was first spoken of by Simon Marius in 1611, but it was already shown as an unidentified object in a star atlas by al-Sufi in the year 964. The discovery of M32 is credited to Le Gentil in 1749, whereas the fainter companion M110 was charted by Messier in 1773 (though it was not added to his catalogue until recently). Its discovery is often credited to Caroline Herschel in 1783.

Numerous studies of the Andromeda galaxy with large reflectors have led to the discovery in it of many single objects like those known in the Milky Way: novae, variable stars of δ Cephei and β Lyrae type, giant stars of early and late spectral types, galactic and globular clusters, gaseous and even planetary nebulae. In the early 1940's W. Baade, using the 100-inch reflector at Mount Wilson, first resolved the central parts of M31, and its neighbor galaxies M32 and M110, into single stars. This photographic achievement finally proved beyond any doubt that galaxies are star systems.

The true structure of the Andromeda galaxy only became known through photography. Smaller telescopes merely reveal the central parts without detail. It is necessary to use an aperture of 30 cm and more, during good viewing conditions, to recognize the spiral arms. However, the true spiral structure still remains hidden, since the plane of M31 is inclined only 16° to our line of sight and therefore we see its NW.-SE. axis considerably shortened. H. C. Arp, and at about the same time N. Richter and O. Weibrecht, rectified good photographs of M31 and thereby found it to have the shape of a logarithmical spiral.

M. Schwarzschild established that the huge mass of the galaxy (estimated at 400 billion solar masses) is rotating so that the material northeast of the nucleus (above and to the left in the picture) is moving away from us. Dark absorption lanes block light from the galaxy's northwest edge, proving that edge to be the one nearest us. In this photograph the length of M31 is just 2°. Microphotometric measurements from long-exposure negatives taken with large reflectors show a length of at least 4°.5. The globular clusters surrounding M31 extend even 1° farther into space.

M110 NGC 205
0ʰ37ᵐ6, +41°25′

Ga, 10ᵐ8, 10′ × 5′
type: Ep/S01

M31 NGC 224
0ʰ40ᵐ0, +41°00′

Ga, 5ᵐ0, 158′ × 50′
type: S3

M32 NGC 221
0ʰ40ᵐ0, +40°36′

Ga, 9ᵐ5, 3′.5 × 2′.7
type: E2

NGC 205
ˣ

M 31
ˣ

M 32
ˣ

ANDROMEDA

+42°

+41°

+40°

0ʰ 45ᵐ   0ʰ 40ᵐ   0ʰ 35ᵐ

Generally north is at the top of the charts. However, in a few cases a different orientation was necessary to include more objects. Coordinates for equinox 1950.0 are marked on each photograph; right ascension is along the chart's bottom edge, and declination along the right-hand side. The positions given in the upper right corner of each chart page are for 1950.0, as are all positions mentioned in the text. Coordinates for 2000.0 are listed in the index of objects beginning on page 238. The charts are arranged in order of 1950.0 right ascension of the field center.

Above each star-field photograph are a finder chart and basic information about the objects. Most of the data are taken from Antonin Becvar's catalogue to his Atlas Coeli. Some of the information given — for example, the dimensions of nebulae, the number of stars in clusters, and distances — should not be taken too literally. Often it will be found that dimensions measured on the photographs do not agree with cited values. Measurements of these uncertain quantities depend on the author's personal judgment, and data given by various observers may differ considerably.

The explanatory text on the lower half of the left-hand pages gives a summary of scientific findings regarding the deep-sky objects in question. For more general information about different kinds of objects, read the continuing essays in this book. In many cases I have described an object from personal observations and have given some hints for locating and identifying it. These comments are intended to help the beginner who is searching for a difficult object with a telescope that does not have a well-aligned equatorial mounting and setting circles.

The picture taking

Three instruments were used to take the original negatives for the chart photographs (the three numbers for each are its clear aperture, mirror diameter, and focal length, respectively).

1. *The Schmidt camera I used at Falkau in the years 1963 to 1973*   *300/450/1000 mm*
2. *The Hamburg Schmidt camera (built by Bernhard Schmidt himself), which I used at Boyden Observatory in South Africa from 1963 to 1966*   *360/440/625 mm*
3. *Celestron 14-inch Schmidt camera used at Falkau, and on the Gamsberg in Namibia (South-West Africa) from 1975 to 1977*   *340/356/600 mm*

Continued

NGC 246

NGC 246 is a planetary nebula with a ring that is not quite closed. It is of considerable size, being about three times larger than the Ring nebula in Lyra (M57, page 199). Although its integrated magnitude (8ᵐ5) suggests easy visibility, its surface brightness, when viewed through a telescope of 3- to 5-inch aperture, is found to be comparatively low due to its large angular size. The nebula looks like a large, pale spot. This relatively nearby planetary (460 pc)

forms an equilateral triangle with the stars φ^1 Ceti (4ᵐ9) and φ^2 Ceti (4ᵐ2) in which NGC 246 is the southern tip.

Also in the field are two faint galaxies, the lenticular NGC 217 and the almost starlike NGC 255.

The trail of a meteor and that of the balloon satellite Echo 2 (1964-4A) frame NGC 246.

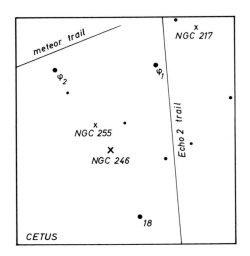

NGC 225
0ʰ45ᵐ2, − 11°45′

Ga, 12ᵐ8, 1′.0 × 1′.0
type: S

NGC 217
0ʰ39ᵐ2, − 10°16′

Ga, 12ᵐ5, 2′.2 × 0′.5
type: Sb

NGC 246
0ʰ44ᵐ6, − 12°09′

Pl, 8ᵐ5, m⋆ = 11.3
4′.1 × 3′.5, type: IIIb

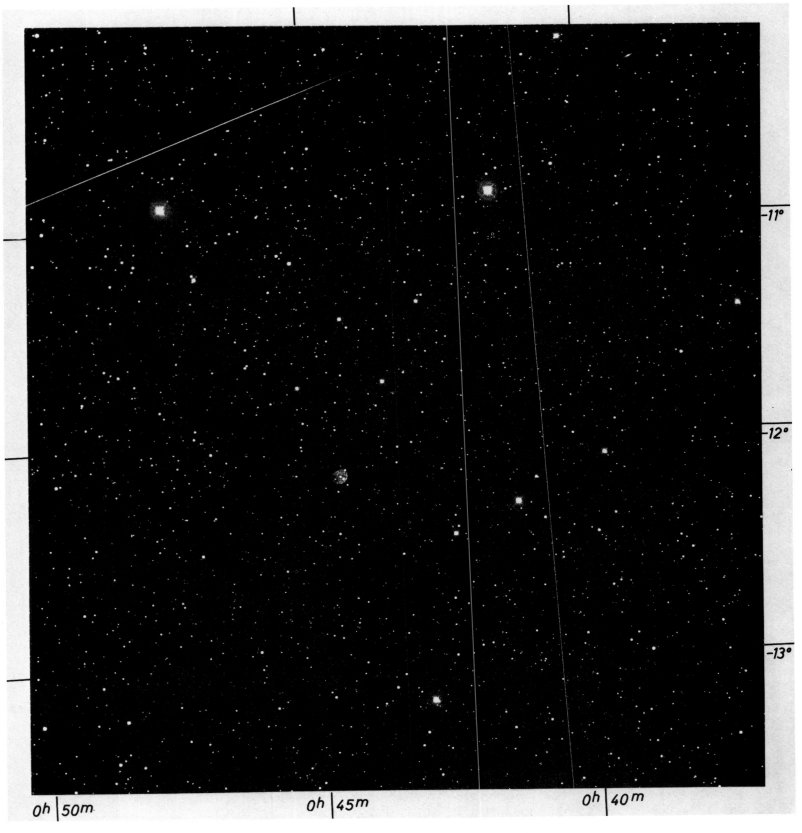

A table showing which photograph was taken with which camera is given on page 246.

The standard exposure time with the first Schmidt camera was 60 minutes for galaxies and faint nebulae, and 20 to 30 minutes for star clusters. Ilford HP5 film was used. A half-hour exposure goes to slightly fainter than magnitude 17 on this emulsion. There were occasional exceptions: Thus, for the Ring nebula M57 in Lyra the exposure time was only five minutes, in order to preserve the ring's dark interior.

At the Boyden Observatory in South Africa, the exposure times were never more than 20 minutes, because of the greater light-gathering power of the Hamburg Schmidt. In 1975, I bought the 14-inch Celestron Schmidt camera. Its great speed (focal ratio f/1.7) but shorter focal length, together with Kodak spectroscopic emulsions, encouraged me to take many color photographs, some of which are shown in this new edition. The photographs on pages 65, 75, 103, 187, and 189 were taken on High Speed Ektachrome. The pictures on pages 40, 53, 60, 82, 110, 179, and 223 were obtained by the three-color composite technique on Kodak 103a-O (7 minutes), 103a-G (10 minutes), and 103a-E (15 to 20 minutes).

All the enlargements for the charts, including the color photographs, were made by myself, in order to control the results from the photographic as well as the astronomical point of view.

A guide to the celestial objects.

Most of the 113 chart photographs in this book show celestial objects that, broadly speaking, can be called stellar systems. Some contain less than a dozen stars, others consist of literally trillions. Members of stellar systems share common physical properties; they are not just accidental groupings. A basic aim of astronomical research is to recognize these common properties, and to trace the origin and evolution of such stellar systems.

Continued on page 26

NGC 247

NGC 247, a galaxy of low surface brightness but considerable size, lies only 3°5 north of the equally large but much brighter galaxy NGC 253 (page 23). Both belong to the Sculptor group. As in NGC 55 (page 13), we can recognize some light and dark structural features, but no prominent spiral arms.

To find NGC 247, start from β Ceti (2^{m}2), swing the telescope 2¾° southward, and wait 3½ minutes without moving the instrument. The motion of the earth will carry the object into the center of the field of view. This is known as the star-drift method. Because of the galaxy's faintness, choose the eyepiece with the lowest magnifying power. The galaxy will then be seen as a pale oval spot without any structure. Its southern position requires observers in high northern latitudes to use a sizable telescope and wait for a dark night and suitable conditions.

Of the other faint galaxies in the field, NGC 175 is the brightest.

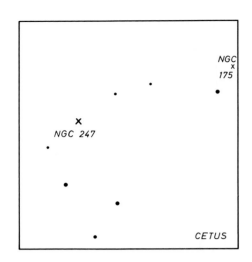

NGC 175
0ʰ34ᵐ9, −20°12′

Ga, 12ᵐ8, 1′.8 × 1′.5
type: Sa

NGC 247
0ʰ44ᵐ6, −21°01′

Ga, 10ᵐ7, 20′.9 × 7′.4
type: SAB(s)d(Vau)

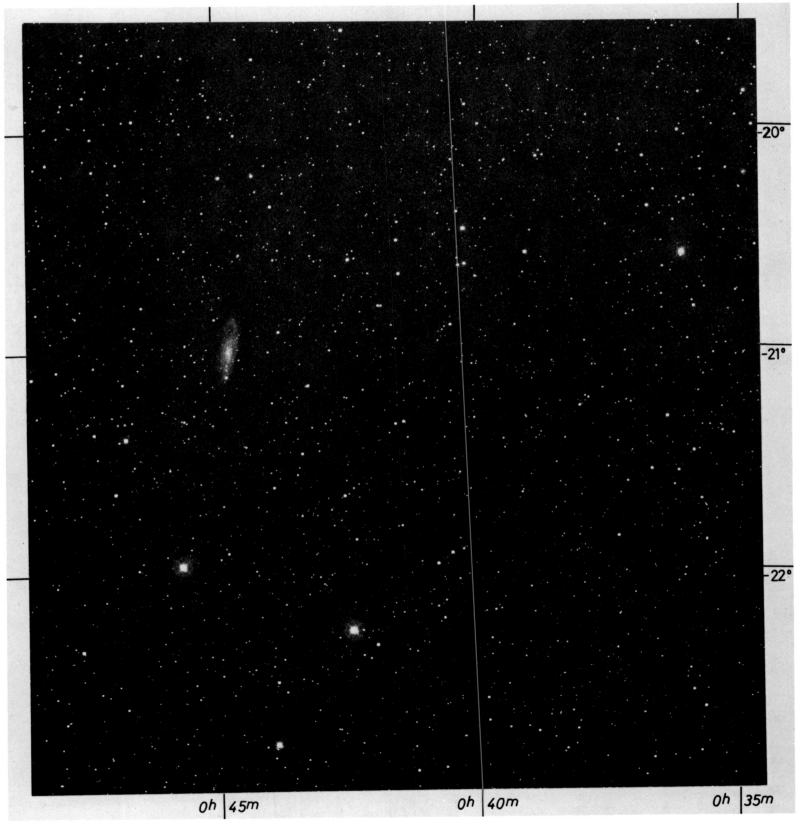

NGC 253 from a 100-inch reflector photograph at Mount Wilson.

NGC 253, NGC 288

NGC 253 is in many respects similar to the galaxy NGC 55, and also belongs to the Sculptor group. The two bear a strong resemblance in type, size, and brightness. Observed through the eyepiece, this object resembles a much smaller version of the Andromeda galaxy. Due to its southerly declination, NGC 253 requires good viewing conditions and at least a 6-inch telescope to be seen really well from higher latitudes of the Northern Hemisphere. The above enlargement shows its richness in structure, brought about by dust clouds, yet spiral arms are still recognizable. G. de Vaucouleurs measured the inclination of the system to the line of sight (12°). He determined that the northwest edge of the galaxy is closest to us while the northeast end is approaching us as the system rotates. NGC 253 is also known as a source of cosmic radio radiation.

NGC 288 is a loose globular cluster, which together with the galaxy makes a very impressive picture on the sparse background. The thin line running through the galaxy is the trail of an Earth satellite, an Agena rocket, 1962 $\beta\tau_6$.

NGC 253

0ʰ45ᵐ1, −25°34′

*Ga, 7ᵐ0, 24′.0 × 6′.3
type: Sc*

NGC 288

0ʰ50ᵐ2, −26°52′

*Gl, 7ᵐ2,
φ = 12′.4, type: X*

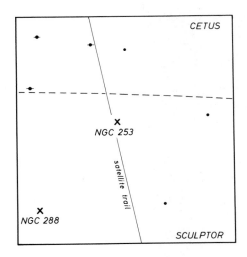

The Large and Small Magellanic Clouds. The bright star at top right is Achernar (α Eridani). The globular clusters 47 Tucanae and NGC 362 can be seen near the SMC. Harvard College Observatory photo.

The two Magellanic Clouds, the smaller of which is pictured on the facing page, are galaxies even though at first glance they look more like irregular clusters. As such they are our two nearest extragalactic neighbors. Together with the Andromeda galaxy and M33 in Triangulum, they belong to the Local Group of galaxies. However, the Clouds are 10 times nearer to us than the Andromeda system, and therefore we are able to study their individual contents more closely than those of any other external galaxies.

Because all objects within a Magellanic Cloud are at nearly the same distance from us, we are able to determine all their absolute magnitudes from their apparent magnitudes, provided that we know the distance of the Cloud or even one of its objects. In the early part of this century, astronomers seized upon this fact to establish the first extragalactic distance scale. In 1912, during her studies of Cepheid variable stars in the Clouds, H. S. Leavitt discovered that the stars' periods were related to their magnitudes; the brighter the Cepheid, the longer its period. This relation seemed quite precise for all Cepheids. When rough absolute magnitudes of Cepheid variables were worked out by H. Shapley in 1922, the distance could then be computed to any nearby galaxy in which these stars could be identified.

Small Magellanic Cloud (SMC)

Over 20 years later, while studying variable stars in globular clusters within M31, W. Baade realized that the classical zero point of the Cepheid period-luminosity relation was off by 1^m3. This correction resulted in a doubling of all the derived distances. Today distances determined by means of the Cepheids should still be considered somewhat approximate, since the absolute magnitude of even one Cepheid is not known with any great accuracy, while interstellar absorption can further complicate the picture.

The distance to the Small Cloud is now set at about 200,000 light-years. Its total mass was derived by F. J. Kerr and G. de Vaucouleurs, through velocity profiles of its 21-cm neutral hydrogen radio emission, as 1.3 billion solar masses — about one percent the mass of the Milky Way.

Two globular clusters are to be found near the SMC, but they are not physically associated with it. NGC 104 = 47 Tucanae is, in apparent size, the second largest globular cluster in the sky, superseded only by ω Centauri (page 147). It is only about 20,000 light-years away from us, while NGC 362 is about twice as far. R. L. Wildey compiled a color-magnitude diagram of 300 stars in NGC 104, and from it derived an intermediate age for this very rich cluster.

NGC 362
1ʰ00ᵐ6, − 71°07'

Gl, 8ᵐ0, Sp: F8
φ = 17'.7, type: III

SMC
Small Magellanic Cloud
0ʰ50ᵐ0, − 73°00'

Ga, 2ᵐ5, 216' × 240'
type: I

NGC 104
47 Tuc
0ʰ21ᵐ9, − 72°21'

Gl, 4ᵐ7, Sp: G3
φ = 44', type: III

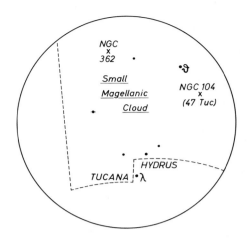

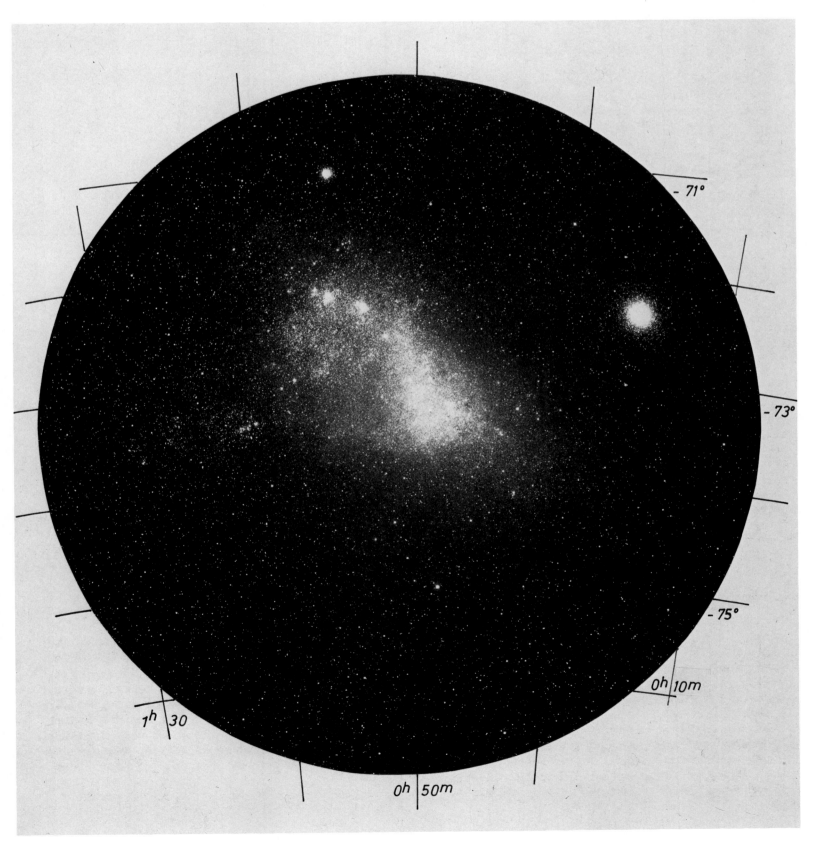

The systems can be divided into two main classes according to their cosmic size. The first group comprises the open or galactic star clusters (Cl) and the globular star clusters (Gl), both of which belong to our Milky Way system. The second class consists of the very remote stellar systems known as galaxies (Ga), enormously larger and richer in stars. They are other Milky Ways, but at such great distances as to superficially resemble nebulae, and they were regarded as such in former times. Many of them are spiral shaped; hence the old term "spiral nebulae."

In addition, there is another class of deep-sky object, which comprises the actual diffuse nebulae (N) and the disk- and ring-shaped planetary nebulae (Pl). The nebulae are great clouds of gas and dust, some luminous and others dark. They often have stars embedded in them. Although the term "stellar system" can be applied to the nebulae only quite loosely, they are very closely connected with the development of stars and clusters. Many diffuse nebulae are "stellar nurseries" in which new stars are being born; the planetary nebulae are clouds of ejected matter surrounding old, dying stars.

Because of the extensive information accompanying each chart photograph, the use of abbreviations has been unavoidable. One purpose of this guide is to explain these abbreviations; it also may help the reader to fully appreciate the contents of this book.

Open or galactic star clusters (Cl)

As the name suggests, an open cluster is a collection of stars that are clearly separable, but are more numerous than the stars in a similar area of the surrounding sky. The members of a cluster are scattered across a more or less circular area, usually concentrated in the center. Without exception, the open star clusters belong to the Milky Way system. They show a distinct tendency to congregate toward the galactic plane; thus, they are mostly found within the star clouds of the Milky Way. The clusters lie at distances between 70 and 10,000 parsecs (pc), and their true diameters range between 1 and 45 pc. (One parsec equals 3.26 light-years).

Continued

NGC 300

After the Andromeda galaxy and M33 in Triangulum, NGC 300 is one of the largest galaxies in the sky. Together with NGC 55, 247 and 253, it belongs to the Sculptor group, and can only be observed to advantage from the Southern Hemisphere. In appearance, it strikingly resembles M33. Both galaxies have small and compact nuclei, and well-shaped spiral arms that, on large-scale photographs, can be resolved into numerous gaseous nebulae and individual bright stars (supergiants).

According to photometric research by G. de Vaucouleurs and J. Page, we see that the central plane of this galaxy is inclined 42° to our line of sight. By measuring the profiles of the galaxy's 21-cm neutral hydrogen emission, R. R. Shobbrock and B. J. Robinson in Australia were able to derive its rotation curve and establish its mass at 25 billion solar masses, using an assumed distance of 1.9 megaparsecs.

NGC 300

0ʰ52ᵐ6, −37°58′

Ga, 8ᵐ7, 30′ × 23′
type: SA(s)cd(Vau)

NGC 300

×

SCULPTOR

−37°

−38°

−39°

1ʰ 00ᵐ   0ʰ 55ᵐ   0ʰ 50ᵐ   0ʰ 45ᵐ

A typical open cluster contains between 20 and 2,200 member stars, though the large clusters are rare. R. J. Trumpler found the average number of members per cluster to be 75. A comparison between different clusters shows not only the diversity in numbers of members, but also great variations in the average magnitudes of the stars, and their concentration. The contrast with which the cluster stands out from its surrounding area depends on the density of background stars and on the concentration of each cluster. These features enabled early classifications of open clusters to be made, quite independently, by R. J. Trumpler and H. Shapley. In this book the Shapley classifications have been adopted, as follows:

OPEN CLUSTER TYPES

Type	Description	Example	Page
g	Very concentrated cluster, standing out prominently from its background	NGC 2158 M93	71 89
f	Concentrated cluster, standing out well from its background	h Persei M37	39 69
e	Cluster with moderate concentration, easily recognizable	NGC 457 M41	31 79
d	Cluster with only slight concentration, easily recognizable	M34 Praesepe	43 95
c	Cluster without noticeable concentration, but clearly recognizable	Pleiades Hyades Coma cluster	51 55 123
a	Cluster giving the impression of an accidental agglomeration of stars, hardly standing out from its background	M73	221

Continued

IC 59 and IC 63

IC 59 and IC 63 are two irregularly shaped emission nebulae in the immediate vicinity of the star γ Cassiopeiae ($1^m6 - 3^m0$). This is an irregular variable star, prototype of the γ Cassiopeiae type, and is of spectral type B0ne. There is no doubt of some connection between the nebulae and the star.

To the right (west) of IC 59 is the triple star ADS 721, with components A = 5^m0, B = 9^m5, and C = 12^m3. A and B form a widely separated pair with a distance of 30″, whereas B and C are close together (0″9). Above this triple star one can see an oval ghost image of γ Cas. More about such ghosts, which occur near bright stars on photographs taken with Schmidt cameras, appears on page 210.

An inconspicuous open star cluster, NGC 381, decorates the top left corner of the photograph. It forms roughly the optical center of the stellar association Cassiopeia I.

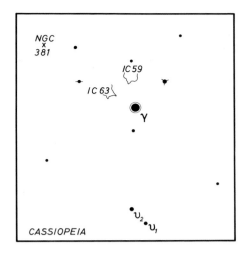

NGC 381
1ʰ05ᵐ2, +61°18'

Cl, 9ᵐ3, 30 ★
φ = 6'.5, type: c

IC 59
0ʰ53ᵐ7, +60°48'

N, 18' × 12', type: e

IC 63
0ʰ56ᵐ4, −60°33'

N, 11' × 11', type: e

Above each chart photograph the following data are given for open clusters: Shapley's type description, the NGC or IC number as listed in Dreyer's New General Catalogue or Index Catalogue, and the M number from Messier's catalogue, if any. In addition, the object's position is given in right ascension and declination for equinox 1950.0. Also the integrated photographic magnitude (m_p) and the apparent diameter (ϕ) are given. These data have been taken from a table of 514 open clusters by H. B. Sawyer Hogg in Handbuch der Physik Volume 53, Astrophysics IV: Stellar Systems, pages 195-205 (1959). Occasionally some data were taken from other sources, such as the Catalogue of Star Clusters and Associations by G. Alter, J. Ruprecht and V. Vanysek, Prague 1958 (with nine supplements in the Czechoslovakian Bulletin of the Astronomical Institutes of Czechoslovakia). This complete card index catalogue in its revised edition, published in 1970 by the Hungarian Academy of Sciences, contains more than 1,000 open star clusters. The number of star members (★) has been taken mainly from the sources cited in the text.

The total magnitude m_p of a cluster can be determined fairly accurately. But the number of star members and the apparent diameter (ϕ) are mostly tentative, because it is difficult to distinguish between true cluster members and background stars. Exceptions are the relatively near clusters (Hyades, Pleiades, Praesepe and Coma star cluster), where the measurable proper motion has made it possible to ascertain which stars are members and which are not. Even so, new members are still being discovered in these clusters.

Luckily, there is a method by which one can establish the physical structure and the history of stars in open clusters. We plot the apparent magnitude versus the spectral type (in clusters with bright stars) or the equivalent color index (in clusters with rather faint stars) on a diagram with rectangular coordinates. The star points will be scattered more or less along two main lines, which correspond to the main sequence and the giant branch in the Hertzsprung-Russell diagram (HRD). Such a graphic presentation of colors and magnitudes of the stars in a cluster is called a color-magnitude diagram (CMD). In fact the CMD is nothing other than an HRD whose ordinate is not absolute magnitude but apparent magnitude.

Continued on page 54

M103 = NGC 581

In the facing photograph of the rich star field surrounding δ Cassiopeiae (2ᵐ7), there are four rather unobtrusive clusters, which together with two more clusters outside the exposed star field (NGC 654 and NGC 663) form, according to S. W. McCuskey and N. Houk, a spatial group at a distance of 2,500 pc.

M103 = NGC 581 is a loose cluster with 60-70 members, which was brought to Messier's notice by Méchain. Without checking it himself, Messier took it as the last object in his catalogue. Its description by J. Herschel as "round and rich" is not borne out by photographs. T. Oja has done some closer research on M103 in connection with the open cluster Tr 1 (Trumpler 1), half of which is just visible at the top edge of the photograph.

NGC 457 is similar in brightness to M103 but has a greater number of stars and is more extended. Nevertheless, this cluster was overlooked by Messier and Méchain. P. Pesch was able to deduce from the color-magnitude diagram of the cluster that it is similar to the double cluster h and χ Persei. The bright star φ Cassiopeiae (5ᵐ0) on its south-western border may or may not be a member of it.

NGC 659 is a small galactic cluster of faint stars, slightly northeast of the quintuple star 44 Cassiopeiae, which is listed in Aitken's Double Star Catalogue as ADS 1344. Its components have magnitudes: A = 5ᵐ8, B = 12ᵐ1, C = 9ᵐ6, and D = 9ᵐ2 (furthermore, D is a spectroscopic binary star).

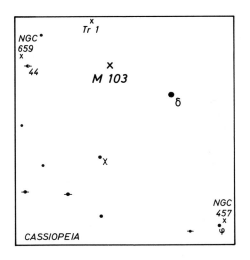

NGC 659

1ʰ40ᵐ8, +60°28′

Cl, 9ᵐ8, 30 ★
φ = 5′, type: d

M103   NGC 581

1ʰ29ᵐ9, +60°27′

Cl, 7ᵐ4, 73 ★
φ = 7′.1, type: d

Tr 1

1ʰ32ᵐ3, +61°02′

Cl, 10ᵐ2, 37 ★
φ = 4′.8, type: d?

NGC 457

1ʰ15ᵐ9, +58°04′

Cl, 7ᵐ5, 100 ★
φ = 12′, type: e

M33
taken from a 2-meter reflector photograph at Karl-Schwarzschild-Sternwarte at Tautenberg near Jena.

M33 = NGC 598

Galaxies like M33, with their obvious spiral structure, give the impression of being rotating objects, and in fact they are. For many galaxies, this has been established by measuring the differential Doppler shift along an axis going through the nucleus. Until this was accomplished, it was impossible to say with certainty whether the ends of the spiral arms point in the direction of the rotation, or the other way. We now know that all the spirals rotate like pinwheels, with their arms trailing.

From their outward appearance, we can differentiate between right-hand and left-hand spirals. However, in order to measure the true direction of rotation it is necessary to know which edge of the galaxy is the front one, because the assumed direction of rotation becomes reversed when front and rear edges are changed around. If the central plane of a galaxy is tilted to the direction of vision enough to make individual details easily recognizable (knots of nebulae, star clusters, clouds of dark material), then the question of which is the front edge can be established by measuring the Doppler effect along various axes. This was possible for the Andromeda galaxy, whereas in M33 the angle of the central plane is 55°, according to G. de Vaucouleurs. Thus it has not been possible so far to establish which edge of M33 is the front one.

For the visual observer M33 is an unrewarding object, unless he or she is satisfied with just finding the galaxy with the aid of binoculars or a comet seeker. Most probably that is why J. L. E. Dreyer thought that several of the starclouds visible some distance away from the center are independent nebulae, and listed them separately in his *New General Catalogue*. One example is NGC 604, the knot situated northeast of the center.

Messier first saw M33 on August 25, 1764.

M33 *NGC 598*

1ʰ31ᵐ1, +30°24'

Ga, 6ᵐ3, 61'.7 × 38'.1
type: Sc

×
M 33

TRIANGULUM | PISCES

+31°

+30°

+29°

1ʰ 35m   1ʰ 30m   1ʰ 25m

M74
200-inch Hale Observatories photograph.

M74 = NGC 628

The field in Pisces portrayed in the facing photograph, and the surrounding areas, offer the observer with a small telescope only a few interesting objects. Of the many distant galaxies there, only NGC 628 = M74 is bright enough for Messier to have seen it — and his ability to find it at all is another proof of his extraordinary powers of observation. To locate this object, a powerful comet seeker used on a dark night gives the best results. Even with a telescope of 15-cm aperture, M74 still remains difficult because its surface brightness is so low. Many observers consider M74 the most difficult Messier object.

The bright star η Piscium (3^m6), ½° south and 5 minutes west, is handy as a reference star. With a larger telescope, one should use only a low-power eyepiece, but even under the best possible conditions nothing can be seen of the spiral structure shown in the photograph.

M74 has a rather bright starlike nucleus. It is a two-armed spiral whose central plane is considerably tilted away from our line of sight (55°). M. S. Roberts, by measuring the profiles of its 21-cm neutral hydrogen emission, was able to ascertain the mass of this galaxy to be 58 billion suns.

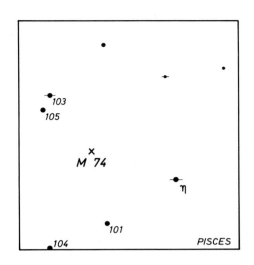

M74 NGC 628
1ʰ34ᵐ0, + 15°32'

Ga, 11ᵐ2, 12' × 12'
type: Sc

PISCES

+17°

+16°

+15°

1h 35m   1h 30m   1h 25m

M76
The two faint stars at the center of the nebula are separated by only 1".5; the fact that they are resolved is testimony to the very great sharpness of this photograph. One of them is the planetary's true core; the other is thought to be most likely a chance superposition in the line of sight.

Photographed by Laird A. Thompson on hypersensitized Ektachrome ASA 400 film with the 3.6-meter f/4.2 Canada-France-Hawaii telescope on Mauna Kea, Hawaii, during excellent seeing. Photograph provided by the Institute for Astronomy, University of Hawaii.

M76 = NGC 650-651

The planetary nebula NGC 650-651 = M76 is sometimes also called the Little Dumbbell nebula, and in fact the facing photograph, despite its small scale, does show it to have a certain similarity to the real Dumbbell nebula M27 (page 213). On exposures with large instruments, the object resembles more the shape of a cork.

W. Herschel saw the planetary in two separate parts, which is why it is listed in Dreyer's catalogue with a double number. M76 was discovered by Méchain on September 5, 1760, and Messier himself observed the object the same year. However, he thought it was a star cluster mixed with nebulosity. Lord Rosse took the object to be a spiral nebu-

la. Only modern photographic exposures have revealed the true nature of M76.

The American astronomers J. H. Cahn and J. B. Kaler concluded in 1971, from all available photometric and radio observations of M76, that the distance to this planetary is about 450 pc.

When searching for M76, one can use φ Persei as a reference star. This star is a spectroscopic double with a period of 126.6 days. One component is an irregular variable of small range.

M76 NGC 650-51
1ʰ38ᵐ8, +51°19′

PI, 12ᵐ2, m⋆ = 16.6,
2ʹ6 × 1ʹ5, type: V

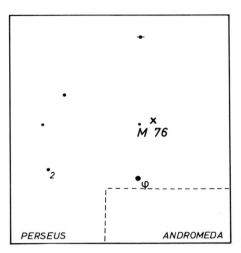

PERSEUS   ANDROMEDA

1ʰ 50m   1ʰ 45m   1ʰ 40m   1ʰ 35m

+52°
+51°
+50°

The Double Cluster, photographed by E. Alt, E. Brodkorb, K. Rihm, and J. Rusche.

h and χ Persei (NGC 869 and 884)

The double star cluster h and χ Persei, one of the "show-pieces" of the northern sky, is quite clearly visible against the background of the Milky Way even with the naked eye. Binoculars or a small telescope show very many stars in the two clusters, and one can even distinguish different colors among them. In a larger instrument, either of the clusters alone fills the whole field of view. It is somewhat surprising that Messier did not put this prominent double object into his catalogue, though he must have known about it.

Both clusters have been the subject of much research, but nevertheless the true number of their physical members has not yet been established. P. T. Oosterhoff has shown that, at the direction and distance (2,250 pc) of the clusters, the proper motion of the background stars due to galactic rotation would be about the same as that observed for the cluster stars. Therefore we are unable to use the proper motion of a star to tell whether it is a member of the cluster or not. In the cluster h there are 340 stars brighter than 15^m5, and

300 in χ. Unfortunately, irregular interstellar absorption clouds are noticeable in the region of the Double Cluster. They show as rather empty patches on the facing photograph.

According to A. R. Sandage, both clusters are among the youngest of their kind (see diagram on page 14), being 1 million years old by his estimate. R. L. Wildey has studied their color-magnitude diagram in connection with the Perseus I association, which surrounds the clusters.

North of h Persei is the star 7 Persei (6^m2), which is sometimes misidentified as χ. It is a wide double star (A = 6^m1, B = 10^m8, distance 70″), which can be separated with a small telescope.

The small open cluster NGC 957, at an estimated distance of 2,290 pc, is apparently associated with h and χ Persei.

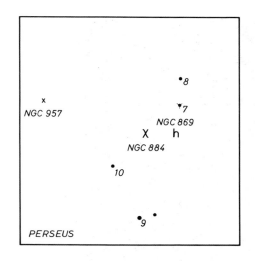

NGC 957

2ʰ28ᵐ9, +57°18'

Cl, 7ᵐ2, 40 ★
φ = 9', type: e

NGC 869

(h Per)

2ʰ15ᵐ5, +56°55'

Cl, 4ᵐ4, 340 ★
42' × 51', type: f

NGC 884

(χ Per)

2ʰ18ᵐ 9, +56°53'

Cl, 4ᵐ7, 300 ★
46' × 55', type: e

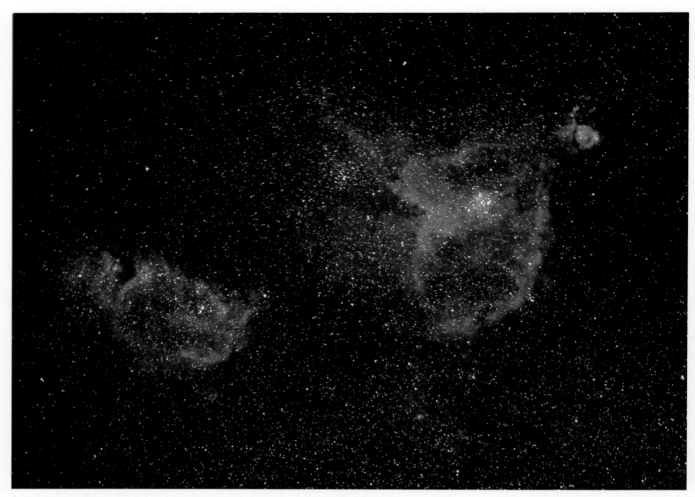

Color photograph by the author, taken with the same instrument as the field opposite.

IC 1805, IC 1848

IC 1805 and IC 1848 were first observed by E. E. Barnard with a 6-inch refractor at Nashville, Tennessee. J. L. E. Dreyer described IC 1805 as "cluster, coarse, extremely large, extended nebulosity following," and IC 1848 as "cluster with faint stars in faint nebulosity." Large wreaths of glowing hydrogen gas surround the open clusters in both objects, but in IC 1805 the cluster itself is hidden in the overexposed center on the facing photograph. In the color picture above this cluster can be easily detected. This photograph was made using the three-color composite technique.

The bright and compact patch of nebulosity at the right edge of the facing star field is IC 1795, where a strong OH (hydroxyl) radio source is located.

At right ascension 2^h32^m6, declination $+59°25'.8$, (7 mm from the lower edge of the facing photograph), the infrared object "Maffei 1" can be seen as a small nebulous patch, and even "Maffei 2" can be suspected 40 minutes of arc to the east, when a careful comparison is made with the 48-inch Palomar Schmidt telescope photograph reproduced in Sky & Telescope, Vol. 41, page 144 (1971). Both are nearby dust-dimmed galaxies, detected in 1968 by the Italian astronomer P. Maffei.

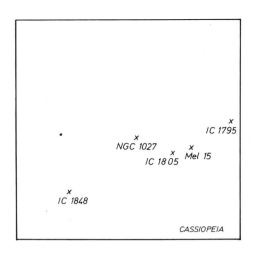

NGC 1027
$2^h38^m8, +61°20'$

Cl, 7^m5, 25 ★
$\phi = 7'$, type: d

IC 1795
$2^h21^m0, +61°40'$

N, $27' \times 13'$

IC 1805
$2^h28^m2, +61°15'$

N, ★ = B0 6^m0,
$150' \times 130'$, type: e

Mel 15
$2^h29^m8, +61°15'$

Cl + N, 7^m0, 30 ★
$\phi = 6'$

IC 1848
$2^h47^m4, +60°30'$

N, ★ = O7 7^m1,
$\phi = 60' \times 30'$, type: e

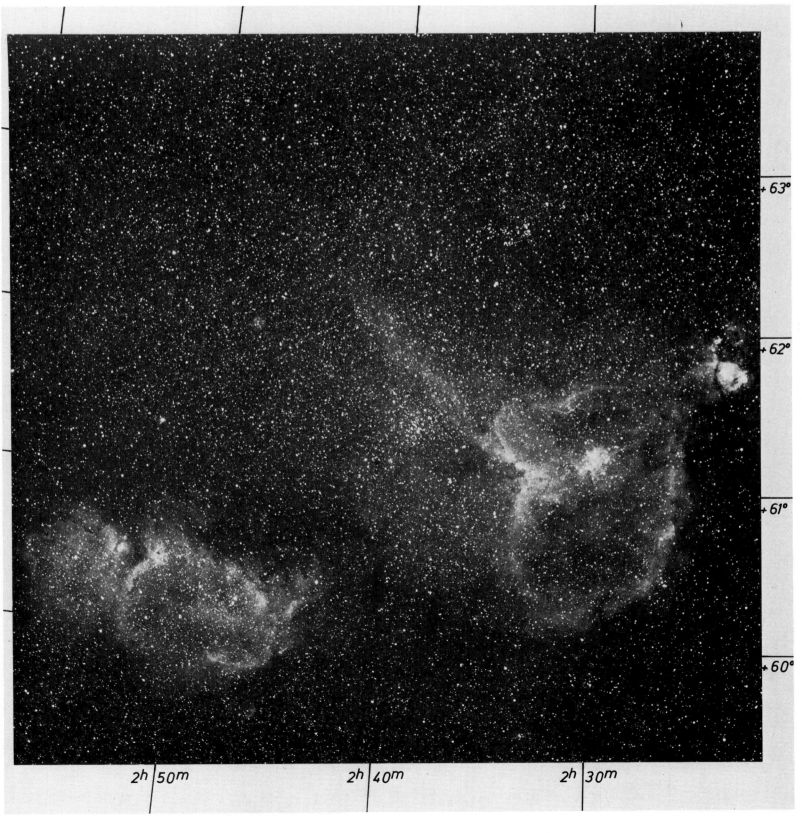

A wide-angle photograph of the star field near M34. The cluster is at the left-hand edge. In the center of the picture is NGC 752, and at bottom right corner M33.

M34 = NGC 1039

M34 is a loose, bright, open cluster, not particularly rich in stars. On a dark night it can just be seen with the naked eye between Algol (β Persei) and γ Andromedae, slightly nearer the former. Among its 70-80 stars are six bright ones of 9th magnitude. With large telescopes and high powers, this cluster merges into the Milky Way. Many of its fainter stars presumably belong to the Milky Way background. Messier discovered M34 on August 25, 1764, and described it as a "cluster of smaller stars."

Though many astronomers have studied this cluster, H. L. Johnson has carried out the most intensive researches. In 1954 he determined its distance as 525 pc from his color-magnitude diagram of 57 member stars. In 1957 he revised this to 440 pc.

About ½° above and to the right of the brightest star in the field (12 Persei, 5^{m}0) is the faint spiral galaxy NGC 1003, which became well-known some years ago, when W. Baade and F. Zwicky observed a supernova in it. This galaxy is difficult for even experienced visual observers to find.

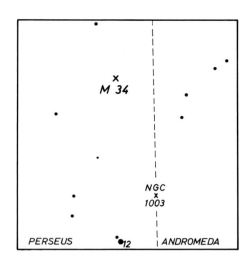

M34 NGC 1039
2h38m8, +42°34'

Cl, 5m5, 80 ★
φ = 30', type: d

NGC 1003
2h36m1, +40°40'

Ga, 12m4, 4'.8 × 1'.5
type: Sc

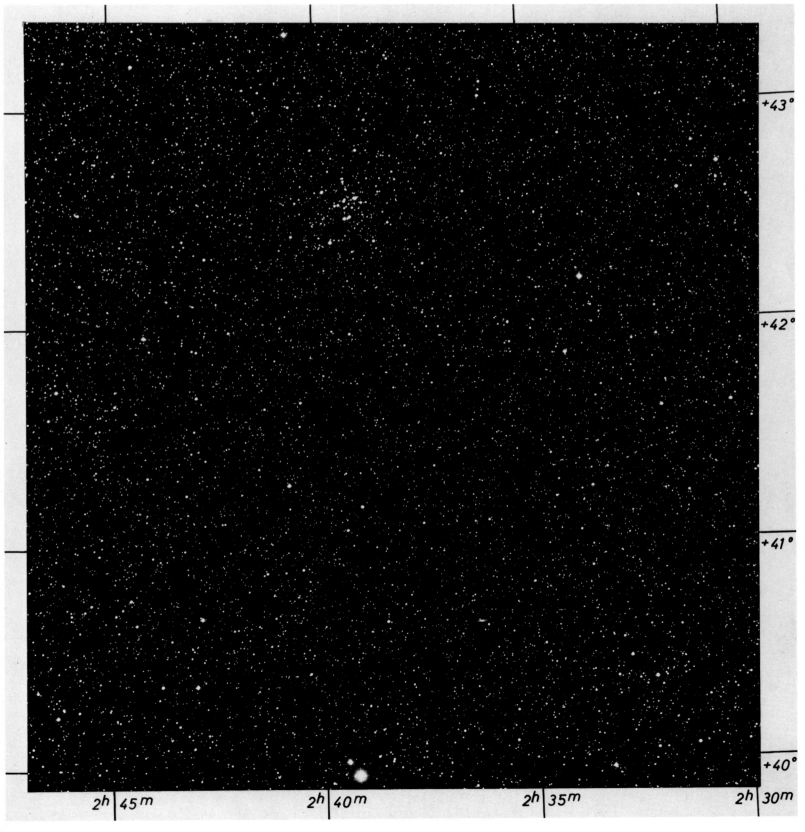

M77
from a Hale Observatories photograph.

M77 = NGC 1068

Within an area of only a few square degrees situated mainly east of δ Ceti (4^{m}0), there are six spiral galaxies brighter than 13^{m}0. The brightest of these is M77 = NGC 1068. It is not recognizably spiral on the facing photograph, but the enlargement above clearly shows a spiral with two main arms and several seemingly smaller ones. Exposures taken with the largest instruments of the area around δ Ceti show at least 45 galaxies. These in fact form a small cluster of galaxies, similar to the richer one in the Virgo area.

In October 1780, Messier described M77 somewhat erroneously as a "cluster of smaller stars embedded in nebulae." The object was originally discovered by Méchain. The star very slightly east of M77, which was observed by Lassell with his 48-inch reflector as slightly nebulous, belongs to the galactic foreground.

E. M. Burbidge, G. R. Burbidge, and K. H. Prendergast studied the inner region of M77 and found that the central plane is tilted 51° to the line of sight, and that its main body contains 27 billion solar masses. In the bright, compact center of the galaxy, M. F. Walker discovered some emission nebulae undergoing considerable expansion. This is a Seyfert galaxy, characterized by mysterious high-energy processes in a bright, tiny nucleus.

The star above the middle of the bottom edge is a double, 84 Ceti = ADS 2046, whose components A = 5^{m}8 and B = 9^{m}0, separated by 4".1, can be resolved in small telescopes.

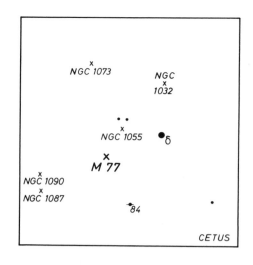

CETUS

NGC 1087
2ʰ43ᵐ9, −0°42′

Ga, 11ᵐ2, 3′.0 × 1′.9
type: Sc

NGC 1055
2ʰ39ᵐ2, +0°16′

Ga, 12ᵐ0, 6′.8 × 2′.2
type: S

M77   NGC 1068
2ʰ40ᵐ3, −0°13′

Ga, 10ᵐ0, 5′.2 × 4′.3
type: Sb

NGC 1090
2ʰ44ᵐ0, −0°27′

Ga, 12ᵐ8, 3′.7 × 1′.5
type: S

NGC 1073
2ʰ41ᵐ2, +1°10′

Ga, 12ᵐ0, 4′.5 × 4′.3
type: S

NGC 1032
2ʰ36ᵐ8, +0°52′

Ga, 13ᵐ0, 1′.8 × 0′.7
type: S

NGC 1097 from a 100-inch reflector photograph at Mount Wilson.

NGC 1097

NGC 1097 is a fine example of a barred spiral galaxy, characterized by two spiral arms coming out from the ends of a more or less oblong central bar and winding around almost as far as the opposing ends of the bar. In the case of NGC 1097, the spiral arms appear in the shape of an "S," leading to its classification as type SB(s)3 by G. de Vaucouleurs. Unfortunately the splendor of its form cannot be observed visually, even with large amateur telescopes. This is indeed an excellent example of the advantage of photographic observation.

According to the work of E. M. Burbidge and G. R. Burbidge, the central part of NGC 1097 has a mass of 13 billion solar masses. Presumably this is about 70% of the whole galaxy. Shortly before the end of the exposure on the facing page, the satellite Pegasus 2 = 1965 — 39 A crossed the field. The fluctuating light trail was caused by the fast rotation of the satellite.

NGC 1097

2^{h}44^{m}3, −30°29′

Ga, 10^{m}6, 7′.9 × 5′.4
type: SB(s)3 (Vau)

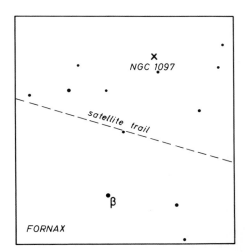

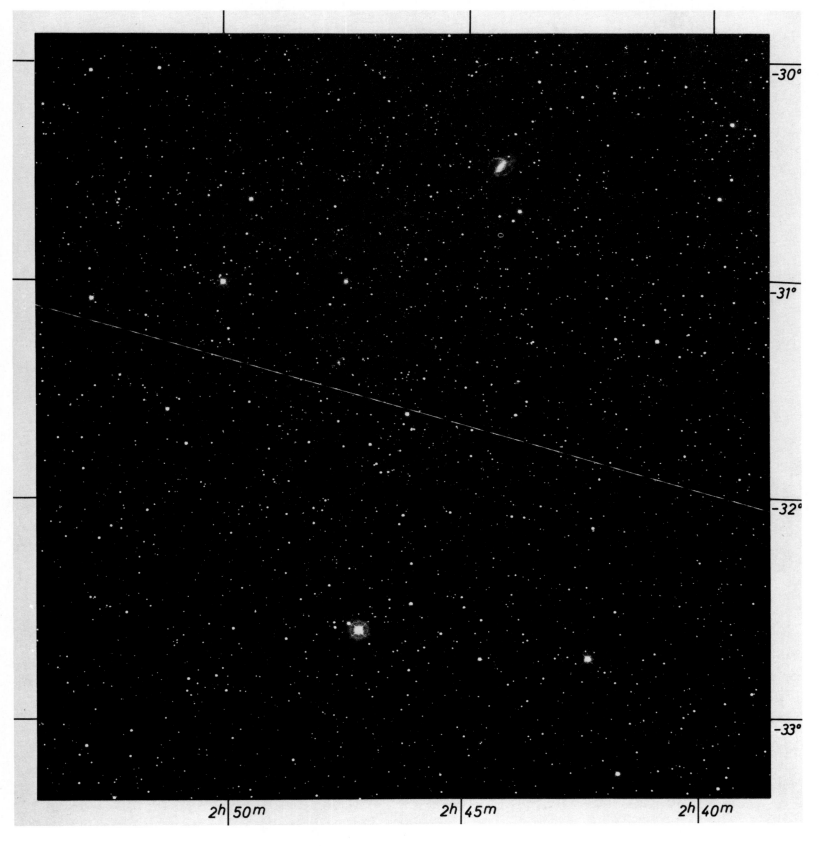

STELLAR ASSOCIATIONS

OB associations, discovered by V. A. Ambartsumian in 1952, are expanding groups of young stars of spectral classes O to B2. The spatial density of stars in an association is much greater than for stars of similar spectral type in the surrounding field. The 12 most significant of the 70 known associations are given below.

Name (IAU Com.)	Name (Morgan/Schmidt)	R.A. 1950.0 Dec.		Dim(pc)	page
Per OB 3	Per III	3^h24^m2	$+49°44'$	170	49
Cam OB 1	Cam I	3 27.6	$+58$ 28	900	
Per OB 2	Per II	3 39.0	$+33$ 16	400	
Aur OB 1	Aur I	5 18.4	$+33$ 49	1430	59
Ori OB 1	Ori I	5 28.9	-02 43	300	
Mon OB 2	Mon II	6 34.5	$+04$ 53	1400	
CMa OB 1	CMa I	7 04.6	-10 23	1315	83
Vel OB 1	Vel I	8 48.2	-44 49	1000	
Sco OB 1	Sco I	16 50.0	-41 52	1400	171
Cyg OB 1	Cyg I	20 15.9	$+37$ 29	1700	
Cep OB 2	Cep II	21 46.4	$+60$ 50	700	
Cep OB 3	Cep III	22 58.4	$+63$ 47	960	

Perseus III Association

Between the bright stars α and δ Persei, the observer with binoculars can easily find a group of about 60 to 70 stars of 5th to 10th magnitude, rather evenly distributed in a field of six square degrees. Such a loose group of physically connected stars is called a stellar association. The most prominent members are young and hot OB stars.

The diameter of the Perseus III association is about 100 parsecs. The proper motions of its stars have two components: a transverse one and a radial one. The transverse motion shifts the whole group in the same direction relative to the background stars, whereas the radial motion is that of the stars away from the center of the association. The whole group is expanding outward; from this it can be deduced that the stars of the Perseus III association have a common origin, as the Hyades do (page 55). Probably some 4 million years ago Perseus III appeared as a star cluster resembling the Pleiades today.

The galactic cluster NGC 1245, 3° southwest of α Persei, looks like a globular cluster, because of its distance and the small scale of the photograph.

Per III Association
3ʰ24ᵐ2, + 49°44'

NGC 1245
3ʰ11ᵐ2, + 47°03'

Cl, 6ᵐ9, 40 ★
φ = 30', type: e

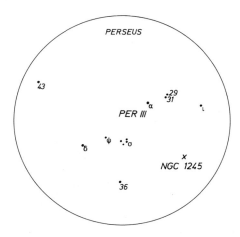

PERSEUS

43

29
31

PER III   α

ι

δ   Ψ   ο

×
NGC 1245

36

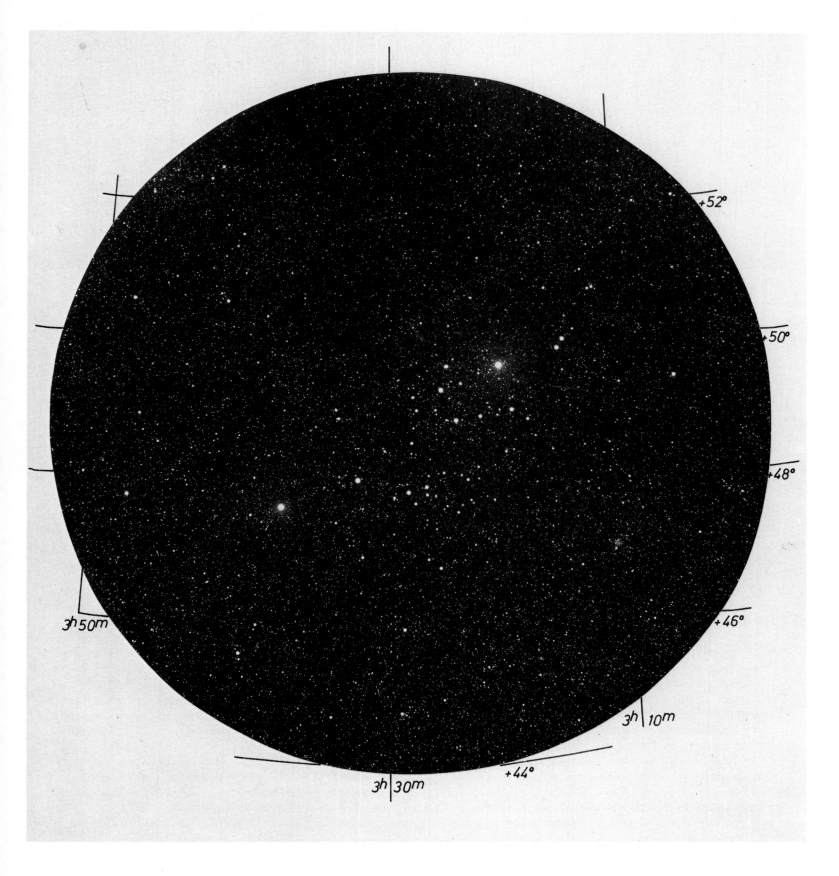

+52°

+50°

+48°

+46°

3ʰ 50ᵐ

3ʰ 10ᵐ

3ʰ 30ᵐ

+44°

The Pleiades. Three-color composite photograph by E. Alt, E. Brodkorb, K. Rihm, and J. Rusche.

M45 (Pleiades)

The Pleiades, perhaps the most impressive of all open clusters in the northern sky, are equally attractive whether viewed with the naked eye or with a small telescope. M45, as the cluster is known, has always been a test of eyesight. Most people can distinguish six stars, but in order to see seven or more exceptionally good eyesight and atmospheric clarity are needed. When I observed the Pleiades at Falkau on clear dark nights, I found that when the cluster was near the horizon it was easier to resolve single stars than when it was nearer to the zenith, where the stars seemed to be embedded in bright nebulosity.

As early as the year 1579, that is, before the introduction of telescopes, Maestlin drew 11 stars correctly. According to Kepler, some observers had even seen 14 stars. For the amateur astrophotographer, the Pleiades are most rewarding, for even an ordinary small camera and an exposure time of half an hour will reveal numerous stars and also show traces of the associated nebulae. The opposite photograph was exposed for 15 minutes.

Few other galactic objects have been studied as intensively as M45. Despite this, or perhaps just for that very reason, some questions have been left unanswered up to this date. The number of its members was given in 1921 by R. J. Trumpler as 246, but we know there are many more, because a study of the proper motions shows that some outlying members are up to 3° from the star Alcyone, the brightest of the Pleiades. We can therefore say with certainty that the cluster extends beyond the field of our photographs.

For many years the distance of the Pleiades was uncertain, as the moving-cluster method that works so well for the Hyades cannot be applied here. Moreover, the cluster lies at the limit of direct trigonometric measurement of parallax. From the orbital motion of the binary star ADS 2755, which belongs to the cluster and has completed more than a full revolution, E. Hertzsprung long ago found a distance of 80 pc. Very accurate color-magnitude diagrams of the Pleiades stars have been constructed by B. Iriarte and by R. I. Mitchell and H. L. Johnson. From these, the distance of the Pleiades is now known with considerable accuracy as 120 pc.

The brighter stars of the Pleiades, all of spectral type $B6$ to $B8$, have an unusually high speed of rotation (150-300 km/sec. at their equators). O. Struve discovered that the star Pleione (28 Tauri) has so rapid a rotation that a gaseous shell is thrown off. Such a shell was in fact spectroscopically observed between 1938 and 1952. Possibly the reflection nebulae visible around the brighter stars of the Pleiades are the result of continuous gaseous expulsions. Alternatively, they may be the last wisps of the nebula from whose material the stars formed. The Pleiades cluster is noteworthy for the large number of flare stars it contains. These are very faint red dwarfs, some as dim as magnitude 20, which occasionally brighten abruptly by up to several magnitudes, and then return to their normal obscurity within minutes or a few hours.

IC 1995 is a small reflection nebula around the double star ADS 2799 (A = $5^{m}9$; B = $6^{m}3$, separation $0\rlap{.}''4$) whose period of 62.3 years was worked out in 1955. It is only possible to separate the two components with large telescopes.

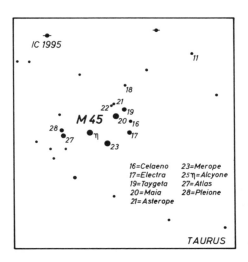

16=Celaeno   23=Merope
17=Electra   25η=Alcyone
19=Taygeta   27=Atlas
20=Maia   28=Pleione
21=Asterope

TAURUS

M45 *Pleiades*
$3^h43^m9, +23°58'$

Cl, 1^m4, 250 ★
$\phi = 120'$, type: c

IC 1995
$3^h47^m3, +25°26'$

N, $2' \times 2'$, Sp: c

NGC 1499 photographed at Lick Observatory. To improve contrast, a red filter was used.

NGC 1499 (California nebula)

Named after the state because of a similarity in shape, the California nebula is almost as large but much fainter than the famous North America nebula. Only its brightest parts can be observed visually, even in large telescopes, and long exposure photographs are required to depict this emission nebula in its entirety.

The nebula is illuminated by the star ξ Persei (4.0, spectrum O7n), and therefore must lie at about the same distance as the star (about 600 pc). Y. Terzian has studied the distribution of the radio emission from the nebula at a frequency of 750 MHz and found a conformity with the distribution of the optical radiation. The gas is estimated to have a mass of 240 suns.

NGC 1499
California nebula

4ʰ00ᵐ1, +36°17'

N, 145' × 40', Sp: e

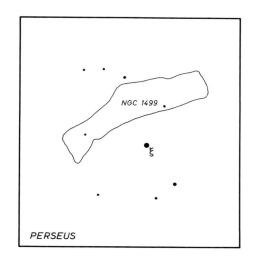

NGC 1499

ξ

PERSEUS

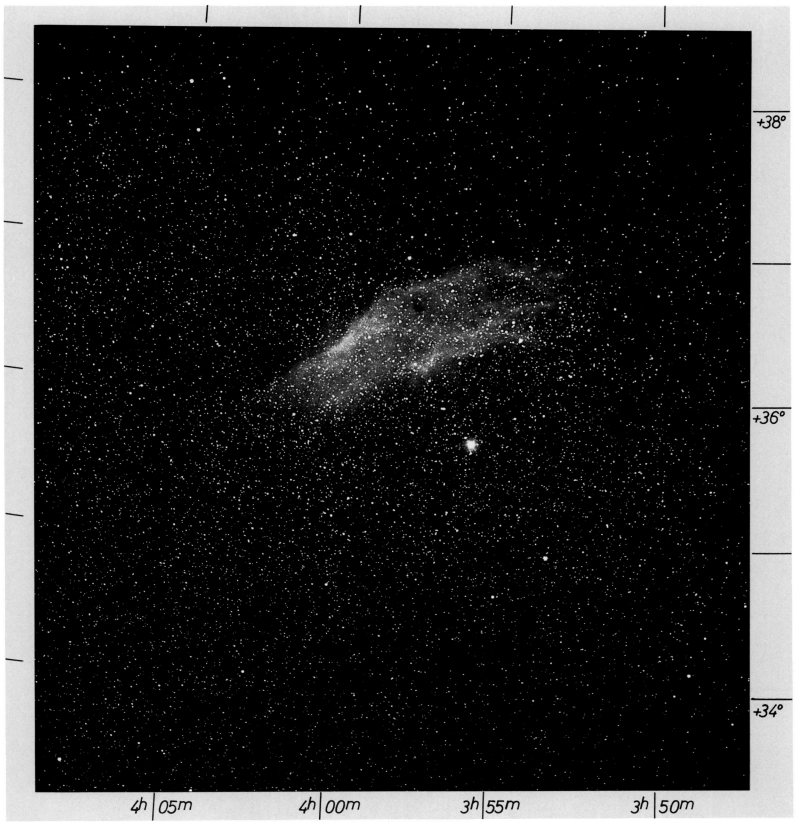

+38°

+36°

+34°

4ʰ|05m   4ʰ|00m   3ʰ|55m   3ʰ|50m

Continued from page 30

The difference in the ordinates between the H-R and color-magnitude diagrams is the distance modulus m-M (apparent magnitude minus absolute magnitude), which is simply a shifting of the zero point, depending entirely on the distance. Even if the distance of only one member of a cluster is known, it is immediately possible to convert the CMD into an H-R diagram. On the other hand, the distance can be derived from the position of the main sequence in the cluster's CMD, assuming that the cluster's stars are similar in chemical and physical structure to those in the vicinity of the Sun, whose positions in the main sequence of the H-R diagram are well known.

Such an assumption cannot always be applied, and another method gives better results. The main sequence of the CMD is compared to its equivalent in the H-R diagram for a nearby cluster whose distance has been firmly established by direct measurements (e.g. trigonometric parallaxes, proper motions with convergent points), as in the case of the Hyades (opposite). Due to the great distances of clusters, compared to stars in the Sun's vicinity, it is necessary to take into careful consideration the effect of interstellar absorption — whether distances are derived from a CMD or from the magnitudes and color indexes of the stars. Because of the irregular distribution of interstellar matter, the amount of absorption cannot be accurately predicted. The farther a cluster is, the greater are the difficulties.

When comparing the color-magnitude diagrams of different clusters, one finds striking variations in the distribution of the spectral types; that is, there are great differences in the color indexes of the stars. On page 14 the diagrams of 11 clusters have been converted into Hertzsprung-Russell diagrams. They have been drawn in such a way that the red ends of their main sequences, containing the dwarf stars of spectral type K and M (color index $+0^m8$ to $+1^m4$), are overlapping.

Continued

Hyades (Mel 25)

The Hyades is the nearest galactic star cluster. Since it is near the star Aldebaran = α Tauri (1^m1), which is not one of its members, it is easily located. Although the field reproduced here has a diameter of nearly 5°, one does not get the impression of seeing a cluster. This is primarily due to the low space density of the Hyades stars and also because we ourselves are situated near the fringe of the cluster, whose nearest stars are 88 light-years from us, the farthest being about 150 light-years away.

The Hyades is a perfect example of a moving star cluster. If one draws arrows on a chart to show the amount and direction of the proper motion of each member star, all these arrows converge toward a point, which J. A. Pearce gives as $\alpha = 6^h7^m2$, $\delta = +9°\,06'$, just east of Betelgeuse (α Orionis). The Hyades stars are traveling together through space on parallel paths with a velocity of 43.2 km/sec, and the observed convergence is the result of perspective. By knowing the convergent point, it is not only possible to establish the distance to the cluster's center, but also to its individual members, so that we get a true picture of the spatial arrangement of the Hyades.

Other Hyades members are far outside the photograph reproduced here. Even in completely different regions of the sky, stars have been found to be moving toward the Hyades convergent point. This physically related group has been named the Taurus stream, and so far 350 members have been counted. Over the years the proper motions of many very faint stars in Taurus have been studied. Thus, in 1962, W. J. Luyten found 45 new Hyades members.

Since accurate distances of the individual stars are known, it has been possible to compile a fairly complete Hertzsprung-Russell diagram of the Hyades. J. Titus and W. W. Morgan found that this agrees well with a corresponding diagram of stars in the vicinity of the Sun. Another equally complete diagram was compiled by H. L. Johnson, R. I. Mitchell, and B. Iriarte, which can be used as the basis to establish the distances and ages of other open clusters.

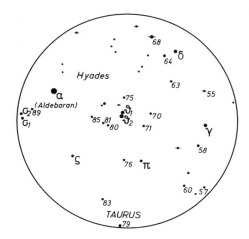

Mel 25 Hyades
$4^h16^m7, +15°31'$

CI, 0^m8, 245★
$\phi = 400'$, type: c

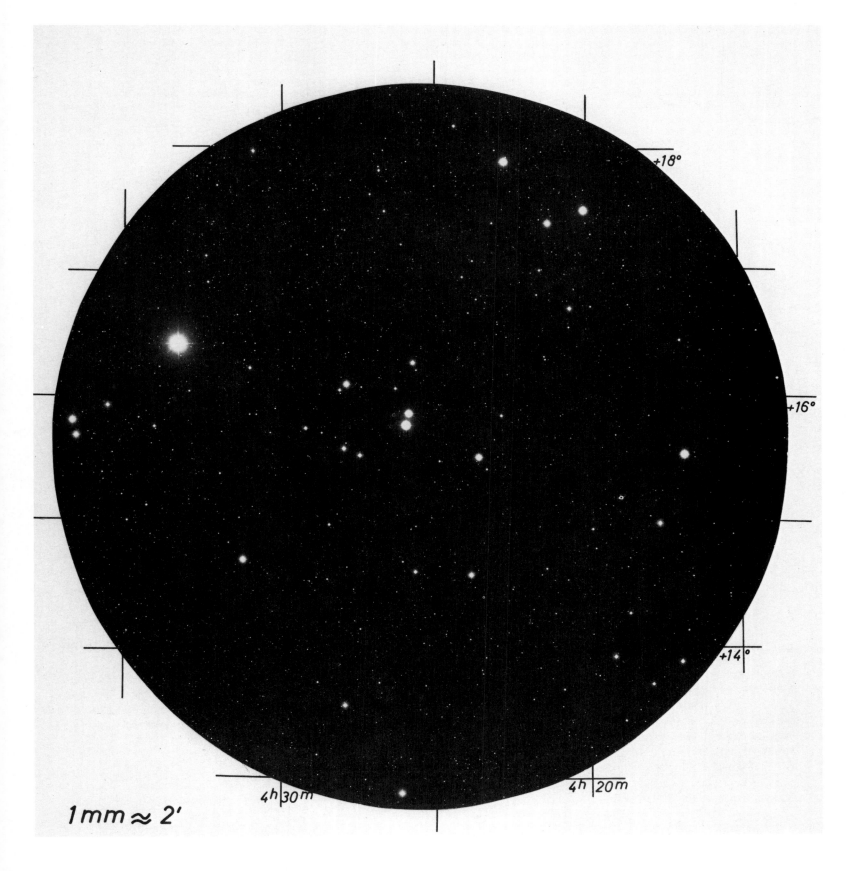

1mm ≈ 2'

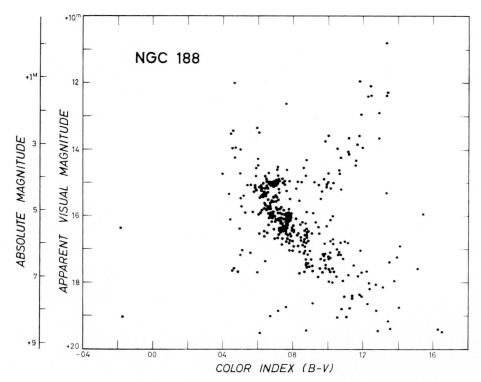

Color-magnitude diagram of star cluster NGC 188
according to A. R. Sandage (*Astrophysical Journal,
135,* pp. 333-348, 1962).
The vertical scale of absolute magnitudes corre-
sponds to a distance of 1,500 parsecs.

*It will be noticed that the main lines of the different clusters run together along the lower part of the main se-
quence, but bend off in a knee at various points toward and into the giant branch. For NGC 188 this takes
place at about the level of stars that are similar to the Sun (spectral type G2), and the bend is S-shaped. In*

Continued

M79 = NGC 1904

M79 in Lepus was discovered by Méchain on October 26,
1780. Messier described this rather concentrated globular
cluster as "a nebula without stars and having a bright
center," but W. Herschel partially resolved the cluster into
individual stars. Like so many other globular clusters, M79
has been studied in great detail. The results for 132
globular clusters have been concisely summarized by G. Alcaino (*Astronomical Journal, 89,* p. 491, 1977). As the most
reliable distance for M79, he cites 11.4 kpc.

Half a degree southwest of M79 is the double star
41 Leporis = ADS 3954, whose components A = 5^m4 and
B = 6^m7 are $3\rlap{.}''2$ from one another. A third star (9^m2) is $61''$
from the primary component A, and to its east. All three can
be detected in a small telescope.

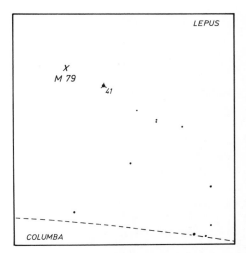

LEPUS

X
M 79

41

COLUMBA

M79 **NGC 1904**

$5^h22^m2, -24°34'$

Gl, 8^m4, Sp: F3
$\phi = 7'.8$, type: V

-24°

-25°

-26°

-27°

5^h 20^m 5^h 15^m

the case of the Coma star cluster, there is a gradual deviation of the main line at spectral type F, and the actual knee is among the A stars. For the Double Cluster h and χ Persei the knee lies at the highest point; it is only slightly bent toward the right. The color-magnitude diagram of NGC 2362 seems to have no knee at all, if one does not regard the gradual right bend as such.

The fact that the different patterns in color-magnitude diagrams have a direct connection with the evolution of clusters was discovered by A. R. Sandage and M. Schwarzschild in 1953 and by H. L. Johnson in 1954. It is believed that when a cluster forms, all its stars are distributed along the main sequence and have almost the same chemical composition. They are all using hydrogen as their thermonuclear fuel. During the later stages of their development they have changed all their available hydrogen into helium. The more massive and brighter a star is, the faster this happens.

The hot blue stars at the top part of the main sequence move quickly into the red giant region of the Hertzsprung-Russell diagram, while the redder stars in the lower parts of the HRD do not move off the main sequence until much later. This is why a knee appears in the main sequence of a stellar cluster. With increasing age, the knee moves farther and farther down the main sequence. This can be seen in the diagram on page 14. From the position of the knee, or "turn-off point," the age of an open cluster can be deduced when its age has not been established by other means. How greatly the ages of a few well-known clusters vary according to different authors, however, is illustrated by the table on page 68.

Continued on page 68

M36 = NGC 1960, M38 = NGC 1912

This Milky Way field in Auriga contains six open clusters, all of which, except NGC 1907, are probably associated, since their distances are all between 850 and 1,400 pc. Messier first saw NGC 1960 = M36 on September 2, 1764, and NGC 1912 = M38 about three weeks later. However, the discovery of both clusters is credited to Le Gentil in 1749. Both M36 and M38 are quite impressive objects even when viewed through a small telescope at low magnification.

M38, the richest cluster in this picture, has, according to G. A. Mills, 340 members and is only surpassed by M37 = NGC 2099 (page 69), which also belongs to the Auriga group. M38 and the smaller, concentrated cluster NGC 1907, which lies ½° to its south, form a double object, similar to the two clusters M35 and NGC 2158 (page 71).

Here, just as in the other case, the unequal distances of the two clusters lead to a noticeable difference in their apparent diameters and concentrations. V. V. Lavdovskij established the distances for M38 and NGC 1907 at 850 and 2,500 pc, respectively.

Few details are known about IC 410 and NGC 1931, two open star clusters involved in reflection nebulae. On our photograph, only the former looks like a cluster. Perhaps these two are very young clusters similar to the Pleiades, in which the gas and dust that gave birth to the stars has not yet completely dissipated. The nebulae can be seen much better on the original negative than on the reproduction. They are difficult to observe visually.

The small anonymous group of stars slightly east of φ Aurigae (5^m3) was named "Stock 8" in 1956.

Stock 8
5ʰ24ᵐ8, +34°25′

Cl, 10ᵐ2, 45 ★
φ = 4′, type: f

IC 410
5ʰ19ᵐ3, +33°28′

Cl + N, 10ᵐ0, 80 ★
φ = 21′, type: c

M36 NGC 1960
5ʰ32ᵐ0, +34°07′

Cl, 6ᵐ5, 88 ★
φ = 16′, type: f

NGC 1931
5ʰ28ᵐ1, +34°13′

N + Cl, 9ᵐ7, 10 ★
3′ × 3′, type: c

NGC 1907
5ʰ24ᵐ7, +35°17′

Cl, 10ᵐ3, 40 ★
φ = 5′, type: f

M38 NGC 1912
5ʰ25ᵐ3, +35°48′

Cl, 7ᵐ0, 340 ★
φ = 18′, type: e

M 38
NGC 1907
M 36
NGC 1931
Stock 8
IC 410
AURIGA

+36°
+35°
+34°
+33°

5ʰ30ᵐ   5ʰ25ᵐ   5ʰ20ᵐ

Three-color composite photograph of the LMC by the author. The Tarantula nebula is the largest of the many red emission nebulae visible in this satellite galaxy of the Milky Way.

Large Magellanic Cloud (LMC)

The Large Magellanic Cloud is a galaxy like the Small Cloud. In the sky they are about 20° apart, but today there is no longer any doubt that the two are physically joined, for F. J. Kerr and G. de Vaucouleurs were able to prove with the aid of radio telescopes that there is a bridge of neutral hydrogen between the two clouds. The distance of the Large Cloud, calculated from the periods of its Cepheid variable stars, has been set at 190,000 light-years, about equal to that of the Small Cloud. Its mass has been set at 5 to 15 billion suns.

Until 1955, it was generally believed that the Large Cloud was an example of the irregular type of galaxies, which is also the impression one gets from the facing photograph. However, the bar-shaped formation in the brightest parts of the Cloud has often led to controversial discussions about its type. In 1955, G. de Vaucouleurs started studying the structure and extent of the Large Cloud. He photographed the area within 20° of the Cloud with an aerial camera of the Aero-Ektar type (17.5-cm focal length), and from photometry of the negatives he found an almost circular nucleus as well as one very long and several shorter spiral arms.

The nucleus has a diameter of about 8°, comparable to the area of the facing picture taken with the Schmidt camera, but the whole cloud can be followed to about 10° from the center. The Small Cloud then becomes its companion.

Practically every common type of object in our own galaxy has been discovered in the Magellanic Clouds in great numbers: single stars of many types, variables, open and globular star clusters, emission nebulae, planetary nebulae, and interstellar absorbing matter. K. G. Henize counted 415 emission nebulae in the Large Cloud and 117 in the Small Cloud. E. M. Lindsay and D. J. Mullan confirmed 65 planetary nebulae in the Large Cloud. The total number of recognized clusters is nearly 900, according to H. Shapley and E. M. Lindsay. Some of the more prominent clusters have been given NGC numbers and are marked on the reference chart.

The brightest emission nebula is NGC 2070 (Tarantula nebula), also known as the 30 Doradus nebula. It is the largest emission nebula known anywhere, with a diameter of some 800 light-years. Radio observations have set its mass at nearly 500,000 suns. At its center is a cluster of over 100 hot supergiant stars.

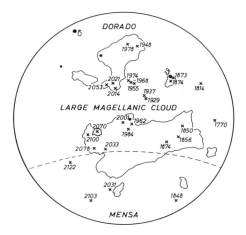

LMC
Large Magellanic Cloud
5ʰ24ᵐ0, −69°08′

Ga, 0ᵐ5, 8° × 8°
type: SB(s)m(Vau)

NGC 2070
Tarantula nebula
5ʰ39ᵐ9, −69°04′

N, 31′ × 30′
Sp: e

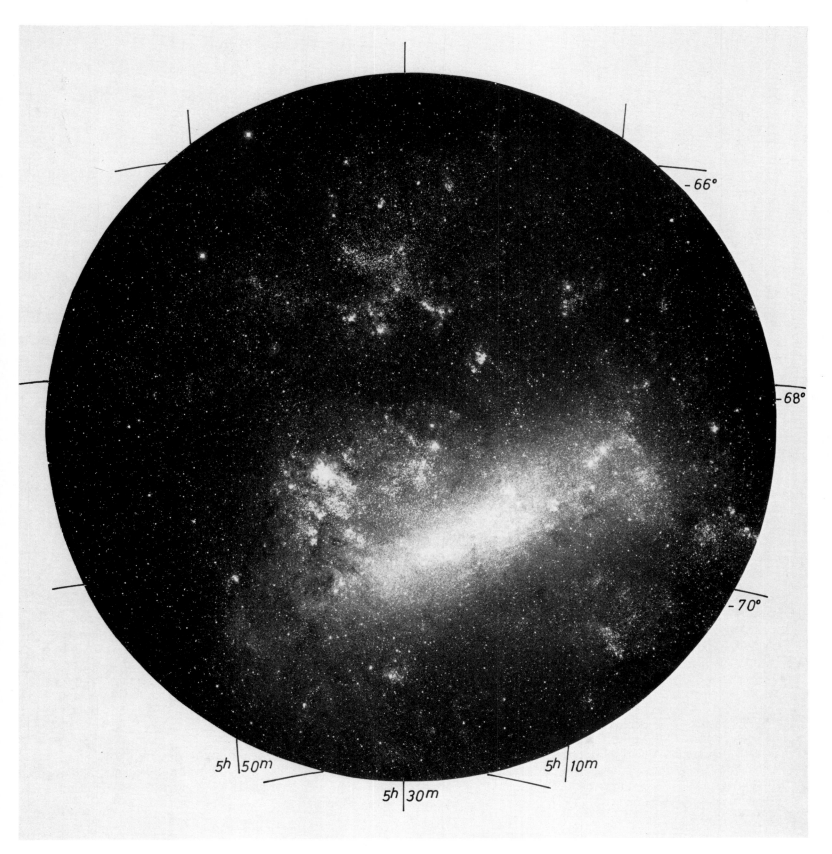

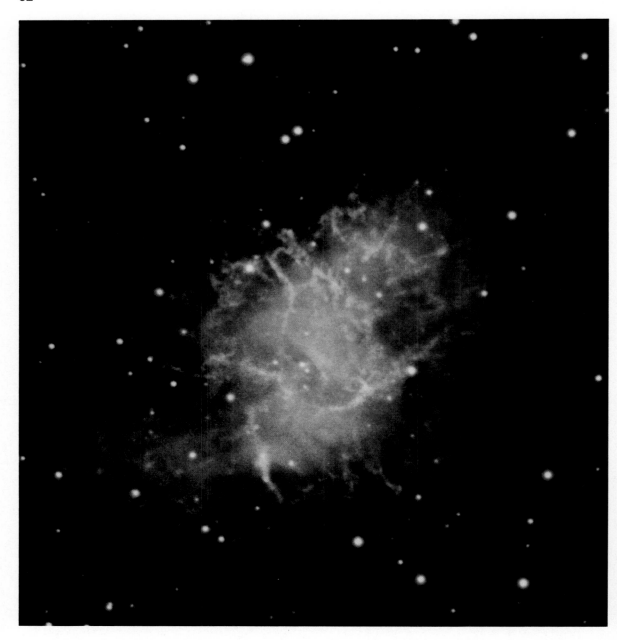

M1
This three-color composite picture was made by the dye-transfer method from three black-and-white exposures taken through color filters with the 36-inch Crossley reflector at Lick Observatory. The reddish filaments shine primarily by hydrogen, sulfur, and nitrogen light, the outlying greenish tendrils by oxygen. The hazy blue is synchrotron radiation.

M1 = NGC 1952 (Crab nebula)

M1, generally known as the Crab nebula, is situated about 1° north and slightly west of ζ Tauri (3^{m}0). The nebula was first seen by J. Bevis in 1731, and Messier found it in 1758 while observing a comet. He described M1 as "being of whitish light and spreading like a flame." Small telescopes show M1 as a faintly luminous oval spot without structure.

In 1921, C. O. Lampland at Lowell Observatory and J. C. Duncan at Mount Wilson Observatory discovered from a comparison of old and new photographs that the Crab nebula is expanding radially. Later studies of the expansion rate indicated that the nebula exploded outward from one spot just 900 years ago. The Crab nebula is, in fact, the debris of a bright supernova seen in the year 1054, mentioned in Chinese and Japanese chronicles, but of which no European record is known.

The real physical research on the Crab nebula did not start until 1942, when W. Baade took some photographs through the 100-inch Mount Wilson telescope with a red hydrogen-alpha filter and discovered a system of filamentary structures extending far beyond the central part of the nebula. These filaments can be seen above.

The central part, which has a continuous spectrum, coincides with the intense radio source Taurus A. The Soviet astronomer I. S. Shklovskij suggested in 1953 that both the optical continuum and the radio emission are synchrotron radiation, caused by the acceleration of very fast electrons in magnetic fields. The existence of these fields was quickly proven by observations that the continuum light is strongly polarized.

A 16th-magnitude star at the center of the Crab nebula was discovered to emit intense pulses of radio energy, light, and X-rays every 0.033 second. This pulsar is a tiny, fantastically dense neutron star with an intense magnetic field; the star rotates at the pulse rate. The neutron star is the stellar remnant of the 1054 supernova, and the gradual slowing of its rotation provides the energy by which the Crab nebula shines. According to V. Trimble, the distance to the Crab nebula is 1,930 pc.

Two minutes in right ascension east of M1 is the double star ADS 4200, whose components A = 7^{m}2 and B = 7^{m}8 are separated by 3″6. They can be easily resolved in moderate-size instruments.

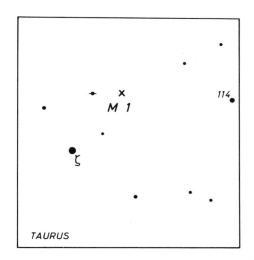

TAURUS

M1   NGC 1952
$5^h31^m5, \ +21°59'$

SNR, $8^m4, \ m_\star = 15.9$
$6' \times 4'$

+22°

+21°

+20°

5ʰ | 35ᵐ   5ʰ | 30ᵐ   5ʰ | 25ᵐ

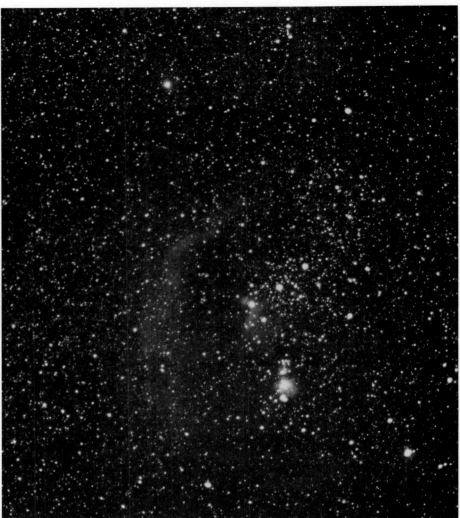

Two views of Orion, by David Healy. *Right:* a 50-mm f/1.8 lens shows most of the constellation in this 10-minute exposure on GAF 500 film (now discontinued). Note the dim red glow of Barnard's Loop surrounding the central portion of the constellation. *Above:* a 135-mm f/2.5 lens captures the Belt and Sword region in this 50-minute exposure on Fujichrome R-100. Compare the nebulae around ζ Orionis with the photographs on pages 66 and 67.

M42 = NGC 1976, M43 = NGC 1982 (Great Orion nebula)

The Orion nebula, situated beneath the middle star ε (1ᵐ8) of Orion's Belt, forms together with the adjoining nebulae and four open star clusters the "Sword" of Orion. Viewed with the naked eye it looks like a diffuse spot, but with binoculars or a small telescope, one can see details of the nebulae and many individual stars. In particular, near the center of the large nebula, which includes both NGC 1976 = M42 and NGC 1982 = M43, one finds the Trapezium, a striking multiple star known as ϑ Orionis or ADS 4186, with its components A = 6ᵐ8, B = 8ᵐ0, C = 5ᵐ4, and D = 6ᵐ9. Above the large nebula (center at declination − 5° 25′) there is a smaller nebula, NGC 1973, -75, -77. It is, however, only an offshoot of the larger nebula and is optically separated by a bridge of nonluminous interstellar matter.

Probably the Orion nebula was known as a diffuse object in antiquity. The first mention of it as a nebula originates from N. Peiresc in the year 1610, and the first full description that included the Trapezium was given by C. Huygens in 1656. Messier entered M42 and M43 into his catalogue on March 4, 1769.

Of the clusters belonging to the nebula, NGC 1981 (declination − 4°28′) is easily recognizable as the most northern in the facing photograph. The cluster NGC 1977 is embedded in nebulosity. The largest cluster, NGC 1976 with 467 members, is draped round the Trapezium in the central part of the nebula, and becomes masked by the nebula after a very short exposure time. This cluster contains variables of the T Tauri type up to spectral type *A*0, from which it was concluded that the cluster and its associated nebula are very young, about one to two million years. By measuring photographic plates showing stars in the region of the large nebula, K. Aa. Strand was able to detect an expansion of the cluster. This led him to surmise an age of only 300,000 years, and together with the radial velocity (3.6 km/sec), a distance of 600 pc. So far it has not been possible to prove whether the nebula is expanding similarly. The fourth cluster, NGC 1980, lies south of the large nebula in the vicinity of ι Orionis (2ᵐ8).

The Orion nebula presents difficult problems for the astrophotographer. Because the brightness diminishes enormously from center to edge, a short exposure shows only a small central portion. On the other hand, though a long exposure shows structural features extending out to the edge of the field, the central part is strongly overexposed and all details there are lost.

The nebula consists mostly of hydrogen and helium, with a couple percent of other gaseous elements and dust. A large part of the hydrogen is excited by the ultraviolet rays emitted by the hot stars, thus making the gas luminous. Only this part of the nebula is visible. In extensive regions around the nebula, dustlike matter is recognizable through its absorbing effect, producing some regions that are particularly poor in faint stars.

NGC 1981
x
NGC 1973-5-7
x

M 43
x
x
M 42
x
NGC 1980

ORION

NGC 1980
5ʰ32ᵐ8, −5°57′

Cl + N, 2ᵐ5, 35★
φ = 14′

M42 NGC 1976
M43 NGC 1982
5ʰ33ᵐ0, −5°21′

N + Cl, 3ᵐ0, 85′ × 60′
Sp: e

NGC 1981
5ʰ32ᵐ8, −4°28′

Cl + N, 8ᵐ0, 45★
φ = 18′

NGC 1973-5-7
5ʰ32ᵐ9, −4°50′

N + Cl, 6ᵐ5, 45′ × 35′
Sp: e

−5°

−6°

5ʰ 35ᵐ

5ʰ 30ᵐ

The ζ Orionis region. Three-color composite print made from plates taken with the 1.2-meter United Kingdom Schmidt camera at Siding Spring, Australia. Photo copyright 1981, The Royal Observatory, Edinburgh.

M78 = NGC 2068 and ζ Orionis

The region around ζ Orionis (2^{m}0) is a particularly interesting skyscape for the observer of nebulae. Here interstellar gas and dust are irregularly dispersed and partly overlapping. Some of the gas shines as luminous nebulae, primarily in the neighborhood of bright stars of early spectral types; it shows an emission spectrum (e in the table on page 67). The dust is observed as dark material, either in front of luminous masses of gas (IC 434) or as regions almost devoid of faint stars, as in the center and lower-left half of the facing picture. It sometimes reflects the light of nearby stars and then shows a continuous spectrum (c in table on page 67). NGC 2024, in close proximity to ζ Orionis, is photographically the most prominent nebula in the picture, but difficult to observe visually. W. Herschel discovered NGC 2024 in 1786 and described it as "a wonderful dark spot divided into three or four parts, and enclosed in mild luminous nebulous matter."

South of ζ Orionis is IC 434, an extensive cloud of gas excited to shine by ultraviolet radiation from σ Orionis (spectrum O9.5), seen in the lower right corner above. Projected onto the gas is a dark cloud, the well-known Horsehead nebula, or B33, the outer edges of which are also illuminated by starlight. The emission nebula NGC 2023 and the star HD 37903 (7^{m}8) are also partially covered by the dust cloud, whereas the gaseous nebula IC 435 and the star HD 38087 (8^{m}2) are outside it. On the other hand, IC 431 and IC 432, north of ζ Orionis, are stars with reflecting dust envelopes surrounding them, similar to the three objects at the northern edge of the field: M78, NGC 2071, and IC 426. M78 = NGC 2068 was discovered by Méchain in 1780.

The physical data on the nebulae shown in the table on page 67 was taken from the Catalogue of Nebulae by S. Cederblad.

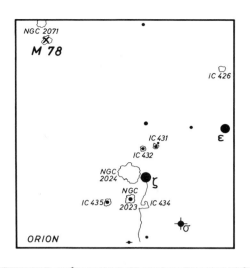

M78 NGC 2068
5ʰ44ᵐ2, +0°12'

N, 8' × 6', Sp: c

Nebula	α	δ	Dim:	Sp:
IC 426	5ʰ34ᵐ3	−0°16'	5'× 5'	c
IC 431	5 37.8	−1 29	5 × 3	c
IC 432	5 38.5	−1 31	8 × 4	c
IC 434	5 38.6	−2 26	60 × 10	c + e
2023	5 39.2	−2 15	10 × 10	c + e
2024	5 39.4	−1 52	30 × 30	e
IC 435	5 40.5	−2 20	4 × 3	e
2071	5 44.6	+0 17	4 × 3	c

OPEN CLUSTER AGES			
Star Cluster (and page)	Millions of years (A. R. Sandage)	Millions of years (W. Lohmann)	Millions of years (G. Linga catalogue)
NGC 2362 (not shown)	0.8	20	25
IC 4665 (not shown)	—	60	36
h + χ Persei (page 39)	1.0	—	5.6 + 3.2
Pleiades (page 51)	20	100	78
M41 (page 79)	60	—	190
M11 (page 197)	60	290	220
Coma cluster (page 123)	300	—	400
M39 (page 229)	—	300	270
Hyades (page 55)	400	1,100	660
Praesepe (page 95)	400	1,500	660
NGC 752 (not shown)	1,000	2,700	1,100
M67 (page 97)	5,000	5,000	3,200
NGC 188 (page 15)	12,000	—	5,000

The ages of open clusters are still not known with great assurance. Ages in the first column are given by A. R. Sandage (Stellar Population, page 46, published by D. J. K. O'Connell, Amsterdam, 1958); data from this source were used for the color-magnitude diagram on page 14. Ages in the second column are from W. Lohmann (Zeitschrift für Astrophysik 42, p. 114-119, 1957). Those in the last column are from a 1981 compilation of open cluster data prepared from critically selected sources by G. Linga of Lund Observatory, Sweden, and should be considered the most up-to-date.

M37 = NGC 2099

The open cluster M37 is situated in Auriga in front of a fairly uniform background of Milky Way stars. M37 is the richest and most beautiful of the three bright clusters in Auriga (see also page 59) and can be resolved into stars with a telescope of 8-cm aperture and a magnification of 40. Near its center is a very striking orange star. Messier discovered M37 on September 2, 1764, and W. Herschel called it a magnificent object. It is true that the observer of this object finds it an inspiring sight.

In 1963, E. Brosterhus compiled a color-magnitude diagram from photographic three-color photometry of 2,291 stars in and around M37. From this he estimated the cluster's age to be about 200 million years and its distance as 1,450 pc. In 1970, G. L. Hagen's critical evaluation of all the data gave 1,400 pc for the distance of M37. However, due to the many faint stars in the Milky Way, the exact number of cluster members is not known.

M37 **NGC 2099**
5ʰ49ᵐ0, +32°33′

Cl, 6ᵐ2, 590 ★
ϕ = 24′, type: f

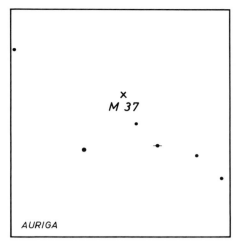

AURIGA

Globular star clusters (Gl)

Unlike an open cluster, a globular cluster is a symmetrical, compact spheroid containing a very large number of stars. Their total numbers are difficult to determine because the inner parts are so concentrated that even the most powerful telescopes can hardly resolve them. Estimates made from photometric measurements put the number of members in some globulars far above 200,000.

As far as a globular cluster is resolvable, we see only its brighter stars. Due to the great distance of these clusters, their dwarf stars are too faint to be seen, and only estimates of their numbers can be made. Because the star density usually decreases smoothly away from the center, an estimate of a globular's diameter should be regarded as a minimum value. Today the known apparent diameters lie between 1 and 65 minutes of arc. Their apparent total magnitudes (m_p) range from 6^m5 to fainter than 13^m0. These physical data, as well as the integrated spectral type (Sp) of the cluster and its classfication by H. Shapley and H. Sawyer Hogg — ranging from I to XII in order of diminishing density — have been taken from a summary report by H. Sawyer Hogg on 125 globular clusters, all those known in 1963. Together with the positions in right ascension and declination for 1950.0, the reader can find all these data above each photograph that contains a globular cluster.

Continued on page 78

M35 and NGC 2158
Photographed by Evered Kreimer of Prescott, Arizona, using a 12½-inch f/7 reflector and chilled High Speed Ektachrome.

M35 = NGC 2168

M35 is a large and bright open star cluster of regular form in the constellation Gemini. Even when viewed through binoculars the cluster is an interesting object, but with a small telescope and low magnification it becomes a very attractive sight.

How to judge the relative distance of two similar objects from their apparent sizes and brightnesses is well shown by M35 and its neighbor, the very concentrated cluster NGC 2158. While M35 is "only" 850 pc from us, NGC 2158 is at a distance of 8,100 pc, or about 10 times farther away. Their angular diameters are 29′ and 4′, respectively. (A similar contrast is shown by the star clusters M38 and NGC 1907, page 59, which are also very different in distance.) In order to see NGC 2158 it is necessary to use a telescope of at least 10-cm aperture.

Here as in Auriga, other small clusters like NGC 2129 and IC 2157 are found in a relatively small sky field.

IC 2157
6ʰ01ᵐ8, +24°02′

Cl, 8ᵐ5, 20 ★
φ = 4′, type: d

M35 NGC 2168
6ʰ05ᵐ7, +24°20′

Cl, 5ᵐ3, 130 ★
φ = 29′, type: e

NGC 2158
6ʰ04ᵐ3, +24°06′

Cl, 12ᵐ5, 40 ★
φ = 4′, type: g

NGC 2129
5ʰ58ᵐ1, +23°18′

Cl, 7ᵐ2, 25 ★
φ = 5′, type: d

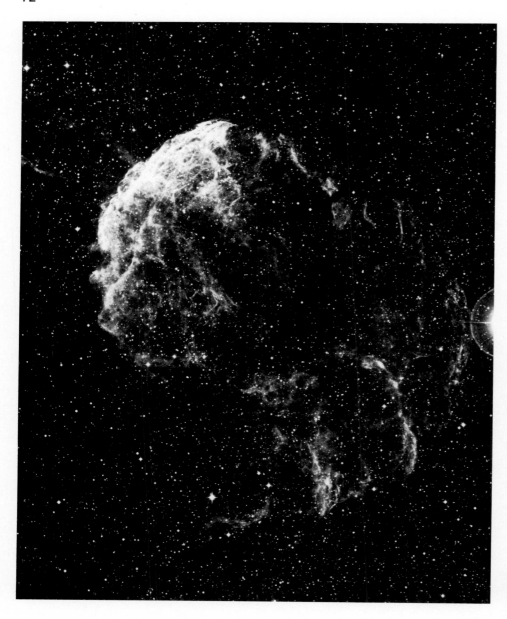

IC 443
from a 48-inch Schmidt camera exposure at Mount Palomar.

IC 443, IC 444

The wreath of filamentary nebulosity known as IC 443 is the remnant of a prehistoric supernova explosion and is rather similar to the great Veil nebula in Cygnus. Radial velocity measurements of IC 433 show that it is expanding with a velocity of 65 km per second. This object is also a well-observed radio source known as 3C 157, whose radio emission is strongest from the regions where the optical filaments are brightest. The pulsar 0611+22 is located only 0°.6 from the center of IC 443, and the X-ray source 2U 0601+21 also appears to be associated with this supernova remnant. According to S. van den Bergh, the distance of IC 443 is still uncertain.

Near the bright star μ Geminorum on the sky, but not associated with it, is the large, faint reflection nebula IC 444, which is illuminated by the 7th-magnitude star GC 8106, spectral class *B9*. Its distance is about 250 pc.

Both IC 443 and IC 444 were discovered independently by M. Wolf in Germany and E. E. Barnard in the United States.

IC 443
6ʰ13ᵐ9, +22°48'

N, 5' × 5', Sp: c

IC 444
6ʰ17ᵐ5, +23°19'

N, 27' × 5', Sp: c

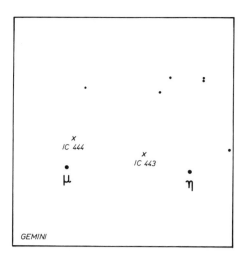

The Rosette nebula, photographed with the 1.34-meter (clear aperture) Schmidt camera at Karl Schwartzschild Observatory, Tautenberg, East Germany. This 80-minute red-light exposure shows many dark globules. Kodak 103a-E film, RG11 filter.

NGC 2237-39 (Rosette nebula)

In the constellation Monoceros, which is not very rich in bright stars, lies NGC 2237-39, generally called the "Rosette nebula." It is an extended emission nebula surrounding the open star cluster NGC 2244.

The Rosette nebula is a birthplace of new stars and perhaps even of star clusters. In 1962, H. L. Johnson compiled a color-magnitude diagram of 46 hot stars in NGC 2244 and found the cluster to be a very young one. Surprisingly enough, the densest part of the nebula is not in the region of the cluster, as is the case in the Orion nebula (page 65). Instead, the dense parts form a misshapen ring around the cluster's center. One gets an impression that the missing

gas from the center has either been blown outward or was used up in the formation of the cluster stars. In the bright northern part of the nebula are thin elongated dark shapes, called "elephant trunks." S. R. Pottasch has suggested that new stars are being born in them. Filaments of neutral hydrogen are cut off and compressed into globules by the hot, expanding ionized hydrogen, and, after contracting further under their own gravity, the globules form into hot stars.

F. D. Kahn and T. K. Menon have studied the physical processes in the nebula, and put the age of the inner ionized zone at only 50,000 years.

NGC 2237-9
Rosette nebula
6ʰ29ᵐ6, +5°05′

N + Cl, 6ᵐ5, 64′ × 61′
Sp: e

NGC 2244
6ʰ29ᵐ7, +4°54′

Cl, 5ᵐ2, 46 ★
φ = 27′, type: c

NGC 2237-9
×
×
NGC 2244

MONOCEROS

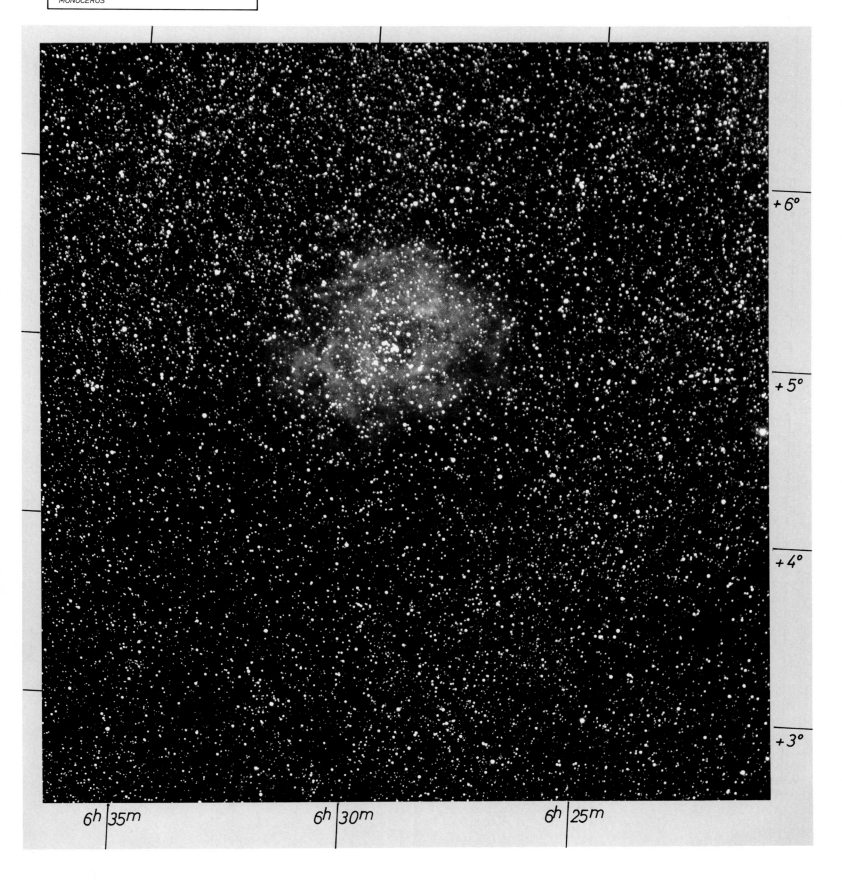

+6°

+5°

+4°

+3°

6ʰ 35ᵐ   6ʰ 30ᵐ   6ʰ 25ᵐ

NGC 2264
Hale Observatories photograph.
Compare with the photo on page 6.

NGC 2264 (Cone nebula), NGC 2261

In this area of Monoceros, the galactic star cluster NGC 2264 is the most prominent object. Its members are mostly grouped south of the brilliant star S Monocerotis (4^{m}7) and are surrounded by extended nebulae, which are excited to shine by the hot O and B stars.

Numerous patches devoid of stars verify that the nebula around S Mon reaches far out into space. Long ago, the German astronomer M. Wolf called attention to "empty" places in this field. On photographs he made counts of stars in different magnitude intervals and thus determined the approximate distance of the obscuring nebula.

S. Vasilevsky, W. L. Sanders, and A. G. A. Balz, Jr., studied the proper motions of 245 stars in NGC 2264 and recognized 140 members, from which they drew a color-magnitude diagram that showed the cluster to be very young. The distance of the cluster is 850 pc, according to M. F. Walker. E. Raimond found from measurements of the radio emission at 21 cm that the total mass of the nebula is 8,000 suns or less, and its age is 5 million years. According to Raimond, the Cone nebula and the nearby Rosette nebula (page 75) together form the center of the associations Mon I and Mon II,

containing one of the largest clouds of neutral hydrogen known in our galaxy.

NGC 2261 is one of the most unusual objects in the sky. Shaped like the tail of a comet, it is known as Hubble's variable nebula. In our picture it can be seen about 1° below center and a little to the left. In the "head" of the nebula is the irregular variable R Monocerotis (10^{m}0 — 13^{m}0), whose fluctuating light directly influences the brightness and apparent shape of the nebula. As star and nebula show the same spectrum, the latter must shine by reflection. From infrared investigations of the nebula, F. J. Low and B. S. Smith deduced the existence of a circumstellar dust cloud around R Monocerotis. They concluded that R Monocerotis is a collapsing protostar that is about to form into a planetary system. Hubble's variable nebula was the first object officially photographed with the 200-inch Hale telescope.

In the field are two other nebulae, NGC 2245 and NGC 2247, and two small open clusters, NGC 2251 and NGC 2259, which are surrounded by nebulae too faint to appear in this reproduction.

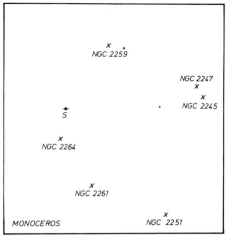

NGC 2259
6ʰ35ᵐ8, +10°55'

Cl, 10ᵐ8, 20 ★
φ = 3', type: d

NGC 2261
Hubble's variable neb.
6ʰ36ᵐ4, +8°46'

N, 10-12ᵐ, Dim: var
type: ce

NGC 2264
Cone nebula
6ʰ38ᵐ2, +9°57'

Cl + N, 4ᵐ4, 140 ★
φ = 30', Dim_N: 60' × 30'
type_Cl: c, type_N: e

NGC 2251
6ʰ32ᵐ0, +8°24'

Cl, 8ᵐ5, 35 ★
φ = 10', type: d

NGC 2247
6ʰ30ᵐ3, +10°23'

N, 8ᵐ5, 4' × 3'
type: c

NGC 2245
6ʰ29ᵐ9, +10°12'

N, m★ = 10.8,
5' × 3',
type: c

Continued from page 70

Globular and open clusters differ not only in appearance but also in physical characteristics. Unlike galactic clusters, globulars are not concentrated toward the galactic plane and can be found in all galactic latitudes. They do, however, concentrate in the direction of our Milky Way system's center. This is partially the effect of our observation point, since the Sun occupies an eccentric position about 10,000 parsecs away from the galactic center. Taken as a whole, the globular clusters form an almost spherical halo around the Milky Way system, being in some respects its outposts.

A number of globular clusters in the constellation Sagittarius are seen from our point of view to lie in front of the galactic center. Other globulars lying behind it are hidden by the extensive dark material in the neighborhood of the center.

The most distant globular clusters are some 50,000 pc away, roughly 1,000 times farther than the nearest open clusters. On the other hand, there are also some globular clusters closer than 5,000 pc, in the range where the most distant open clusters lie. The globular clusters (together with the RR Lyrae stars) are situated far outside the spiral arms of the Milky Way. They consist of ancient Population II stars, whereas the bright stars and open clusters in the spiral arms are of the younger Population I.

Another very striking difference between open and globular clusters is that the latter contain a great number of intrinsically bright variable stars. Their periods of light fluctuation correlate strongly with their absolute magnitudes, or luminosities. Thus the distances of globular clusters can be photometrically established in the same way as was first done with the Cepheid stars in the Small Magellanic Cloud (page 25). Naturally at such great distances the dimming effect of interstellar matter plays an important role, and it is therefore not surprising that there are large discrepancies between distances calculated by different authors.

For the brighter globular clusters, and those nearer to us, color-magnitude diagrams give an idea of their ages and development, and also provide a check on the distances derived from variable stars. These diagrams show only slight differences from globular to globular, but they are quite unlike color-magnitude diagrams of open clusters. There is no red bottom part of the main sequence in diagrams of globular clusters, because the yellow and red dwarfs are not observable individually at such great distances. The upper region of the main sequence is curtailed, similar to the older open clusters. After an S-shaped knee is formed, a well-defined giant branch extends to the extreme red giants and, unlike in the open clusters, is completely populated along its length. The yellow and blue giant stars form a generally clear-cut, almost horizontal branch in the diagram, on which the pulsating variables also lie. From the position of the knee in the diagrams of globular clusters, we can deduce that the globulars are extremely old, older than the open clusters M67 and NGC 188 (see page 14). It has not yet been possible, even for the few globulars with well-defined color-magnitude diagrams, to derive an age sequence from the minor differences in their main sequences.

A table of all globular clusters appearing in this book, with their sizes and brightnesses, can be found on page 140.

M41 = NGC 2287

If one points a stationary telescope 4° south of Sirius, in about two minutes diurnal motion will dramatically carry the galactic star cluster M41 into sight. This cluster is an extended, bright, and fairly rich object, particularly suitable for the novice observer with binoculars. In the cluster's center one can see a remarkable red star. A. N. Cox carried out a very intensive study of M41. In the color-magnitude diagram that he compiled, some red giant stars are seen to have already departed from the very prominent main sequence.

The cluster's distance as found by him is 750 pc. H. L. Johnson later found 650 pc.

In the top left corner of our photograph we find two wide double stars: π Canis Majoris = ADS 5602 with components A = 4^m6 and B = 9^m5, $11\overset{''}{.}6$ apart, and 17 Canis Majoris = ADS 5585, with a distance between A = 5^m8 and B = 10^m0 of $44\overset{''}{.}4$.

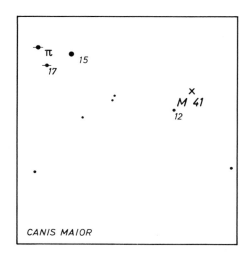

CANIS MAIOR

M41   NGC 2287
6ʰ44ᵐ9, − 20°42′

Cl, 5ᵐ0, 100 ★
φ = 32′, type: e

6ʰ 50m   6ʰ 45m

-20°

-21°

-22°

Galaxies (Ga)

In 1924, Edwin Hubble succeeded in resolving the outer sections of the spiral arms of M33 in Triangulum (page 33), and in the Andromeda galaxy M31 (page 17), into individual stars. In 1944, Walter Baade did likewise with the central parts of M31 and its elliptical companion M110 (page 16). Thus the question of the nature of "spiral nebulae," which had been debated for more than a century, was finally settled.

We now know with certainty that these bodies do not belong to our Milky Way but are independent stellar systems, comparable to our galaxy in size, shape, structure, and number of stars. Today the term "spiral nebula" is little used for these extragalactic stellar systems; they are simply called galaxies.

For many years, our knowledge of galaxies was closely linked with the operation of the first large American reflectors — the 100-inch Hooker telescope, the 120-inch Shane telescope, and the 200-inch Hale telescope. Undoubtedly, without these instruments, our knowledge of galaxies would have grown at a much slower pace. Because of their construction, the Milky Way, which until the beginning of the 20th century was regarded as being the whole universe, lost that position and was recognized as just a tiny unit in the immensity of space.

The first photographs taken with the 100-inch telescope at Mount Wilson showed a large number of galaxies, averaging 100 in an area the size of the full Moon. A photographic survey of the entire sky was not possible with the small field of view of this telescope. So at first, only specially selected fields of the sky were photographed. Partial surveys were carried out by H. Shapley and his associates, who concluded that there were about 500,000 galaxies down to magnitude 18.0. Hubble, at Mount Wilson (1934), surveyed 1,283 fields (about 2 percent of the total sky area) and found 43,201 galaxies down to magnitude 20.0. After the completion of the 48-inch Schmidt camera at Palomar Observatory (aperture 48 inches, focal length 121 inches), which could record fields of 6.5 by 6.5 degrees with perfect images, it was possible to obtain a

Continued on page 86

M50 = NGC 2323

The open star cluster M50 is not very impressive. However, it is easily recognized in this Monoceros field because of the evenly distributed faint field stars. Messier discovered this cluster on August 5, 1772, but the first observation of M50 goes back to G. D. Cassini in 1711. To find it easily, look about midway between Sirius and Procyon for the star 19 Monocerotis (5ᵐ0), then go 4° south, where the cluster can be seen in a small telescope.

The number given for its members varies between 80 and 150. A. A. Hoag and his associates carried out a photoelectric three-color photometric survey of M50 (and 69 other open clusters), and compiled its color-magnitude diagram. The cluster's distance is given as 700 — 800 pc.

The weak, diffuse cluster at the bottom left edge of the picture is NGC 2335.

M50   NGC 2323
$7^h00^m5, -8°16'$

Cl, 7^m2, 120 ★
$\phi = 16'$, type: e

NGC 2335
$7^h04^m2, -10°00'$

Cl, 9^m1, 35 ★
$\phi = 12'$, type: f

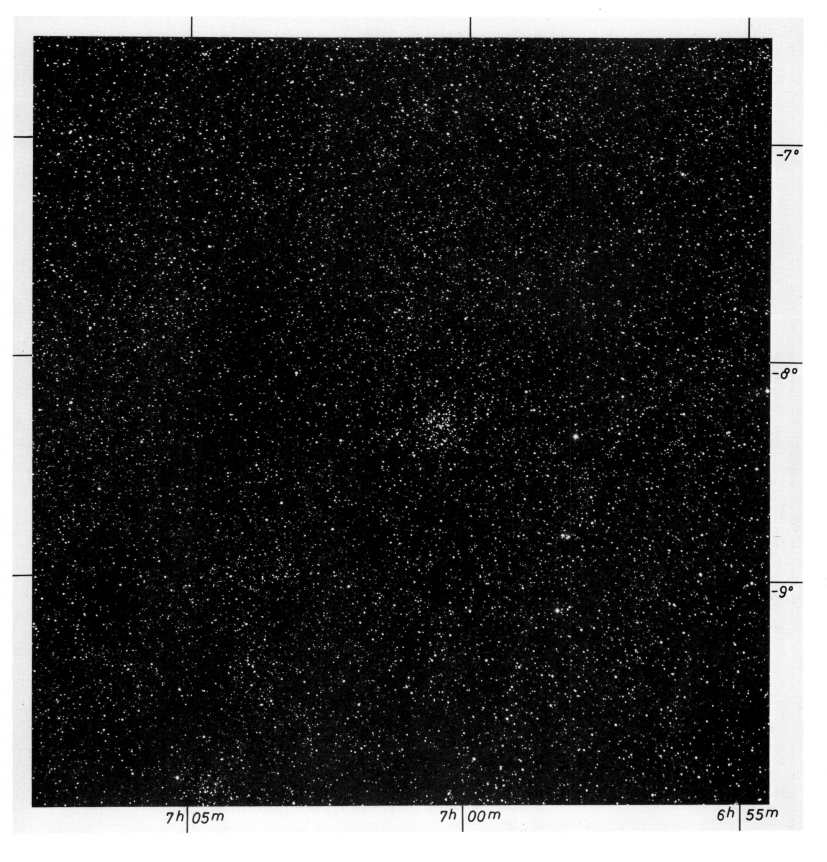

NGC 2335
x

MONOCEROS

M 50
x

-7°

-8°

-9°

7h 05m   7h 00m   6h 55m

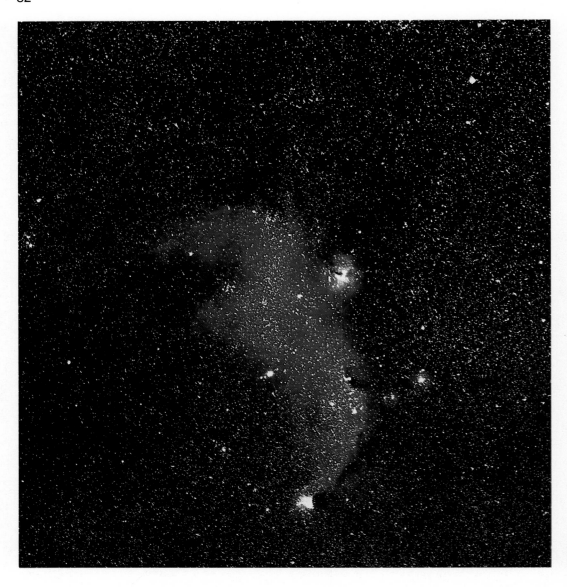

IC 2177
Photographed by the author.

IC 2177

When comparing the photograph on the facing page with the finder chart, the numbering of the objects may seem confusing. This is not surprising, since the NGC numbers were assigned in the 19th century from visual observations alone, whereas IC 2177 is a later discovery made photographically.

There are no problems with open star clusters like NGC 2335 and NGC 2343, as the visual and photographic impressions are nearly the same. IC 2177 is an H II region of more than 3° extent. J. L. E. Dreyer described it as "pretty bright, irregular round," evidently referring to the bright round nebula near right ascension 7^h02^m5, declination $-10°.3$. In A. Becvar's *Atlas Coeli Catalogue,* the size of IC 2177 is given as only 85 x 25 minutes of arc, a very small part of the real extent of the nebula.

On the other hand, NGC 2327 was placed by Dreyer at right ascension 7^h01^m9, declination $-11°14'$. On the photograph there is only an unremarkable star cluster in the faint nebulosity here, yet the very conspicuous bright emission nebula at the tip of the lower edge was not numbered by Dreyer. This is now known as Cederblad 90.

MONOCEROS

x
NGC 2335

x
NGC 2343

x
IC 2177

x
NGC 2327

x
CED 90

CANIS MAIOR

NGC 2335
$7^h04^m2, -10°00'$

CI, 9^m1, 35 ★
$\phi = 12'$, type: f

IC 2177
$7^h03^m1, -10°29'$

N, $85' \times 25'$, type: e
$m_\star = 7.1$, Sp: B0p

NGC 2343
$7^h05^m9, -10°34'$

CI, 8^m0, 15 ★
$\phi = 7'$

NGC 2327
$7^h01^m9, -11°14'$

CI + N, $\phi = 20'$

-10°

-11°

-12°

7^h 10^m 7^h 05^m 7^h 00^m

NGC 2403   Photograph from Hale Observatories

NGC 2403

If you turn your telescope about 10 minutes of right ascension west of the star 51 Camelopardalis (6^{m}0), the bright galaxy NGC 2403 will come into the field of view. This spiral system shows external similarities to the galaxy M33 in Triangulum (page 33); however, its central plane is slightly more inclined to our line of sight. NGC 2403 is relatively near to us and belongs to a group of at least seven other neighboring galaxies called the M81 group. NGC 2403, though, is near the edge of this group and stands rather isolated in this sparse field.

M. S. Roberts found from his studies of the radio emission at 21 cm that the neutral hydrogen in NGC 2403 and four other galaxies amounts on an average to 7 percent of their total mass. The above enlargement taken with the 200-inch Hale telescope shows the spiral arms of the stellar system, and star clouds in which Cepheid variable stars with periods of 18 to 54 days have been discovered — the first such stars ever found in a galaxy outside the Local Group.

NGC 2403

7ʰ32ᵐ0, +65°43'

Ga, 10ᵐ2, 15'5 × 9'5
type: Sc

CAMELOPARDALIS

NGC
×
2403

51

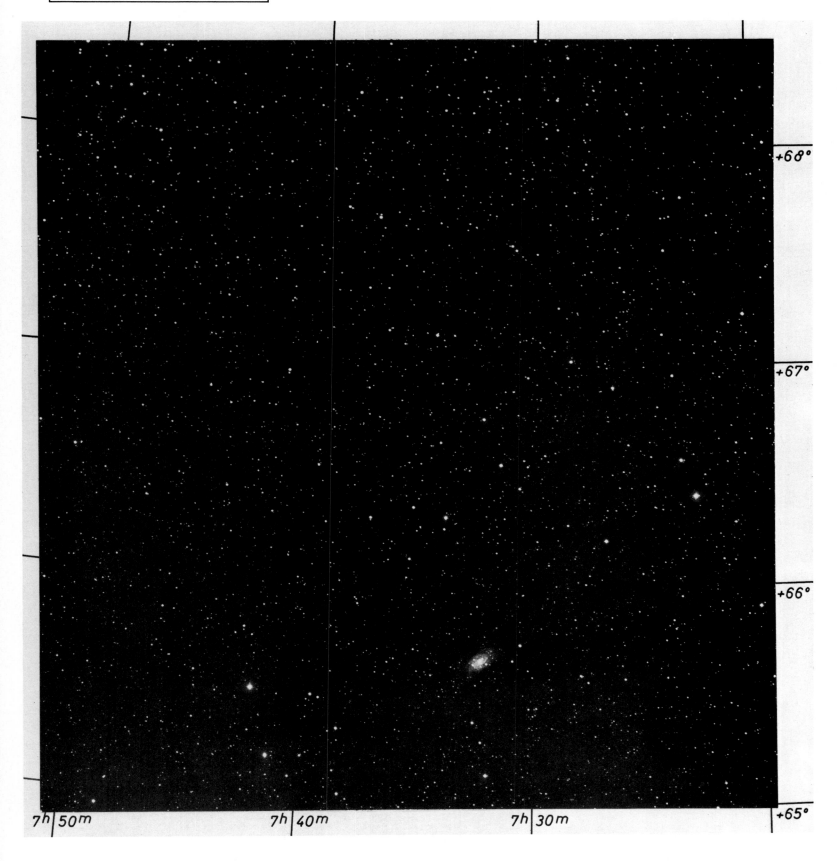

+68°

+67°

+66°

+65°

7ʰ 50m   7ʰ 40m   7ʰ 30m

photographic record of all galaxies to magnitude 20 as far south as −33° declination. These photographs were published in 1954 by the National Geographic Society and California Institute of Technology under the title National Geographic Society-Palomar Observatory Sky Survey. *Today the total number of galaxies to magnitude 20.0 over the whole sky is estimated at 20 million, a number just equal to the stars down to magnitude 20 in our Milky Way.*

Extensive lists of galaxies have been compiled from the Palomar Sky Survey *photographs by W. Baade in the United States and B. A. Vorontzov-Velyaminov in the U.S.S.R. A later work is the* Uppsala General Catalogue of Galaxies *by P. Nilson (1973), which contains data on 12,921 galaxies north of −2° 30′ declination, including all brighter than magnitude 14.5.*

The late 1970's saw the near completion of a similar, but deeper, photographic survey of the southern heavens from −17° to −90° declination, undertaken jointly by the European Southern Observatory in Chile and by British astronomers at Mount Stromlo Observatory in Australia. The former mapped the sky in blue light to magnitude 21 with a 1-meter Schmidt telescope, the latter in blue light to magnitude 23 with a 1.2-meter Schmidt. The gain in limiting magnitude over the Palomar survey was achieved by improved photographic emulsions and hypersensitization.

Even the very few galaxies that are plotted on the index map inside the cover of this book reveal that galaxies are practically absent in those regions of the sky through which the Milky Way runs. The reason for this apparently uneven distribution is the absorption of light by interstellar matter, whose densest parts form dark clouds within the Milky Way. Thus, our view from the Earth of the extragalactic world behind the Milky Way is blocked. However, there are also regions outside the Milky Way band where the distribution of galaxies is distinctly uneven. For instance, there are striking agglomerations of galaxies within the constellations Coma, Virgo, Ursa Major, and Leo. The largest of these, the Virgo cluster of galaxies, is fully described in words and pictures on pages 116 to 129. Clustering of galaxies appears to be the rule rather than the exception throughout the universe.

Continued

M46 = NGC 2437, NGC 2422 (M47)

M46 is one of the most beautiful star clusters in the constellation Puppis, the stern of the ship Argo. This open cluster was discovered by Messier on February 19, 1771. On the northern fringe of the cluster is the planetary nebula NGC 2438, discovered by W. Herschel, seen here only as a small round spot. In large-scale pictures, it resembles a ring nebula similar to the well-known M57 in Lyra (page 199). The nebula is not associated with the cluster, as their distances from us are 850 and 1,700 pc, respectively.

As in many other regions of the Milky Way, here several clusters are found close together. NGC 2422, though not as rich as M46, is noteworthy not only for some bright stars

of magnitude 6, but also for Messier's historic mistake, by which he listed this cluster as M47 in his catalogue, describing it as east of 2 Puppis (6ᵐ1) instead of west. Of course later M47 could not be found in the place he gave. The cluster NGC 2423 north of NGC 2422 is quite insignificant and can be easily overlooked on this photograph.

M. J. Smyth and K. Nandy in 1962 carried out an extensive photometric study of all three clusters. Judging from the color-magnitude diagrams, NGC 2422 and M46 are young clusters, being about 20 million years old, but NGC 2423 is much older, with an estimated age of 300 million years.

NGC 2423

7ʰ34ᵐ8, − 13°45′

Cl, 6ᵐ9, 80 ★
φ = 19′, type: d

M46   NGC 2437

7ʰ39ᵐ6, − 14°42′

Cl, 6ᵐ6, 220 ★
φ = 27′, type: f

NGC 2438

7ʰ39ᵐ6, − 14°36′

Pl, 11ᵐ3, m★ = 16.8
φ = 68″, type: IV

NGC 2422

7ʰ34ᵐ3, − 14°22′

Cl, 4ᵐ5, 80 ★
φ = 30′, type: d

Photographs taken with large reflectors not only reveal vast numbers of galaxies, but show their very different shapes and sizes. The enlargements in this book give only a first indication of the richness of the structure within individual galaxies. Of the millions of galaxies that have been photographed, only a few hundred are near enough to us to reveal much detail. A good idea of the diverse shapes of galaxies is given by A. R. Sandage's photographic work The Hubble Atlas of Galaxies (Carnegie Institution of Washington, Publication 618, 1961). That volume contains 187 specially selected enlargements, some of which have been reproduced in this book. We find that some galaxies are irregular in structure, others are smoothly round or elliptical, and yet other galaxies show a more or less well-proportioned spiral or pinwheel form. Among these we see some that are lenticular or spindle-shaped and, lastly, some whose odd appearance defies description. We must remember that in those stellar systems seen nearly edge on, spiral arms and other structural features become partly or wholly lost through foreshortening. Astronomers have tried to bring some kind of systematic order to the many different kinds of galaxies by classifying them into groups, though it is very difficult to relate physical features to considerations like age and degree of evolutionary development. Hubble's early general classification has been adapted for this book; it is described below.

GALAXY TYPES

Hubble Type	Definition	Example	Page
E0-E7	Elliptical galaxies; the number denotes the degree of ellipticity, with E0 being round and E7 the most elongated.	3379 (E0)	105
		221 (E2)	17
		4621 (E5)	129
S0, Sa, Sb, Sc	Spiral-shaped galaxies whose spiral arms are attached to the central mass. S0 is barely distinguishable from an elliptical galaxy, Sa has tightly wound arms, and Sc loosely wound arms.	4594 (Sa)	131
		3031 (Sb)	101
		5457 (Sc)	155
SB0, SBa, SBb, SBc	Spiral-shaped galaxies whose spiral arms are attached to the ends of a central bar.	3384 (SBa)	105
		3351 (SBb)	105
		3992 (SBc)	113
I (also Irr)	Galaxies of irregular structure.	3034 (I)	101

Continued

M93 = NGC 2447

Messier discovered the very concentrated open star cluster M93 on March 20, 1781, and later it was also observed by W. Herschel. As is the case with so many open clusters, estimates of the number of members vary widely, ranging in this case from 63 to 186. As the power of our instruments increases, so will the number of observed stars, and, moreover, no cluster has a sharply defined boundary. In the case of M93, the problem of taking a census of the cluster is made even more difficult by the density of background stars. In 1959, W. Becker compiled a color-magnitude diagram of 104 stars in M93; and found from this a distance of 1,100 pc.

In the bottom left-hand corner of our photograph one can see NGC 2467. The small cluster Collinder 164 is embedded in this emission nebula, also called Cederblad 103, which is photographically very bright. In 1957, H. Haffner, while probing the southern sky, discovered a triple cluster, now called Haffner 18a, 18b, and 18c, just north of NGC 2467.

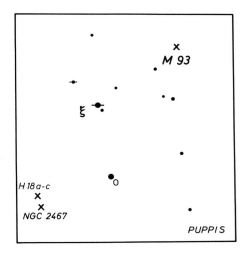

H18 a, b, c
7ʰ51ᵐ8, −26°10′

Cl, m_p: ?, 35 ★
5′ × 5′, type: g

M93 NGC 2447
7ʰ42ᵐ4, −23°45′

Cl, 6ᵐ0, 104 ★
φ = 13′, type: g

NGC 2467
7ʰ51ᵐ3, −26°16′

N + Cl, 7ᵐ2, 25 ★
φ = 12′, Sp: e

90

Other types of galaxies with peculiarities of structure that disqualify them from any of the above groups are marked with a "p" (=peculiar). Many galaxies, especially those fainter than magnitude 12, are so distant and have such small angular diameters that even the largest telescopes cannot provide exact classifications. In these cases, less detailed classifications are given, such as E, S, and SB.

A very comprehensive two-dimensional classification has been compiled by G. de Vaucouleurs. In particular, he has taken into account the numerous modifications of structure that lie between the true spirals (SA) and the barred spirals (SB); these intermediate varieties he symbolizes by SAB. Occasionally additional symbols are added in brackets to specify the spiral's shape: (s) = S-shaped spiral, (r) = spiral arms in the form of a ring, and (rs) = midway between the first two. G. de Vaucouleurs shows the degree in which a spiral can be resolved by the letters a, ab, b, bc, c, cd and d. The symbol m stands for absolute resolvability right up to the irregular type. In this book, we have used de Vaucouleur's classification symbols for five bright galaxies, since in these particular cases Hubble's type definition is incomplete.

For all the galaxies in this book, the following physical data are given in addition to the description and position (due to the large number of objects, partly in the form of a separate table): the apparent photographic total magnitude (mp), the largest and smallest apparent dimensions in minutes of arc (Dim), and the type of structure. The main source for these data was the Reference Catalogue of Bright Galaxies by G. and A. de Vaucouleurs (1964), containing 2,599 objects to as faint as magnitude 13.0. G. de Vaucouleurs and H. Corwin, Jr., in 1976 published a Second Reference Catalogue of Bright Galaxies with information on 4,364 systems. The text presents other data, such as distances of nearer galaxies, inclination of the central plane to the line of sight, and in some cases the total mass. The mass of a galaxy can sometimes be derived from the differential radial velocity of its Hα line (optical method) or the 21-cm line (radio method) of neutral hydrogen along a profile of the galaxy. When plotted on a graph, these velocities yield the galaxy's rotation curve. Masses found in this manner refer only to material between the core and the outermost point where radial velocities are determined; the true total mass of the galaxy may be substantially larger.

NGC 2548 (M48)

The inconspicuous galactic star cluster NGC 2548 = M48 is one of the "lost" Messier objects, and is reproduced here for that very reason. West of the cluster and beyond the confines of the field are the stars 27, 28 and ζ Monocerotis, which, on old charts, form the end of the Unicorn's tail.

As was common in his day, Messier measured the positions of each of his newly discovered objects with respect to nearby bright stars. He must thereby have made a mistake in the case of NGC 2548, giving a position *north* of those three stars when, in fact, it was the same distance *south*. In the position given by Messier for M48, there is no object that could have been reached by his instruments. NGC 2548 and M48 can therefore be considered identical.

From his three-color photometry of 30 stars in the cluster, P. Pesch drew a color-magnitude diagram and a second one of the color differences, and found the distance to be 630 pc. In its loose structure and its age, NGC 2548 bears a resemblance to Praesepe (page 95).

M48 NGC 2548
$8^h11^m2,\ -5°38'$

Cl, 5^m5, 80 ★
$\phi = 30'$, type: f

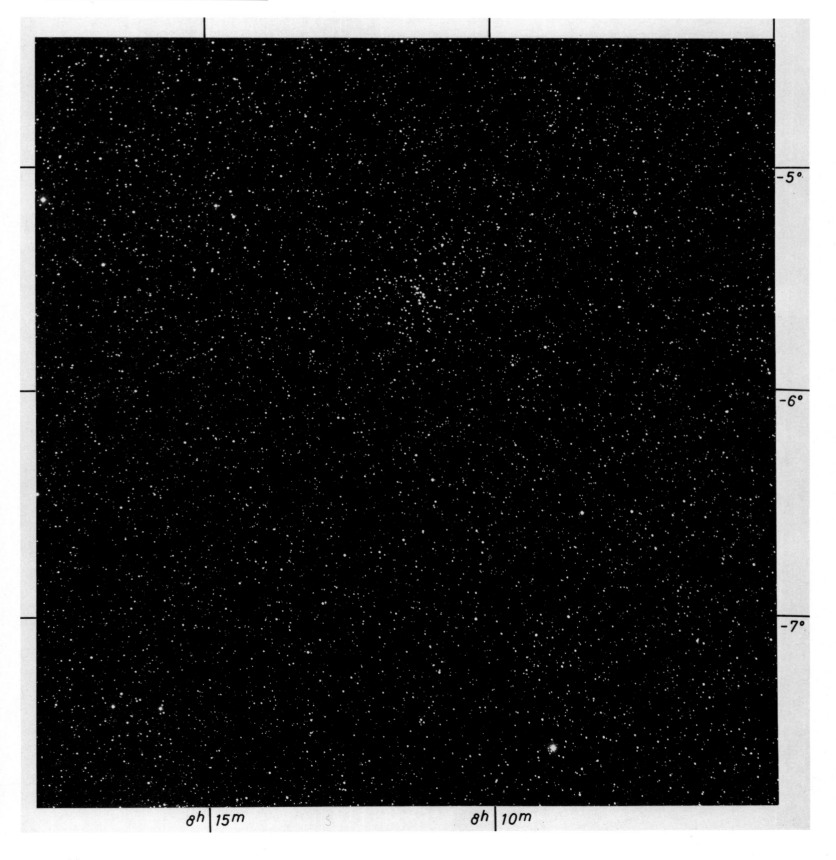

The Gum nebula region, exposed with a
40-mm lens for 4 hours 27 minutes on
Kodak IIa-E with a Schott RG 645 filter.
Photograph by J. C. Brandt *et al.*

Gum nebula

The Gum nebula, named after its 1952 discoverer, the Australian astronomer Colin Gum, is probably the biggest H II region in the sky. Its diameter is at least 35°, and its full size may exceed 60° by 30°, extending over the constellations of Puppis and Vela. The photograph above shows the huge hydrogen cloud between Sirius (upper-right corner) and the Coal Sack (lower-left corner). In the facing picture only the central part of the Gum nebula with its curling filaments can be seen, but this is overexposed in the photograph at top.

The object that stimulates the central part of the Gum nebula to shine may be the pulsar PSR 0833-45, which emits radio and optical pulses with a period of 0.09 sec. Pulsars are neutron stars, remnants of supernovae. It can be estimated from the slowdown of the period that the supernova explosion occurred about 11,000 years ago. At that time the supernova may have blazed up to apparent magnitude -10, or 6 magnitudes brighter than Venus at its greatest light.

The distance of the Gum nebula has been found to be 460 pc, from investigations of the pulsar and the stars ζ Puppis (*O5f*) and γ Velorum (*WC8 + O7*).

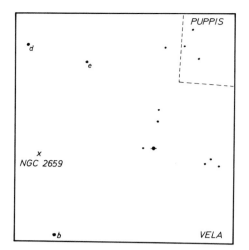

Gum nebula
8ʰ30ᵐ, − 44°

N, O5f + WC8
40° × 30°

NGC 2659
8ʰ40ᵐ9, − 44°46′

Cl, 9ᵐ7, 40 ★
φ = 10′

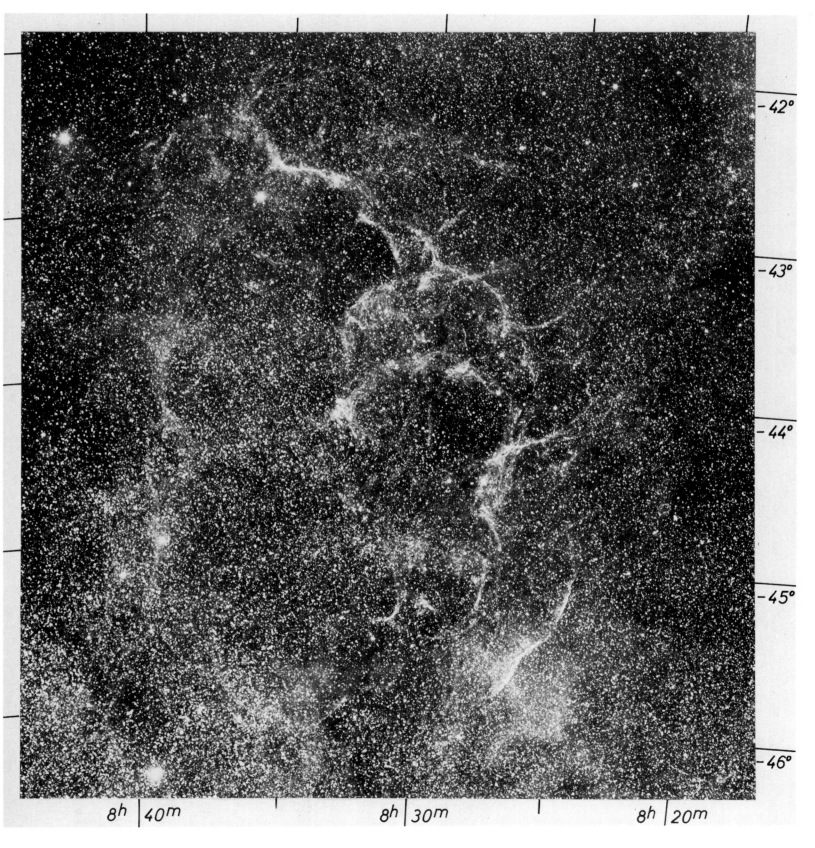

Gaseous nebulae and dust clouds (N)

It has been known for over 50 years that the space between the stars of our galaxy is not empty, but is filled with very tenuous gas and dust. Both are referred to as "interstellar matter."

Understanding the distribution of interstellar matter in space has become very important in the last 30 years because of the great increase in the accuracy of photometric measurement of stars. The interstellar medium, which seems to exist everywhere in our galaxy, absorbs the starlight in two ways: The dust absorbs light at all wavelengths, but more in the violet and blue than in the red and yellow, while the gas absorbs selectively, only at certain wavelengths. As a result, the interstellar dust makes it difficult to calculate distances and absolute magnitudes of stars.

Gas and dust are generally found together, but they cause different optical phenomena. Gas produces particularly impressive appearances in the neighborhood of a luminous and very hot star of spectral type B3 or earlier. The atoms of the gas become excited by the strong ultraviolet radiation of the star, and emit light at certain wavelengths. In this case we observe an emission-line spectrum (symbol e). A beautiful example is the Orion nebula (page 65). At present, about 1,000 nebulae with emission lines are known. They are most frequently located near the plane of our galaxy, and show more or less chaotic structure.

In addition to observing emission nebulae, we can detect the gaseous constituent of the interstellar matter by means of its absorption features. In the spectra of many stars, J. Hartmann and others found that the H and K lines of ionized calcium do not have the same Doppler shift as the other lines in their spectra. This demonstrated the existence of calcium gas between us and these stars, since the gas does not show the same motion as the stars. Later on, interstellar lines of other elements were also detected. The investigation of celestial radio radiation led to the discovery of clouds of cold neutral hydrogen (H I regions) in interstellar space, and later a variety of other elements and chemical compounds in these same regions.

Continued on page 132

M44 = NGC 2632 (Praesepe)

M44 is an open star cluster very near to us. It is well known by the name of Praesepe or the Beehive. Hipparchus called this object "the small cloud" but he had in fact recognized it as a star cluster. Galileo was able to resolve the cluster with his telescope and counted up to 30 individual stars. Because of Praesepe's large angular size, it is advisable to use a telescope with a small magnification and wide field.

Praesepe provides an excellent test for the transparency of the atmosphere. Since it is not possible to resolve the cluster with the naked eye, we see it as a pale fuzzy patch, which gets more and more indistinct the hazier our atmosphere becomes.

Because of its loose structure, Praesepe has often been compared with the Hyades (page 55). An old but very accurate color-magnitude diagram by H. Haffner and O. Heckmann shows that there is in fact a similarity in the main sequences, but in Praesepe quite a number of stars are located a little above the otherwise very narrow and sharply defined main sequence. This suggests that there is a large percentage of unresolved close double stars in this cluster. The distance has been given as 160 pc.

W. J. Klein-Wassink determined the proper motions of 600 stars in the field of the Praesepe cluster and thus identified 200 of its members. From their proper motions and radial velocities, one can deduce that Praesepe moves in the same direction as the Hyades in space, and thus also belongs to the Taurus stream (page 54).

N. M. Artjuchina made an intensive study of the proper motions of 2,372 stars in the vicinity, some as faint as $13^{m}4$, and found there are members as far as 3° away from the center of Praesepe. This means that the cluster extends far beyond the limits of the field shown here.

M44 NGC 2632
Praesepe
8ʰ37ᵐ5, +19°52′

Cl, 3ᵐ9, 211★
φ = 90′, type: d

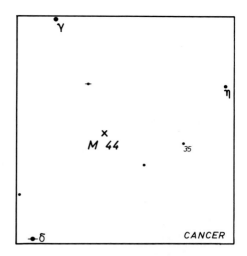

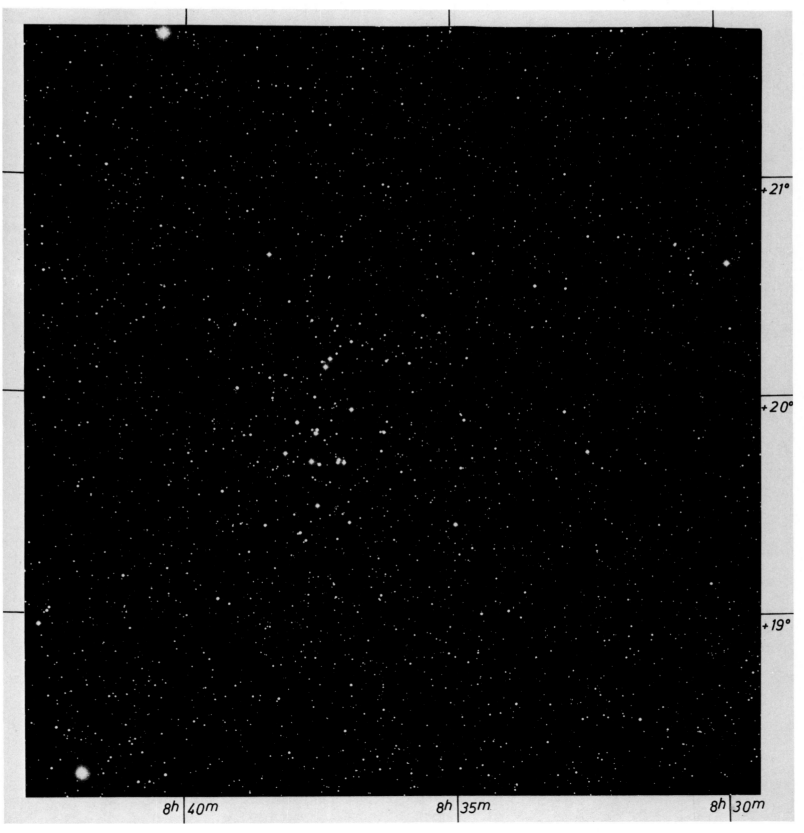

M67 from a 200-inch Hale telescope photograph.

M67 = NGC 2682

Eight degrees south of Praesepe (page 95), within the constellation Cancer, is the open star cluster M67. This object is easily found by pinpointing α Cancri (4^{m}3), then moving the instrument about four Moon diameters to the west. As the integrated visual brightness of the cluster, made up of stars ranging from 8^{m}5 to 15^{m}0 or fainter, is only 6^{m}1, just at the naked eye limit, it is necessary to use binoculars or a small telescope to observe it. However, with a 6-inch telescope and a magnification of 40, the cluster becomes a splendid object with many stars, as can be seen in the above enlargement.

Many papers have been written about M67. O. J. Eggen and A. R. Sandage made photoelectric three-color measurements of 130 stars and compiled a color-magnitude diagram, which is shown together with that of other clusters in the diagram on page 14. From this it can be seen that M67 is one of the oldest clusters known. Its distance is between 800 and 1,000 pc.

C. A. Murray and E. D. Clements measured the proper motions of all stars to as faint as 16^{m}5 in an extensive region around M67. They found members as far as 19′ from the center of the cluster. For the central part a diameter of about 12′ with bright stars was ascertained, with a halo of fainter stars to an approximate diameter of 38′. This structure, combining starry center and halo, can be seen particularly well on the picture, because this region has very few faint stars.

M67 NGC 2682
8ʰ48ᵐ3, +12°00'

CI, 7ᵐ4, 200 ★
φ = 38', type: f

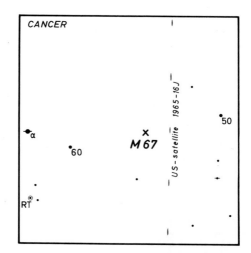

NGC 2903
photographed at Lick Observatory.

NGC 2903

The galaxy NGC 2903 has a total magnitude of 9.1, and so was bright enough for Messier to have seen it, but he listed neither this nor about a dozen equally bright galaxies. On the other hand, some much fainter galaxies in the constellations Coma and Virgo are listed in his catalogue. We may infer that Messier did not conduct a systematic search for "nebulae" and star clusters, and that most of his discoveries are accidental byproducts of his successful comet observations.

NGC 2903 is situated 1.5 degrees south of λ Leonis (4^{m}3), from which it can be easily found. Even in medium-size telescopes, the star system remains a featureless spot. Photography with large telescopes reveals rich structure in the central regions, a mass of star clouds and dark matter to which two spiral arms are attached. The above exposure, made with the 36-inch Crossley reflector at Lick Observatory, shows some resemblance of this galaxy to NGC 253.

Together with other galaxies, NGC 2903 was studied spectrographically by E. M. Burbidge, G. R. Burbidge, and K. H. Prendergast. By placing the spectrograph slit at various points along the long diameter, variation in the line shift of Hα was measured and thereby also the variation of radial velocity along that diameter. From this study, the rotation curve for the system could be drawn. Assuming the galaxy's distance to be 7 Mpc, a total mass of 43 billion solar masses was derived.

The trail seen in the bottom left corner is that of an unidentified Earth satellite.

NGC 2903
9ʰ29ᵐ3, +21°44'

Ga, 10ᵐ3, 11.5 × 5.6
type: Sc

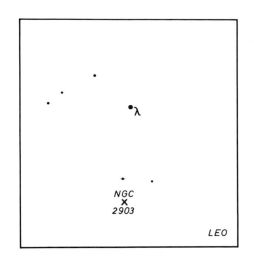

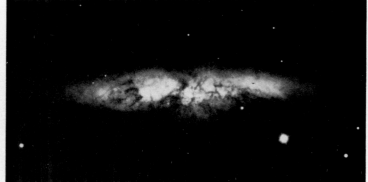

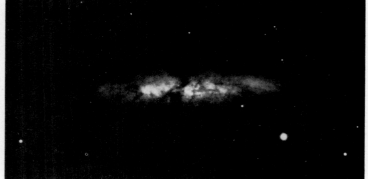

M81
photographed with the 200-inch Hale telescope at Palomar Mountain.

M82
taken in red light; exposure time, 30, 5, and 2 minutes (Hale Observatories photographs). For further information see below.

M81 = NGC 3031, M82 = NGC 3034

The two bright galaxies M81 and M82 were discovered by the Berlin astronomer J. E. Bode in 1774. According to Messier, M81 is oval with a bright center and is easily recognizable, whereas M82 is described as faint but large. Lord Rosse compared M81 to the Andromeda nebula (page 17), and in fact the above enlargement does show a remarkable similarity with M31, particularly in the distribution of light and dark patches, though not so much in the spiral arms.

Since 1962, M82 has been the subject of special interest to astronomers. C. R. Lynds and A. R. Sandage discovered, from photographs in Hα light and from spectra, extensive hydrogen filaments, which show a radial expansion from the center of this irregular galaxy chiefly toward the minor axis at a speed of 1,000 km/sec. This led to the assumption that an explosion must have taken place in the central regions some 1.5 million years ago. More recent work, however, has cast doubt on the popular picture of M82 as an "exploding galaxy;" it may merely be an especially gas- and dust-ridden system with unusual internal motions. A. Elvius measured strong radio radiation and polarization in the central area, which indicates that electrons are being accelerated in strong magnetic fields to nearly the speed of light. Synchrotron radiation results, as in the Crab nebula (page 63). Many properties of this system are as yet unexplained.

The galaxy M81 seems to have been affected by events in M82. H. Arp discovered an extraordinary feature: an arc of a faint, broad ring around the side of M81 that faces M82. In order to make this visible, three exposures were taken with the 48-inch Schmidt camera at Palomar Mountain and printed on top of each other. It is assumed that the luminosity is caused by synchrotron radiation of electrons that originate from M82 and are accelerated in a magnetic field around M81.

Two other faint galaxies, NGC 3077 and NGC 2976, can be easily found on the photograph with the aid of the finder chart.

NGC 2976
9ʰ43ᵐ2, +68°08′

Ga, 11ᵐ2, 4′.4 × 2′.0
type: Sc

M81   NGC 3031
9ʰ51ᵐ5, +69°18′

Ga, 8ᵐ9, 24′.0 × 13′.2
type: Sb

NGC 3077
9ʰ59ᵐ4, +68°58′

Ga, 11ᵐ4, 3′.2 × 2′.4
type: Io

M82   NGC 3034
9ʰ51ᵐ9, +69°56′

Ga, 9ᵐ4, 8′.9 × 2′.6
type: Io

URSA MAIOR

M 82

M 81

NGC 3077

NGC 2976

10ʰ 10m   10ʰ 00m   9ʰ 50m

The Southern Cross region of the Milky Way. The Cross is standing upright at lower center; the η Carinae nebula is near the right edge.

At lower right center, surrounding λ Centauri, is the nebula IC 2944, with the bright cluster NGC 3766 visible above it (see page 111). Just below β Crucis lies the tight $\varkappa$ Crucis cluster (page 135). Farther south lies the Coalsack, in which faint dust-reddened stars can be seen. The bright stars at lower left are α and β Centauri; note the difference in their colors.

The bright object at upper left is ω Centauri (page 147). The field of the peculiar galaxy NGC 5128 (page 145) lies above it on the top edge. Many more deep-sky objects in this photograph can be identified with the aid of a star atlas. Three-color composite photograph by E. Alt, E. Brodkorb, K. Rihm, and J. Rusche.

NGC 3372 (η Carinae)

Eta Carinae is a perplexing variable star in the southern sky, whose historical behavior is not completely known, for astronomical observatories developed rather late in the Southern Hemisphere. Halley saw this star from St. Helena in 1677, and estimated it to be $4^{m}\!.0$. Almost a hundred years later Lacaille observed the star to be about two magnitudes brighter, and, early in the 19th century, η Carinae briefly became almost as bright as Sirius. The star faded to magnitude 8 before 1900, but by 1978 had brightened again to 6.2. Formerly, η Carinae was often called "Nova Carinae 1843" because that was the year it was brightest. However, it is quite unlike any ordinary nova, because of its prolonged brightness and extremely high intrinsic luminosity at maximum. Current variable star catalogues classify η Carinae as a unique variable.

In 1968, η Carinae was discovered to be the brightest infrared source outside of our solar system, as observed at wavelengths of 10 and 20 microns.

Some prominent dark clouds can be seen in front of the η Carinae nebula, such as the one shaped like a bean in the southern part, and a small S-shaped ribbon in the northern part, which is called the "keyhole." Due to overexposure on our picture it is only seen as two dots.

The open star cluster NGC 3293, at upper right and partly surrounded by reflection nebulae, lies at a distance of only 460 pc and appears to have no connection with η Carinae. This is also true of the nebula NGC 3324.

A. D. Thackeray at Radcliffe Observatory, Pretoria, South Africa, studied the spectrum of η Carinae and its surrounding nebulae, and found a similarity with some more recent novae. G. R. Burbidge even predicts that η Carinae is going to explode as a supernova. He estimates its mass to be nearly 100 suns and its distance as 1,100 pc.

NGC 3293

$10^h31^m5, -57°58'$

CI + N, 7^m5, 50 ★
$\phi = 8'$, type: d

NGC 3372

(η Car)

$10^h43^m1, -59°25'$

N, 4^m8, $m_\star = 8.0$
85' × 80', type: e

NGC 3324

$10^h35^m5, -58°22'$

N, 8^m4
$\phi = 15' × 14'$, type: e

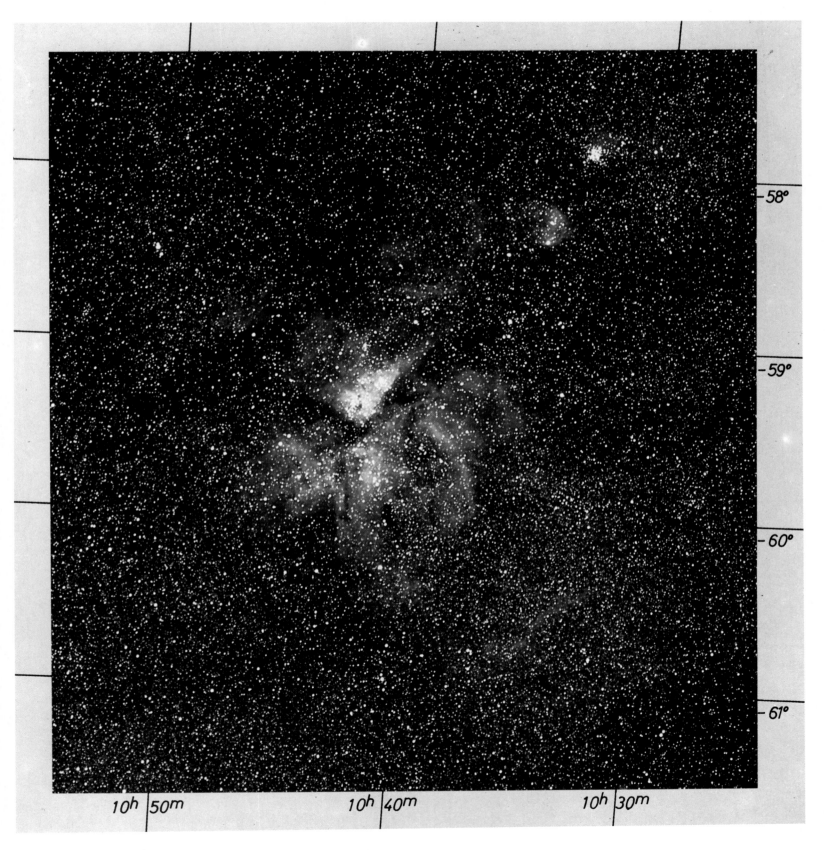

M96 from a 200-inch Hale telescope photograph.

M95 is a type SBb galaxy; that is, a barred spiral with small resolvability, arms attached to the ends of the central bar.

M95 = NGC 3351, M96 = NGC 3368, M105 = NGC 3379

The three bright galaxies M95, M96, and M105, together with five other fainter galaxies, are on the western edge of a great swarm of galaxies stretching through the constellations Leo, Virgo, and Coma. In the facing photograph, we see the central area of the loose Leo group. Of the many thousands of galaxies in the Leo-Virgo-Coma region, Messier listed 21 that he accidentally discovered while following a comet in 1779. Of these, more than half were first seen by Méchain, who passed them on to Messier.

M95, M96, and M105 are bunched together within an area slightly larger than a square degree, and in a medium-size telescope with a wide-angle eyepiece all three can be seen together as pale nebulous patches. Exposures taken with large telescopes show M95 and M96 to be spiral structures, as can be seen by the above enlargements. M105, on the other hand, is an elliptical type and appears featureless even in large telescopes.

G. de Vaucouleurs found that M96's central plane is inclined 35° to the line of sight, and he deduced that the galaxy is rotating with the spiral arms trailing. H. Spinrad carried out an interesting mathematical experiment with M105, attempting to simulate this galaxy's spectrum by selecting the proper mixture of stars of different spectral types. He found in this way that the stellar population of M105 resembles that of a medium-age open star cluster with a large excess of red dwarf stars.

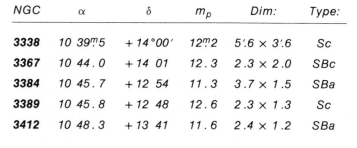

M105 NGC 3379
10ʰ45ᵐ2, +12°51′

Ga, 10ᵐ8, 2′.4 × 2′.1
type: E

M95 NGC 3351
10ʰ41ᵐ3, +11°58′

Ga, 11ᵐ5, 6′.3 × 4′.5
type: SBb

M96 NGC 3368
10ʰ44ᵐ2, +12°05′

Ga, 10ᵐ4, 5′.4 × 3′.8
type: Sa

NGC	α	δ	m_p	Dim:	Type:
3338	10 39ᵐ5	+14°00′	12ᵐ2	5′.6 × 3′.6	Sc
3367	10 44.0	+14 01	12.3	2.3 × 2.0	SBc
3384	10 45.7	+12 54	11.3	3.7 × 1.5	SBa
3389	10 45.8	+12 48	12.6	2.3 × 1.3	Sc
3412	10 48.3	+13 41	11.6	2.4 × 1.2	SBa

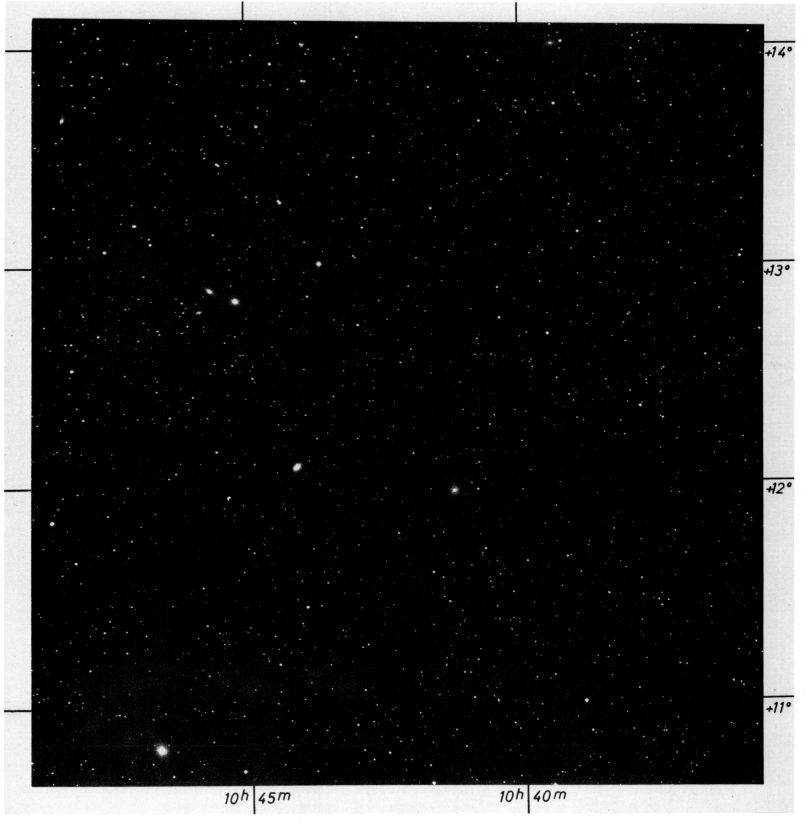

A larger view of the central region of the facing chart photo, showing M97 and M108. Thirty-minute exposure by Evered Kreimer with a 12½-inch f/7 reflector on chilled ASA 160 Ektachrome.

M97 = NGC 3587, M108 = NGC 3556

In the center of our photograph we see M108, whose central plane, according to G. de Vaucouleurs, is inclined only 8° to the line of sight. Because of this slight inclination, E. M. Burbidge, G. R. Burbidge, and K. H. Prendergast were able to establish the rotation curve successfully by observing Doppler shifts of the hydrogen-alpha emission line. They found the galaxy's mass to be 14 billion solar masses, assuming a distance of 10.3 Mpc. In its structure this galaxy resembles NGC 253 (page 23).

About ¾° beneath and to the left of the photograph's center we see the planetary nebula NGC 3587 = M97, discovered by Méchain on February 16, 1781. At first W. Herschel thought that M97 was a star cluster that could not be resolved due to its great distance. In the spring of 1848 the imaginative Lord Rosse drew a sketch of M97 in which the

object resembled the face of an owl, and consequently it became known as the "Owl nebula." On the enlargement above, one can see two dark "cavities" in the otherwise evenly distributed gas of the nebula. In order to see these, it is necessary to use a reflector of at least 20-cm aperture.

R. Minkowski and L. H. Aller studied M97 thoroughly with the 200-inch Hale telescope. They found an average density of 43 electrons per cubic centimeter in the nebula. The distance is given as 550 pc by J. H. Cahn and J. B. Kaler, and as 270 by Haywood Smith, Jr.

The diametric, unusually long beam from the image of star β Ursae Majoris (2^m1) was caused by a temporary misalignment of the correction plate in my Schmidt camera.

M108 NGC 3556
11ʰ08ᵐ7, +55°57′

Ga, 11ᵐ0, 8ʹ3 × 2ʹ1
type: Sb

M97 NGC 3587
Owl nebula
11ʰ12ᵐ0, +55°18′

Pl, 12ᵐ0, m⋆ = 14.3
φ = 200′, type: IIIa

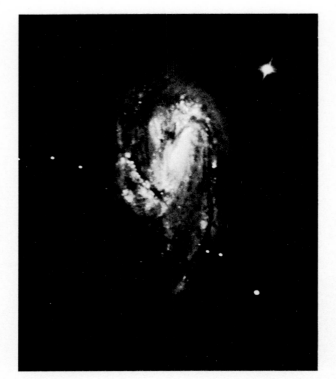

M66   Both pictures taken with the 100-inch Hooker reflector at Mount Wilson.   **M65**

The field shown here is another region in the Leo galaxy cluster (compare with page 105). A clump of three bright galaxies can be easily found by using the star drift method, starting from 73 Leonis (5^{m}5). All three galaxies can be seen together in the same low-power field. M65 and M66, both of type Sb, resemble the Andromeda galaxy (page 17). The third and most northern galaxy, NGC 3628, is also of type Sb, but is oriented so nearly edge on that broad absorption lanes are projected onto the central bulge. In a reflector of 20-cm aperture, the three galaxies appear to be quite bright but structureless.

M65 = NGC 3623, M66 = NGC 3627

E. M. Burbidge, G. R. Burbidge, and K. H. Prendergast used their spectrographic method successfully to measure the rotation of M65, for which G. de Vaucouleurs had found the central plane to be inclined only 15° to the line of sight. It was thus deduced that the total mass of the galaxy is 250 billion solar masses, assuming the distance to be 9.3 Mpc. When a galaxy is as inclined as this one, there is a clear criterion for establishing which is its nearer edge: The brighter and less reddened part of the central bulge is the one superimposed on the farther side, because the part nearest to us is weakened by absorption due to dark clouds in the central plane.

NGC 3593
11ʰ12ᵐ0, +13°06'

Ga, 12ᵐ4, 4'.5 × 1'.5
type: Sb

M65 NGC 3623
11ʰ16ᵐ3, +13°23'

Ga, 10ᵐ5, 8'.1 × 2'.5
type: Sb

NGC 3628
11ʰ17ᵐ7, +13°53'

Ga, 11ᵐ3, 14'.4 × 2'.7
type: Sb

M66 NGC 3627
11ʰ17ᵐ6, +13°17'

Ga, 9ᵐ9, 7'.8 × 3'.6
type: Sb

IC 2944, which surrounds 3rd magnitude λ Centauri and the open cluster IC 2948. The decrease in star density to the south and west of the field is due to interstellar obscuring matter. Three-color composite photograph by the author.

IC 2944

IC 2944, an ionized-hydrogen region in the Carina spiral arm of our galaxy, is situated in the Carina-Centaurus section of the Milky Way. The field is midway between η Carinae and the Coalsack, which is next to the Southern Cross. λ Centauri can be found on the color photograph in the upper third of the nebula. Detailed photographs of IC 2944, taken with the 24-inch Schmidt camera at Cerro Tololo, and explained by B. J. Bok of Steward Observatory in Arizona, can be found in *Sky & Telescope,* January, 1970, page 21.

Both the small nebulae IC 2872 and the unnamed southern one might be parts of the main nebula driven off by a supernova explosion long ago. Since IC 2944 is nearer than the Crab nebula (page 63), investigations should be made as to whether the nebula is expanding or not.

The loose and irregular galactic star cluster IC 2948 lies in the densest part of IC 2944. NGC 3766 is a very rich and concentrated star cluster, similar to M37 in Auriga (page 69).

NGC 3766
11ʰ34ᵐ2, − 61°19′

Cl, 5ᵐ1, 60 ★
φ = 10′, type: g

IC 2872
11ʰ26ᵐ1, − 62°40′

N, 5′ × 2′

IC 2948
11ʰ36ᵐ2, − 63°15′

Cl, 25 ★
φ = 15′, type: c

IC 2944
11ʰ33ᵐ5, − 62°44′

N, ★ = B9 3ᵐ34,
60′ × 36′, type: c

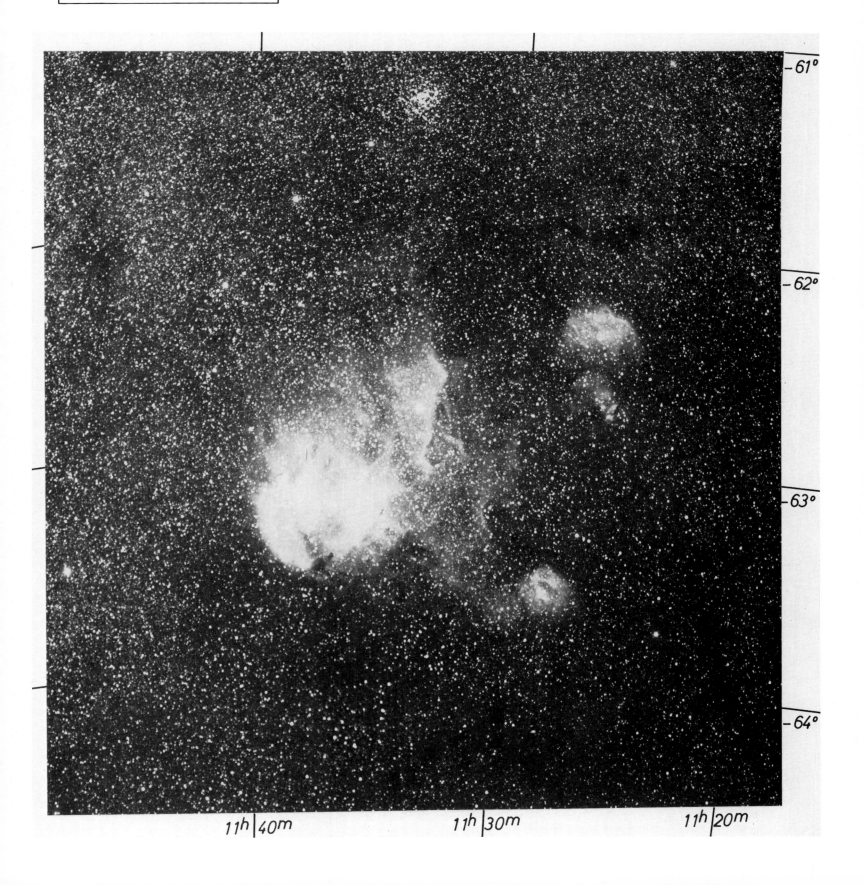

112

NGC 3992. Lick Observatory photograph with the 120-inch Shane reflector.

M109 = NGC 3992

North and south of the bright star γ Ursae Majoris (2ᵐ4), which marks the bottom of the Big Dipper's bowl, there are many faint galaxies. Together with the systems around M108 (page 107) they form the northern part of the extensive Ursa Major group of galaxies, centered between the stars γ Ursae Majoris and β Canum Venaticorum.

The two brightest of these galaxies are NGC 3953 and NGC 3992 = M109, in the southern part of our photograph.

The former is an Sc spiral like M31, whereas M109 is a barred spiral. In the northern part of the photograph are three galaxies with NGC numbers, but the sharp-eyed reader can spot other galaxies fainter than 13ᵐ0. To help him or her get the utmost from the photograph, seven of these fainter objects are marked by small circles on the finder chart. These galaxies form a local clustering within a larger group, like the dense central gathering found in the Virgo cluster of galaxies.

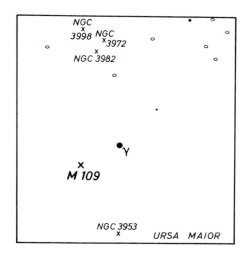

NGC 3998
11ʰ55ᵐ3, +55°44′

Ga, 11ᵐ6, 1ʹ9 × 1ʹ4
type: Ep

NGC 3972
11ʰ53ᵐ2, +55°35′

Ga, 13ᵐ0, 3ʹ7 × 3ʹ1
type: S

M109   NGC 3992
11ʰ55ᵐ0, +53°39′

Ga, 11ᵐ2, 6ʹ9 × 4ʹ5
type: SBc

NGC 3982
11ʰ53ᵐ9, +55°24′

Ga, 11ᵐ8, 2ʹ0 × 1ʹ7
type: Sc

NGC 3953
11ʰ51ᵐ2, +52°37′

Ga, 11ᵐ5, 5ʹ9 × 3ʹ0
type: Sc

M106,
a type Sb spiral. U. S. Naval Observatory
photograph.

M106 = NGC 4258

On the border between the constellations Ursa Major and Canes Venatici we find M106, a spiral system amid a group of fainter galaxies, of which only the brightest are listed on the following page. These are only a small part of the very extensive Ursa Major cluster. According to F. Zwicky, this cluster of galaxies is spread over an area between right ascension 11^h and 13^h and declinations $+20°$ to $+60°$, and has 211 members not fainter than 13^m0, the brightest being NGC 4826 = M64 (page 139).

When comparing the above enlargement with the facing photograph, one can see an extended halo surrounding the main body of M106 in the latter picture, where a slight indication of a continuation of the spiral is visible. This appearance cannot be seen on the large-scale photograph, but many more details of the complex spiral structure can be seen. Apart from two well-defined spiral arms on the periphery, there are indications of other short arms, which fail to show the spiral pattern. E. M. Burbidge, G. R. Burbidge, and K. H. Prendergast scanned the long axis of M106 with the slit of a spectrograph and derived a curve for the galaxy's rotation. From this, the mass of the galaxy amounts to 160 billion solar masses, assuming the distance to be 7 Mpc. M106 is a cosmic radio source.

In the facing field one can recognize many faint galaxies with the aid of a magnifier.

M106   NGC 4258
12ʰ16ᵐ5, +47°35′

Ga, 10ᵐ2, 18′6 × 7′6
type: Sb

NGC	α	δ	mₚ	Dim:	Type:
4096	12ʰ03ᵐ5	+47°45′	12ᵐ2	6′2 × 1′7	Sc
4144	12 07.5	+46 44	12.4	5.1 × 1.1	S
4217	12 13.3	+47 22	11.9	5.0 × 1.4	S
4220	12 13.7	+48 10	12.4	3.0 × 0.9	Sc
4242	12 14.9	+45 54	11.8	4.4 × 3.4	Sb
4346	12 21ᵐ0	+47 16	12.4	2.3 × 0.9	SBa

M100 (NGC 4321) 60-minute exposure taken with the 200-inch Hale telescope on Kodak 103aD film with a GG 14 filter.

Virgo cluster of galaxies

The field on the facing page shows a section of the north-western part of the vast swarm of galaxies known as the Virgo cluster. Five other sections of the inner part of the Virgo cluster can be seen on pages 119, 121, 125, 127, and 129. A reference chart for the whole cluster appears on page 118.

Besides the three bright galaxies M98, M99, and M100, numerous fainter systems can be found in the facing picture. Fourteen of these, including the three Messier objects just mentioned, are listed on page 120 with their physical data, but a keen observer can easily find other galaxies, all fainter than 13^m0, which have been captured on this photograph.

M99 and M100 are typical many-armed spirals seen nearly face on. The above enlargement of M100 shows a counter-clockwise rotating system with numerous star clouds and dark patches. The two main arms are symmetrically attached to the nucleus. M99 rotates to the right and its two main spiral arms begin at two points on the core 120° apart. From a spectrographic analysis of numerous galaxies in the Virgo cluster, W. W. Morgan found that the spectrum of a typical member resembles that of an open star cluster, and becomes redder toward the center of the Virgo cluster.

On page 118 is a general map of the Virgo cluster galaxies, which are pictured on pages 117, 119, 121, 125, 127, and 129. Physical data for these galaxies can be found on pages 120 and 128.

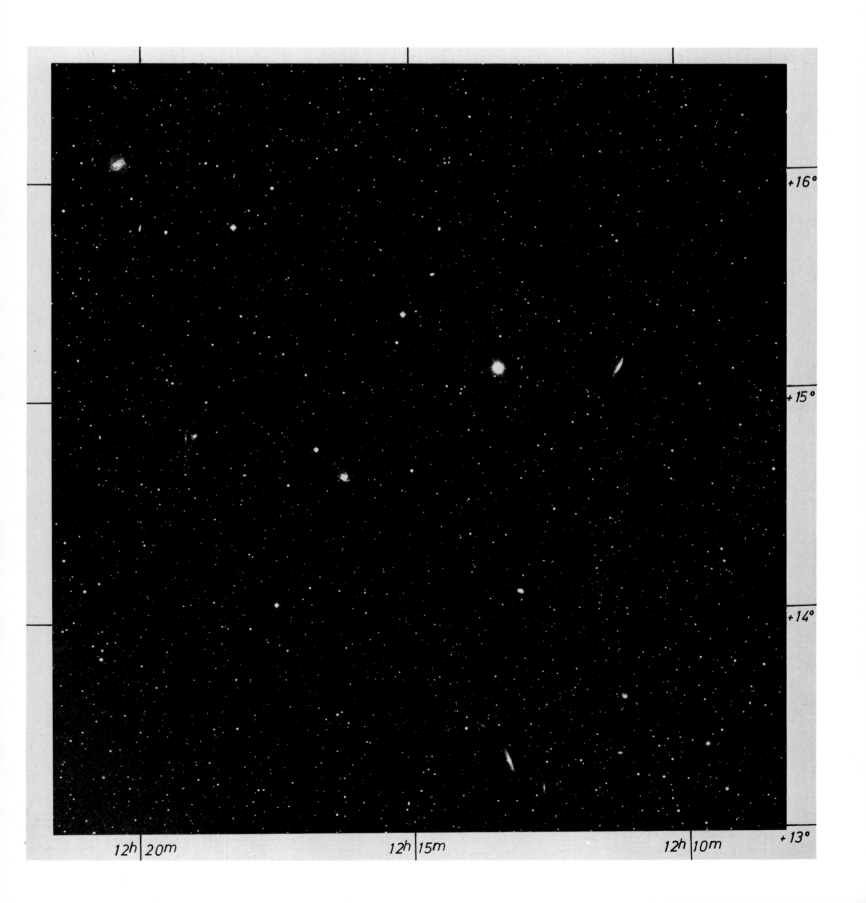

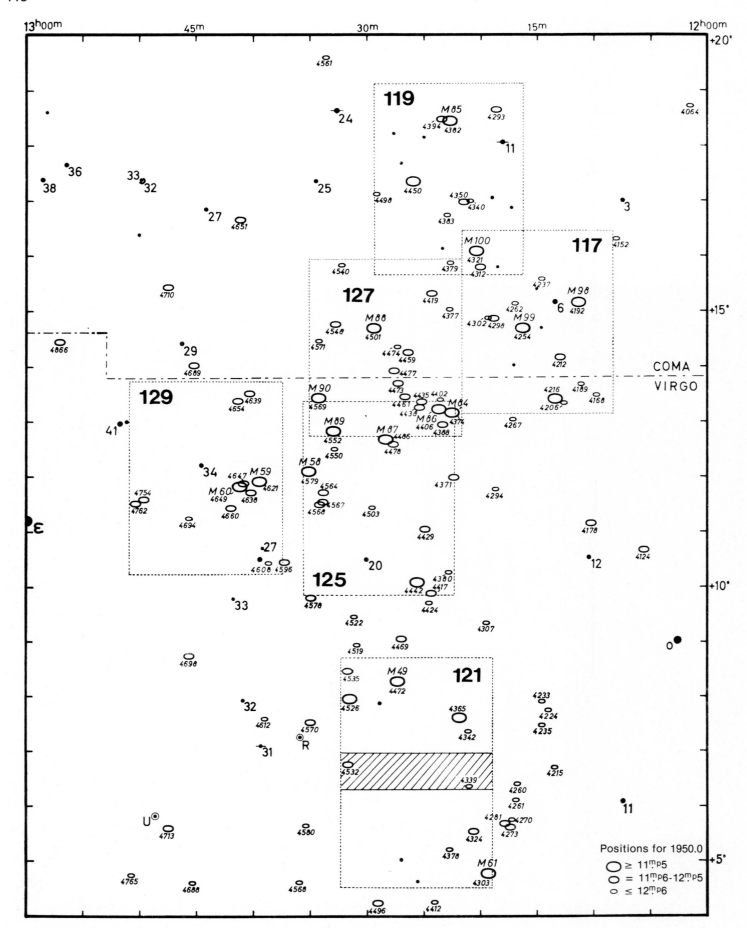

Finding chart for the Virgo Cluster of Galaxies
Areas covered by the photographs on pages 117, 119, 121, 125, 127, and 129 are indicated.
Physical data are on pages 120 and 128.

Although the field on page 109 is in Leo and the one on this page is in Coma, the galaxies in both these fields belong to the Virgo cluster. The facing reference chart shows the six sections photographed in the inner part of the cluster, whose center, according to R. Okroy, lies at $\alpha = 12^h27^m$, $\delta = +12° 36'$, in the neighborhood of M87 (page 125). According to Okroy, the angular extent of the Virgo cluster is still debatable. There are signs that the cluster is spread out over an enormous sky area (between 10^h and 15^h45^m in right ascension, and $-3°$ and $+20°$ in declination), in which there are about 13,500 galaxies down to 15^m7.

Whether all galaxies shown on page 118 belong to the Virgo cluster is debatable. For instance, one distance calculation for M86 places it considerably nearer than the average distance for the cluster.

Two of the brightest galaxies in the field below are M85 = NGC 4382 and M100 = NGC 4321. The latter has already been portrayed and described on page 116. Nine additional galaxies are listed on page 120.

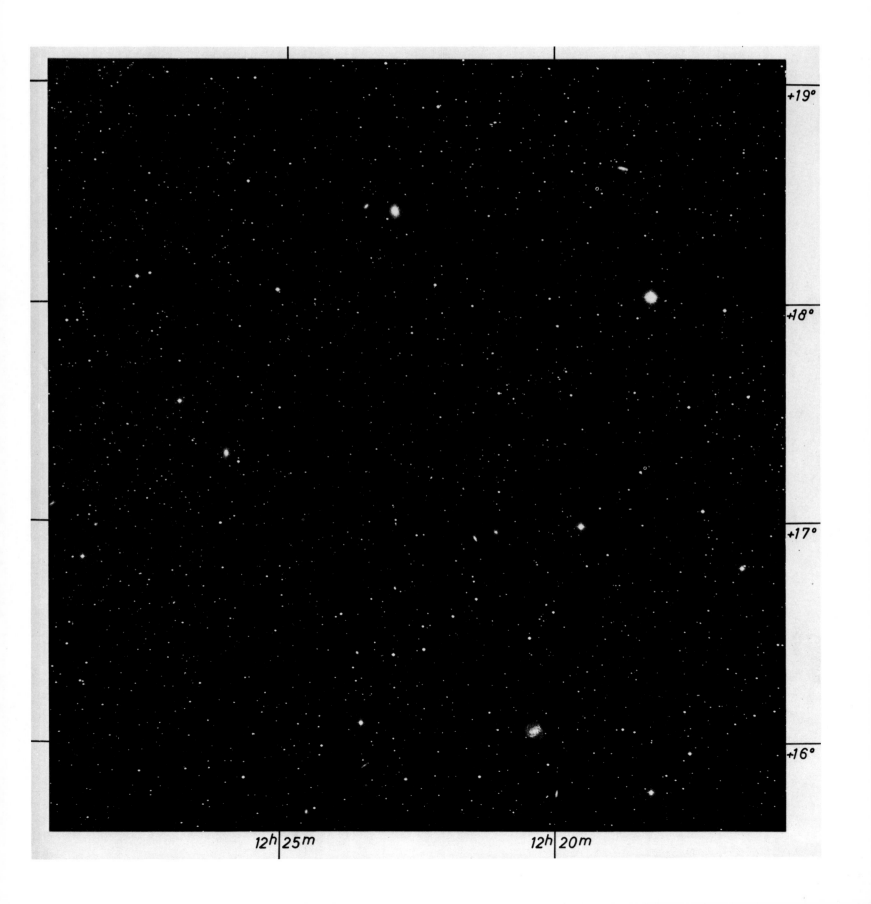

Galaxy Data
for pages 117, 119, 121, 125, 127 and 129 (Virgo cluster of galaxies).

NGC		R.A. 1950.0 Dec.		m_p	Dim:	type	page
4168		12^{h}09^{m}8	+ 13° 29′	12^{m}8	1′.4 × 1′.3	E	117
4189		12 11 .2	+ 13 42	13 .0	2.2 × 1.9	Sb	117
4192	= M98	12 11 .3	+ 15 11	11 .4	8.1 × 2.5	Sb	117
4206		12 12 .8	+ 13 20	13 .0	4.5 × 0.9	Sb	117
4212		12 13 .1	+ 14 11	12 .1	2.6 × 1.6	Sc	117
4216		12 13 .4	+ 13 25	11 .3	7.6 × 1.6	Sb	117
4237		12 14 .7	+ 15 36	12 .6	1.8 × 1.2	Sb	117
4254	= M99	12 16 .3	+ 14 42	10 .5	5.2 × 4.8	Sc	117
4262		12 17 .0	+ 15 09	12 .6	1.3 × 1.2	E	117
4267		12 17 .2	+ 13 03	12 .6	2.4 × 2.1	E	117
4293		12 18 .7	+ 18 40	11 .7	4.6 × 1.8	Sa	119
4298		12 19 .0	+ 14 53	12 .5	3.0 × 1.6	Sc	117
4302		12 19 .2	+ 14 53	13 .2	1.2 × 1.1	S	117
4303	= M61	12 19 .4	+ 4 45	10 .4	5.5 × 5.0	SBc	121
4312		12 20 .0	+ 15 49	12 .5	3.4 × 0.9	S0	117, 119
4321	= M100	12 20 .4	+ 16 06	10 .8	6.3 × 6.0	Sc	117, 119
4324		12 20 .6	+ 5 31	12 .5	1.9 × 0.9	Sb	121
4340		12 21 .0	+ 17 00	13 .0	3.1 × 2.4	SB0	119
4342		12 21 .1	+ 7 22	12 .8	1.0 × 0.5	E	121
4350		12 21 .4	+ 16 58	12 .0	2.3 × 0.7	S	119
4365		12 22 .0	+ 7 36	11 .0	3.6 × 2.5	E	121
4371		12 22 .4	+ 11 59	12 .1	2.4 × 1.6	SBa	125
4374	= M84	12 22 .6	+ 13 10	10 .9	2.6 × 2.1	E	125, 127
4377		12 22 .7	+ 15 02	12 .9	1.3 × 1.1	E	127
4378		12 22 .8	+ 5 12	12 .8	2.9 × 2.6	Sa	121
4379		12 22 .8	+ 15 53	13 .0	1.2 × 1.1	E	119, 127
4380		12 22 .9	+ 10 17	12 .8	3.6 × 2.0	S	125
4382	= M85	12 22 .8	+ 18 28	10 .5	4.6 × 3.2	E	119
4383		12 23 .0	+ 16 45	12 .9	1.6 × 0.8	E	119
4388		12 23 .3	+ 12 56	12 .2	4.6 × 1.0	S	125, 127
4394		12 23 .4	+ 18 29	12 .2	3.5 × 3.0	SBb	119
4402		12 23 .6	+ 13 24	13 .1	3.8 × 1.0	S	125
4406	= M86	12 23 .7	+ 13 13	10 .9	3.4 × 2.4	E	125, 127
4417		12 24 .3	+ 9 52	12 .3	2.6 × 0.8	E	125
4419		12 24 .4	+ 15 19	12 .2	2.8 × 0.9	Sc	127
4424		12 24 .6	+ 9 42	12 .6	3.1 × 1.5	S	125
4429		12 24 .9	+ 11 23	11 .7	3.7 × 1.5	Sa	125
4435		12 25 .2	+ 13 21	11 .8	1.6 × 1.0	E	125, 127
4438		12 25 .3	+ 13 17	11 .9	7.1 × 2.8	Sb	125, 127
4442		12 25 .6	+ 10 05	11 .4	3.2 × 1.2	SBa	125
4450		12 25 .9	+ 17 21	11 .4	3.7 × 2.6	Sb	119
4459		12 26 .5	+ 14 15	11 .9	1.9 × 1.3	E	127
4461		12 26 .6	+ 13 28	12 .4	2.9 × 1.1	S	127
4472	= M49	12 27 .3	+ 8 16	10 .1	4.8 × 3.9	E	121
4473		12 27 .3	+ 13 42	11 .7	2.4 × 1.3	E	127
4474		12 27 .4	+ 14 21	12 .9	1.7 × 0.7	E	127
4477		12 27 .6	+ 13 55	11 .8	3.0 × 2.5	SBa	127
4478		12 27 .8	+ 12 36	12 .5	1.2 × 1.1	E	125
4486	= M87	12 28 .3	+ 12 40	10 .7	3.8 × 3.5	E0p	125
4498		12 29 .2	+ 17 08	13 .1	2.3 × 1.3	Sb	119
4501	= M88	12 29 .5	+ 14 42	10 .9	6.0 × 3.3	Sc	127
4503		12 29 .6	+ 11 27	12 .8	2.3 × 1.0	E	125
4522		12 31 .2	+ 9 27	12 .9	3.6 × 1.0	S	125
4526		12 31 .6	+ 7 58	10 .7	5.4 × 1.5	Sa	121
4535		12 31 .8	+ 8 28	11 .1	6.5 × 4.5	SB	121

Continued on page 128

This field shows a section from the southern part of the inner Virgo cluster, presented in two separate halves in order to remove a strip containing no bright galaxies. Thus it was possible to get two Messier objects, M49 and M61, onto the one page (see key chart on page 118).

M49 is a source of radio radiation, like so many other elliptical galaxies. C. J. van Houten examined the brightness distribution along the major axis of this and 14 other elliptical galaxies. J. L. Sérsic determined the diameters of the H II regions in M61 and eight other Virgo galaxies and found their size was related to the galaxies' type.

Data regarding eight galaxies in this field are listed on the opposite page. A faint trail of an unidentified Earth satellite crosses the top part of the photograph.

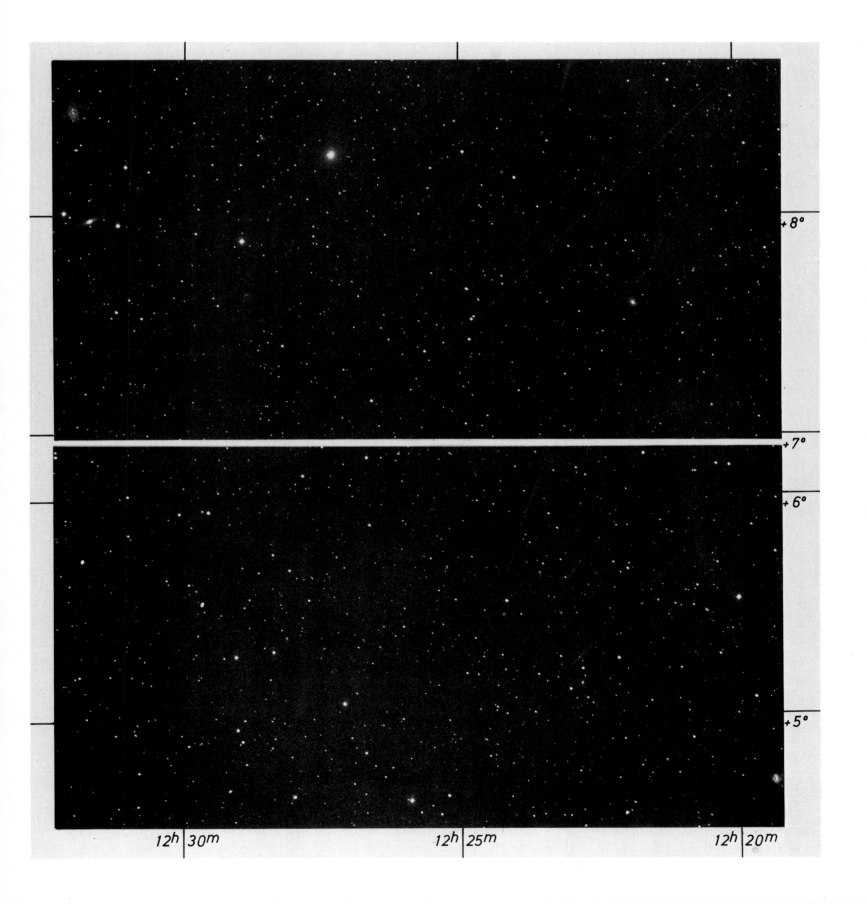

NGC 4565 is one of the most "on edge" galaxies in the sky. 200-inch Hale telescope photograph.

NGC 891 in Andromeda for comparison. The dust lane divides the nucleus almost exactly. 200-inch Hale telescope photograph.

Coma star cluster = Mel 111

In the northwestern part of the constellation Coma Berenices there is a group of widely scattered stars with magnitudes between 5 and 10, called the "Coma star cluster." This galactic cluster can be seen with the naked eye as a dim patch when the transparency of the atmosphere is good. It should not be confused with the Coma cluster of very distant galaxies in the same constellation, which is often referred to in astronomical literature as "the Coma cluster," but whose center lies at $\alpha = 12^h57^m3$, $\delta = +28°24'$. The Coma star cluster, though known in very ancient times, was first listed by P. J. Melotte in his catalogue in 1915, and thus has the number Mel 111.

R. J. Trumpler was the first to examine the cluster thoroughly. From the proper motion of its members, he calculated its distance to be 75 pc. H. F. Weaver has compiled a color-magnitude diagram, in which the stars forming the main sequence show much more dispersion than their counterparts in the Praesepe (page 95). Different estimates of the apparent diameter range from 4° to 8°.

Our photograph shows a number of brighter galaxies, which have no association with the Coma cluster of galaxies. The most impressive of these is NGC 4565 (shown above on a larger scale), which is well known for its spindle form, conspicuous central bulge, and long, narrow absorption lane. G. de Vaucouleurs determined that its central plane is tilted only 4° to our line of sight.

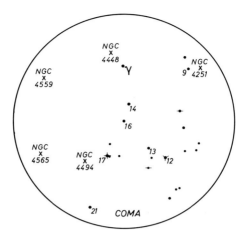

NGC 4559

12ʰ33ᵐ5, +28°14′

Ga, 10ᵐ7, 9′.3 × 3′.9
type: Sc

NGC 4448

12ʰ25ᵐ8, +28°54′

Ga, 11ᵐ9, 3′.5 × 1′.3
type: Sb

Mel 111

12ʰ22ᵐ6, +26°24′

Cl, 2ᵐ9, 47 ★
φ = 360′, type: c

NGC 4565

12ʰ33ᵐ9, +26°16′

Ga, 10ᵐ7, 15′.5 × 2′.1
type: Sb

NGC 4494

12ʰ28ᵐ9, +26°03′

Ga, 10ᵐ9, 2′.2 × 1′.6
type: E

NGC 4251

12ʰ15ᵐ7, +28°27′

Ga, 11ᵐ6, 2′.5 × 0′.9
type: Sa

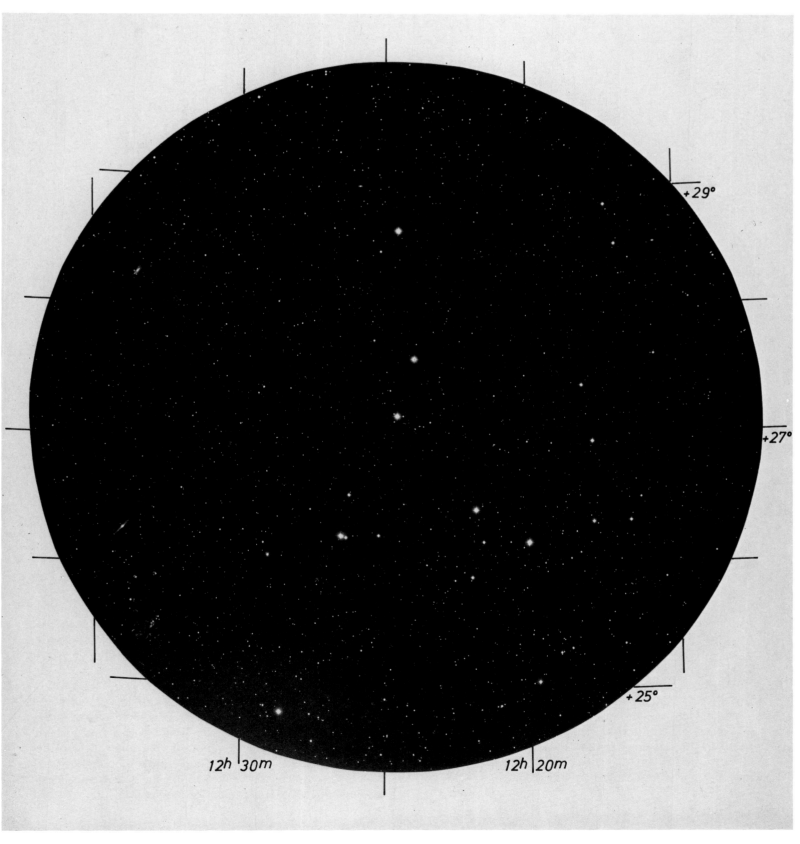

M87 (NGC 4486)
from a 45-minute exposure at Cerro Tololo. The small diffuse spots are some of the 4,000 globular clusters that surround the galaxy like a shell. In our own galaxy about 130 globular clusters are known.

Virgo cluster of galaxies, continued

The center of the Virgo cluster lies here on the border between Virgo and Coma. The following position for the center (southwest of M87) is generally accepted as the best: $\alpha = 12^h\ 27^m$, $\delta = +12°\ 36'$. F. Zwicky, E. Herzog, and P. Wild catalogued all galaxies down to 15^m7, and also all clearly defined clusters of galaxies containing more than 50 single objects brighter than 18^m0, within the area $\alpha = 7^h05^m$ to $18^h\ 16^m$, and $\delta = -3°$ to $+14°\ 30'$. Our field lies inside their catalogue field No. 70, in which there are 84 galaxies down to 15^m7 and seven clusters to which belong a total of 1,387 galaxies. In one small section of 20' radius around the center of the Virgo cluster, 484 galaxies have been counted.

The survey showed that there is a pronounced tendency to form local condensations within the Virgo cluster. However, whether one can talk about cluster formation within the larger cluster of galaxies has been questioned by F. Zwicky.

In the opposite picture are six Messier objects, the most interesting being M87 = NGC 4486, of which a large-scale photograph is reproduced above. In the halo of this giant elliptical galaxy we see numerous bright spots, which are globular clusters forming a cloud surrounding the system. According to an estimate by M. Smith and W. E. Harris, there are about 4,000 globular clusters around M87.

M87 has been identified as the intense radio source Virgo A. In 1954 W. Baade and R. Minkowski, while examining a blue plate taken with the 200-inch telescope, discovered a blue streak of matter that starts from the nucleus and runs out to the northwest. Because the light of the blue jet is highly polarized, it is probably synchrotron radiation. In 1966 H. C. Arp discovered a counterjet with a position angle of about 110° and a length of 35″.

The innermost core of M87, from which the jets arise, is the site of mysterious high-energy processes, perhaps resulting from material falling into a massive black hole. According to J. C. Brandt and R. G. Roosen, the galaxy is exceptionally massive (2.7 trillion solar masses). The distance of M87 is 13.6 Mpc according to de Vaucouleurs (1975); Sandage and Tammann found 19.5 Mpc (1974).

Not infrequently two galaxies not only seem to be but undoubtedly are in close proximity to each other. An example is NGC 4567/4568 at the left edge of the picture below (see also NGC 4490/4485 on page 137).

To identify the various galaxies, use the reference chart on page 118; the respective physical data can be found on pages 120 and 128.

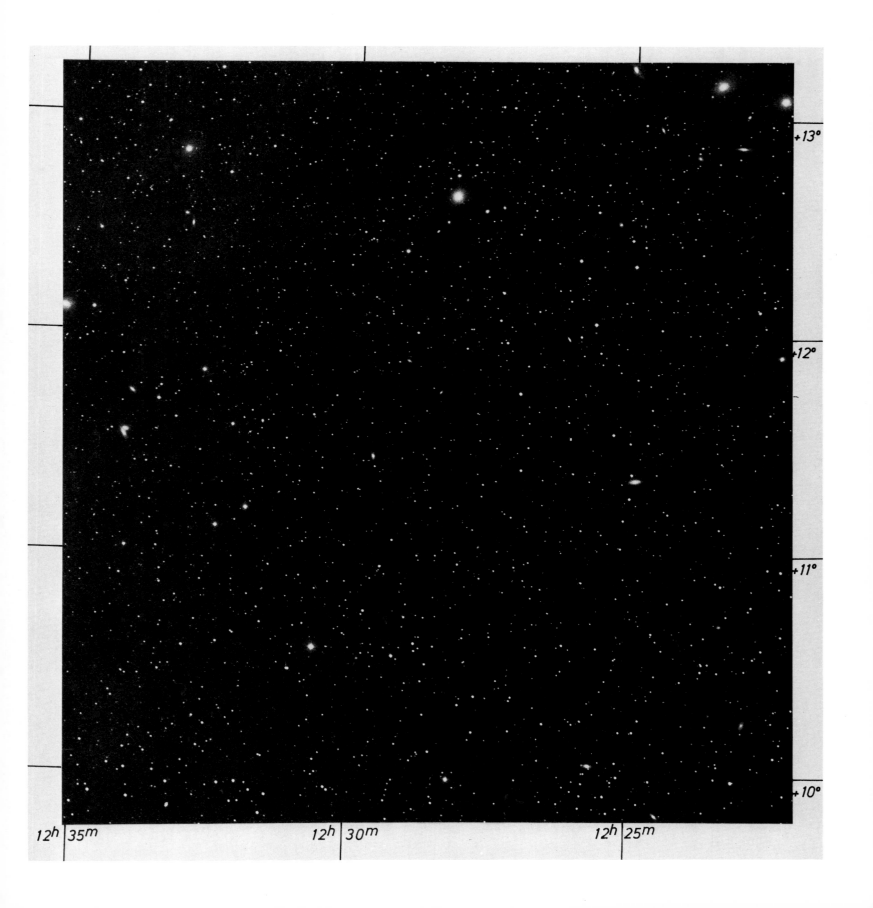

M90 (NGC 4569)
Exposure of 30 minutes, taken with the 200-inch Hale telescope on Kodak 103aO film with a WG2 filter.

Virgo cluster of galaxies, continued

On the facing page we can see the northern continuation of the central area of the Virgo cluster pictured on page 125. The two photographs overlap about ¾° in declination. Here too we find a considerable accumulation of brighter (down to 13^{m}0) galaxies, as well as fainter ones. With a magnifying glass it is possible to detect quite a number of galaxies that are not listed on page 118.

The photographs of the central Virgo areas here and on page 125 show perhaps better than any other in this album the great efficiency of the Falkau Schmidt camera, though it is a very modest piece of equipment indeed, compared with large observatory reflectors.

Of the five Messier objects in the field, M84, M86, and M89 have already been pictured on page 125. Now added are two type Sb galaxies: M88 = NGC 4501, a spiral galaxy in the center of the photograph which resembles the Andromeda nebula (page 17), and M90 = NGC 4569, with its central plane strongly inclined to the line of vision. Both of these systems, as well as the bright giant elliptical galaxy M86 = NGC 4406 at the bottom of the photograph, were included in W. W. Morgan's comparison between galaxy spectra in the Virgo cluster and spectra of open star clusters.

For finder chart, see page 118.
Physical data for galaxies are on pages 120 and 128.

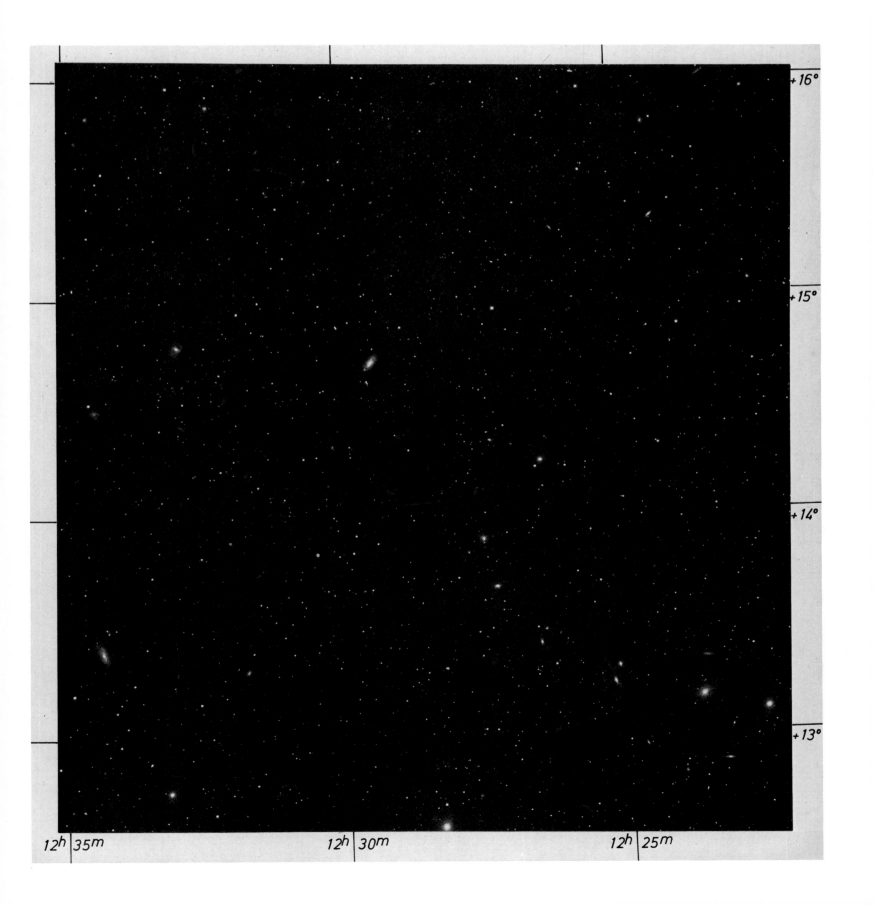

128

Continued from page 120

NGC		R.A. 1950.0 Dec.		m_p	Dim:	type	page
4540		12h32m3	+ 15°50′	12m9	1′.6 × 1′.2	S	127
4548		12 32 .9	+ 14 46	11.9	4.8 × 3.9	SBb	127
4550		12 32 .9	+ 12 30	12.7	2.5 × 0.6	Sa	125
4552	= M89	12 33 .1	+ 12 50	11.3	2.0 × 2.0	E	125, 127
4564		12 34 .0	+ 11 43	12.1	2.0 × 0.7	E	125
4567		12 34 .0	+ 11 32	12.3	2.5 × 1.6	S	125
4568		12 34 .1	+ 11 31	12.2	4.1 × 1.7	S	125
4569	= M90	12 34 .3	+ 13 26	11.2	7.1 × 3.3	Sc	127
4571		12 34 .3	+ 14 28	12.8	3.2 × 2.9	Sc	127
4578		12 35 .0	+ 9 45	12.5	2.6 × 1.9	E	125
4579	= M58	12 35 .1	+ 12 05	11.0	4.5 × 3.7	SBc	125
4608		12 38 .7	+ 10 26	12.7	2.2 × 1.6	S	129
4621	= M59	12 39 .5	+ 11 55	11.4	2.6 × 1.6	E	129
4638		12 40 .2	+ 11 43	12.2	1.4 × 0.6	E	129
4639		12 40 .3	+ 13 31	12.3	2.0 × 1.4	Sc	129
4647		12 41 .0	+ 11 51	12.0	2.5 × 2.1	Sc	129
4649	= M60	12 41 .1	+ 11 49	10.6	3.4 × 2.8	E	129
4654		12 41 .4	+ 13 23	11.7	4.1 × 2.3	Sb	129
4660		12 42 .0	+ 11 26	12.3	1.6 × 0.8	E	129
4694		12 45 .7	+ 11 15	12.6	2.1 × 0.9	E	129
4754		12 49 .7	+ 11 35	12.0	3.2 × 1.6	SBa	129
4762		12 50 .4	+ 11 31	11.8	5.6 × 0.8	Sa	129

Virgo cluster of galaxies, continued

The eastern section of the central area of the Virgo cluster comprises 11 listed galaxies, with which the two bright elliptical stellar systems M59 and M60 were included by C. J. van Houten in his study of galaxy structure (see page 121).

As the photograph shows, M60 has a companion at a distance of only 2′.5: the Sc galaxy NGC 4647. One finds many such double galaxies in the Virgo cluster, for instance NGC 4567/4568 on page 125.

T. Page measured the radial velocities in each of 35 double galaxies that are presumably binary systems and tried to derive the total mass of both components, assuming that they were revolving in Keplerian orbits around each other. For the pairs that he examined, he found an average of 80 billion solar masses for each component, a figure quite consistent with that derived by other methods. Higher figures were found by S. Smith, who used the radial velocities of 32 galaxies in the Virgo cluster to calculate a total mass for the central cluster of 100 trillion solar masses. At that time (1936) it was thought that the Virgo cluster had about 500 member galaxies, and this assumption led to an average of 200 billion solar masses for each galaxy.

Recent estimates of the total mass of the Virgo cluster have produced both higher and lower figures. Probably the figure given here is too small, since M87 (page 125) alone has nearly 3 trillion solar masses. So far it has not been possible to explain why the total mass of a cluster of galaxies seems to exceed the sum of the masses of the member galaxies.

M104 from a photograph by the 200-inch Hale telescope.

M104 = NGC 4594

In southern Virgo there is a multitude of galaxies, predominantly faint ones. They are separated from the large Virgo cluster (pages 117 to 129) and form its southern outliers, in the area between $\alpha = 12^h30^m$ and 13^h30^m, $\delta = 0°$ and $-20°$. The brightest galaxy in this region is M104, having a marked superficial similarity to Saturn, which with its ring system is the most symmetrical object in the sky. M104 was discovered by Méchain on April 9, 1780, and because of its appearance, is often called the "Sombrero nebula." The extensive lens-shaped nucleus, which becomes diffuse toward the edges, is surrounded by a disk of dark nebulosity and star clouds, whose central plane, according to G. de Vaucouleurs, is tilted 6° to the line of sight.

The large-scale view above shows a thin band of absorbing matter that forms the rim of the disk and projects onto the nucleus and even onto the halo, which extends far out into space. Some faint, slightly diffuse light spots in the halo are said to be globular clusters. Due to the great foreshortening it is difficult to ascertain the type of the system, except that it is certainly a spiral. (O. Struve has written a popular report about the difficulties of establishing the types of galaxies.)

M104 NGC 4594
Sombrero galaxy
12ʰ37ᵐ3, − 11°21′

Ga, 8ᵐ1, 6′.9 × 2′.5
type: Sa

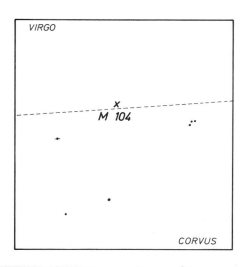

Continued from page 94

The dust component of the interstellar matter is most striking when it occurs in large, relatively dense clouds, so that it partly or totally absorbs the light of the stars behind. Such objects are called "dark nebulae." The most conspicuous example is the Coalsack in the constellation of the Southern Cross (page 134). This one shows rather sharp boundaries, but some other dark nebulae are only detected by a deficiency of stars in certain areas. An example of this can be easily seen in the different densities of faint stars on the two sides of the western part of the Veil nebula in Cygnus (NGC 6960, page 218). As gas expands from an ancient supernova explosion, it is sweeping aside dark matter, allowing more background stars to be seen. Dark nebulae are generally located quite close to the galactic plane.

We can also see dust directly in the form of luminous clouds, when it lies near a bright star and reflects the light of that star. Such a reflection nebula shows a continuous spectrum (symbol c), and is less impressive in integrated light than most of the emission nebulae. Some of the most beautiful reflection nebulae are the wisps and streaks of nebulosity around the brighter members of the Pleiades (page 51).

For every nebula pictured on the chart photos, the description and position, as well as apparent photographic total magnitude m_N, dimensions in minutes of arc (Dim), and type, are given above the photograph. Open star clusters are embedded in many gaseous nebulae; data for these are given separately.

Continued on page 158

M68 = NGC 4590

After M79 (page 57), the next globular cluster in order of right ascension that has a Messier number is M68, more than seven hours to the east. On the other hand, there are no less than 27 Messier globular clusters within the next nine hours of right ascension. This indicates the asymmetric distribution of the globulars on the celestial sphere.

In fact, 50 of the 119 globular clusters listed in H. B. Sawyer Hogg's catalogue are inside a circle of 20° radius around the galactic center in Sagittarius. This asymmetric effect is caused by the eccentric position of the Sun, which is about 9,000 pc from the galactic center toward the direction of the boundary between Gemini and Auriga. In reality, the globular clusters are fairly evenly distributed in a wide, almost spherical halo around the galactic nucleus. In 1917 H. Shapley was the first to realize that the asymmetry of the globular clusters was an indication of the Sun's eccentric position. Shapley also carried out a comprehensive survey of M68. According to W. E. Harris (1976), the distance of M68 is 9,600 pc.

Through a telescope of 10-cm aperture, M68 looks like a pale, somewhat speckled disk. Messier discovered this object in 1780 and mentioned the 6th magnitude star to its southwest. This star was later recognized as a binary, ADS 8612 (A = 5^{m}4, B = 12^{m}2, distance 1˝3).

M68   NGC 4590
12ʰ36ᵐ8, −26°29′

Gl, 9ᵐ1, Sp: A6
φ = 9′.8, type: X

M 68

HYDRA

−25°

−26°

−27°

−28°

12ʰ 45ᵐ   12ʰ 40ᵐ   12ʰ 35ᵐ

The Southern Cross
with Coalsack and surrounding parts of the Milky Way.

NGC 4755 (Kappa Crucis)

The picture on the right shows a section of the constellation Crux, the famous Southern Cross. The bright star above center is β Crucis (1ᵐ5). It is situated on the eastern arm of the crosspiece. The lower part of the picture shows a section of the Coalsack, a huge dark cloud that blots out great numbers of background Milky Way stars and thus stands out conspicuously. The picture above, taken through an Astro-Tessar lens of 25-cm focal length, shows the large extent of the Coalsack, together with the whole constellation Crux and surrounding parts of the Milky Way. The brilliant double star α Crucis, on the right of the Coalsack (1ᵐ6 and 2ᵐ1, separation 4″3) is a physical pair with a long period. In the head of the Cross is γ Crucis (1ᵐ6), of nearly the same visual brightness as β Crucis, but of spectral type M4. Because of its redness, this star appears fainter on the blue-sensitive plate.

Near β Crucis are three open clusters, grouped along a gentle curve, which show interesting differences in structure. The cluster H7 = Tr 20 (on the right) is a loose, irregular collection of faint stars, inserted by R. J. Trumpler into his catalogue in 1930. NGC 4755, to the lower left of β Crucis, is very bright and concentrated, with the star Kappa Crucis (6ᵐ1) in its center. This is a young cluster similar to h and χ Persei (page 39). Its distance from us is 850 pc, according to G. L. Hagen. NGC 4852, completely unlike the former two clusters, is a scattered grouping of a few relatively bright stars.

The corrector plate of the Hamburg Schmidt camera, which incidentally was built by Bernhard Schmidt himself, and with which this photograph was taken at the Boyden Observatory in South Africa, has left its customary reflex or ghost image, this time of β Crucis, near the boundary of the Coalsack.

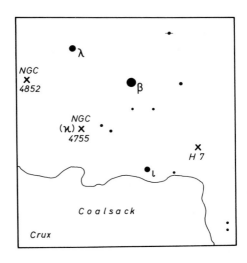

H7 = Tr 20
12ʰ35ᵐ9, − 60°20'

Cl, 10ᵐ1, 200★
φ = 10', type: c

NGC 4755
(× Cru)
12ʰ50ᵐ6, − 60°05'

Cl, 5ᵐ2, 50★
φ = 12', type: g

NGC 4852
12ʰ57ᵐ1, − 59°20'

Cl, 8ᵐ9, 40★
φ = 11', type: d

M94
taken by the 200-inch Hale telescope.

NGC 4485 and 4490
likewise by the 200-inch telescope.

M94 = NGC 4736

Slightly northwest of α Canum Venaticorum lie a number of brighter galaxies, which together with the systems on page 143 form the southern fringe of the Ursa Major group. Apart from M94 = NGC 4736, discovered by Méchain on March 22, 1781, the field also includes the double galaxy NGC 4485 and NGC 4490 (upper right corner) and two fainter objects near the center of the photograph.

M94 is a multiarmed spiral with some dark patches and an extended central lens. Although the central plane of this galaxy is tilted only 35° out of the plane of the sky, E. M. Burbidge and G. R. Burbidge successfully determined the rotation curve and from this deduced a total mass of 29 billion solar masses (on the assumption that the distance is 10 Mpc). Later these figures were confirmed by R. Duflot, who found the inclination to be 42°.

In the double system NGC 4485/4490, T. Page found a bridge of material between the two components, which seems to indicate a physical connection. But according to a spectrographic examination by F. Bertola, such an assumption is very doubtful, due to the considerable difference in the radial velocities of the two components.

The photograph has been "decorated" by three satellites. The bright interrupted trail was made by the rocket of the Russian satellite quintet Cosmos 71-75 (time, 22h25m UT; magnitude, 3.5-6.0; semiperiod, 4.0 sec.; height, 550 km). The continuous weak trail from southwest to northeast was drawn by Cosmos 97 about 21h53m UT. The third trail, parallel to the left edge, shows flashes of about 6 sec semiperiod, and possibly belongs to satellite 1965-27 D, the heat shield of the U. S. satellite "Snapshot."

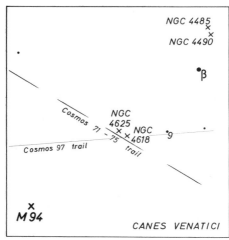

CANES VENATICI

NGC 4625
12ʰ39ᵐ5, +41°33′

Ga, 13ᵐ0, 1ʹ5 × 1ʹ4
type: Sc

NGC 4490
12ʰ28ᵐ3, +41°55′

Ga, 10ᵐ5, 5ʹ4 × 2ʹ7
type: Sc

M94   NGC 4736
12ʰ48ᵐ6, +41°23′

Ga, 9ᵐ0, 7ʹ4 × 5ʹ9
type: Sb

NGC 4618
12ʰ39ᵐ2, +41°25′

Ga, 11ᵐ5, 3ʹ4 × 2ʹ8
type: SB

NGC 4485
12ʰ28ᵐ2, +41°58′

Ga, 12ᵐ9, 1ʹ8 × 1ʹ1
type: Sc

Two exposures of M64
taken in 1910 by G. W. Ritchey with the 60-inch reflector on Mount Wilson. The exposure time on the left was 4 hours, on the right 8 hours.

M64 = NGC 4826

M64 was discovered by J. E. Bode on April 4, 1779. It is easy to find this bright but not very large galaxy with a telescope. Pinpoint the star 35 Comae (5^m1) about ½° south of the finder's crosswires and stop the driving motor; the galaxy will drift into the field of vision after about two minutes.

M64 is richer in detail than one would imagine from the appearance in the facing photograph. The two pictures above, both of M64, were taken in 1910 by Ritchey with the 60-inch reflector at Mount Wilson, shortly after it had been installed. This instrument caused quite a stir at the time because of its high photographic effectiveness and image quality. The photograph at the upper left was exposed for four hours, and the other for twice that time, over three consecutive nights. At first you may think these are two different objects! The extremely long exposure time has brought out an elliptical halo, thereby doubling the apparent size of the galaxy, and has drowned out both the compact dark clouds north of the central lens and the thin spiral arms.

In 1943 E. Hubble established the direction of rotation of M64 and 14 other galaxies, and found M64 to be a right-handed system.

COMA BERENICES

M 64

M64 NGC 4826

12ʰ54ᵐ3, +21°47'

Ga, 8ᵐ0, 7'4 × 4'2
type: Sb

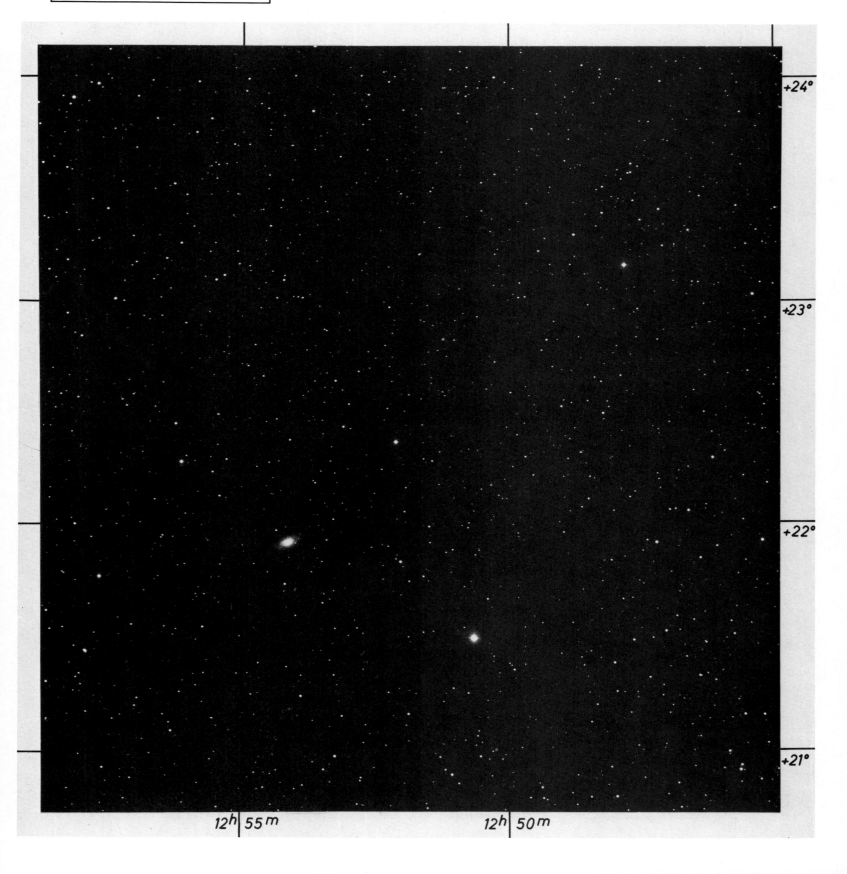

+24°

+23°

+22°

+21°

12ʰ 55m   12ʰ 50m

GLOBULAR CLUSTERS IN THIS BOOK

The apparent diameter (φ) of a globular cluster on a photograph depends largely on the size of the telescope, sensitivity of emulsion, and exposure time. As the years progress, the published figures for the same cluster grow larger and larger. Sizes given in older catalogues should be regarded with reservation!

M	NGC	R.A. 1950.0 Dec.		φ	m_p	page	M	NGC	R.A. 1950.0 Dec.		φ	m_p	page
	104	$00^h21^m.9$	$-72°21'$	44.0	4.7	25		6453	$17^h48^m.0$	$-34°37'$	3.6	11.4	183
	288	50.2	$-26\ 52$	12.4	7.2	23		6544	18 04.3	$-25\ 01$	1.0	11.0	187
	362	01 00.6	$-71\ 07$	17.7	8.0	25	28	6626	21.5	$-24\ 54$	15.0	8.5	193
79	1904	05 22.2	$-24\ 34$	7.8	8.4	57	69	6637	28.1	$-32\ 23$	3.8	8.9	195
68	4590	12 36.8	$-26\ 29$	9.8	9.1	133		6638	27.9	$-25\ 32$	2.2	10.2	193
53	5024	13 10.5	$+18\ 26$	14.4	8.7	141		6652	32.5	$-33\ 02$	2.3	9.8	195
	5053	13.9	$+17\ 57$	8.9	10.9	141	22	6656	33.3	$-23\ 58$	17.0	6.5	193
	5139	23.8	$-47\ 03$	65.0	4.2	147	70	6681	40.0	$-32\ 21$	4.1	9.0	195
3	5272	39.9	$+38\ 38$	18.6	7.2	153		6712	50.3	$-08\ 47$	4.2	10.5	197
5	5904	15 16.0	$+02\ 16$	19.9	7.0	159	54	6715	52.0	$-30\ 32$	5.5	8.7	201
80	6093	16 14.1	$-22\ 52$	5.1	8.4	161	56	6779	19 14.9	$+30\ 05$	5.0	9.6	203
4	6121	20.6	$-26\ 24$	22.8	7.4	163	55	6809	36.9	$-31\ 03$	14.8	7.1	205
	6144	24.2	$-25\ 56$	6.2	10.8	163	71	6838	51.5	$+18\ 39$	6.1	8.3	211
107	6171	29.7	$-12\ 57$	7.8	10.1	165	75	6864	20 03.2	$-22\ 04$	4.6	9.5	215
13	6205	39.9	$+36\ 33$	23.2	6.8	167	72	6981	50.7	$-12\ 44$	5.1	10.2	221
12	6218	44.6	$-01\ 52$	12.2	8.0	169	15	7078	21 27.6	$+11\ 57$	12.3	7.3	225
10	6254	54.5	$-04\ 02$	12.2	7.6	169	2	7089	30.9	$-01\ 03$	11.7	7.3	231
62	6266	58.1	$-30\ 03$	6.3	8.2	173	30	7099	37.5	$-23\ 25$	8.9	8.6	233
19	6273	59.5	$-26\ 11$	5.3	8.3	173							
9	6333	17 16.2	$-18\ 28$	5.5	8.9	177							
92	6341	15.6	$+43\ 12$	12.2	7.3	175							
	6342	18.2	$-19\ 32$	1.3	11.4	177							
	6356	20.7	$-17\ 46$	3.5	9.7	177							
	6366	25.1	$-05\ 02$	5.8	12.1	181							
14	6402	35.0	$-03\ 13$	6.7	9.4	181							

M53 = NGC 5024

M53 is a globular star cluster about 1° northeast of α Comae ($4^m.0$). At first glance, this very rich cluster looks like a miniature of M3 (page 153). However, its distance (18.6 kpc) is nearly twice that of M3, while its angular diameter is almost as great (14'.4 and 18'.6, respectively). Thus it is actually even bigger than M3. Messier first saw the object on February 26, 1777, but J. E. Bode had already discovered M53 in 1775. Using a telescope with a 15-cm aperture and a magnification of 200x, I saw this cluster as a pale, mottled spot with a few individual stars near the edge.

J. Cuffey prepared a color-magnitude diagram of M53 from a very comprehensive two-color photometric study of 569 stars brighter than $18^m.5$ and within a radius of 26'. This showed the absence of blue giants. Later, on a plate ex-posed for only 30 seconds, Cuffey found 64 yellow and red giants in the central area.

In the position $\alpha = 13^h14^m$, $\delta = +18°$ on the facing picture, we see a weak granular spot, which forms a low isosceles triangle with M53 and α Comae. This spot is not a fault in the film but the image of the loose globular cluster NGC 5053. This object has a radius of 8'.9, and its brightest stars are as faint as magnitude 15.

α Comae is the close binary ADS 8804, consisting of two stars of $5^m.2$; the orbital period is only 26 years. Another double star, ADS 8841, can be found south of NGC 5053 (A = $6^m.6$, B = $10^m.2$, distance = 6".4).

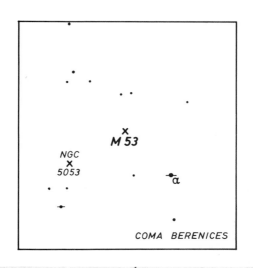

COMA BERENICES

M53   NGC 5024

$13^h10^m5, +18°26'$

Gl, 8^m7, Sp: F4
$\phi = 14'.4$, type: V

NGC 5053

$13^h13^m9, +17°57'$

Gl, 10^m9, Sp: ?
$\phi = 8'.9$, type: XI

M63
Photographed by the 100-inch Hooker telescope at Mount Wilson.

M63 = NGC 5055

M63 belongs to that rare type of galaxy having a large number of spiral arms. However, these are resolved into many star clouds, making it difficult to trace their course. This is shown clearly in the large-scale view above; on the facing photograph, structure is only visible near the edge of the galaxy.

Méchain discovered M63 on June 14, 1779, and passed his findings on to Messier. The latter described it as a faint nebula and mentioned the 8th-magnitude star just west of it. M63 can easily be found by looking at a point one-third of the way from α Canum Venaticorum ($2^m 8$) to η Ursae Majoris ($1^m 9$), the tip of the tail of the Great Bear. At a point two-thirds of the way, we find the conspicuous galaxy M51 (page 149). Perhaps yet an easier way to locate M63 is with the aid of the two stars 19 CVn ($5^m 7$) and 20 CVn ($4^m 7$), which are just below the center of our field.

The complicated spiral structure of M63 has invited a large number of investigations. G. de Vaucouleurs found a 30° inclination of the central plane to the line of sight, and a clockwise rotation. E. M. Burbidge, G. R. Burbidge, and K. H. Prendergast were able to draw a rotation curve, and found the total mass of this galaxy to be 55 billion solar masses, if its distance is 7.4 Mpc. In the course of a detailed photometric study of M63, R. A. Fish found a somewhat larger inclination, 36°.8.

The satellite trail just below M63 was possibly made by the rocket of the Russian satellite Cosmos 110. The latter carried two dogs for 22 days in space and brought them back to Earth unharmed. The rocket reentered the Earth's atmosphere a few days after this photograph was taken on April 29, 1966.

M63   NGC 5055
$13^h13^m5,\ +42°17'$

Ga, $10^m5,\ 10'.2 \times 6'.0$
type: Sb

M 63
×
Rocket Cosmos 110 trail (?)

•18
•20
•23   •19

CANES VENATICI

13h 20m   13h 15m   13h 10m   13h 05m

NGC 5128, photographed in yellow light by R. J. Dufour and S. van den Bergh with the 4-meter telescope at the Cerro Tololo Inter-American Observatory.

NGC 5128

One of the most curious stellar systems of the southern sky is NGC 5128. As the picture above clearly shows, it presents an almost circular disk and halo, upon which is projected an irregular dark absorption zone. In 1949 it was discovered that this galaxy is identical with the very strong radio source Centaurus A. To explain this radio emission, W. Baade and R. Minkowski proposed that NGC 5128 consists of two galaxies in collision. However, it is now generally agreed that NGC 5128 and most other radio galaxies are not colliding pairs but abnormal single systems.

In 1959 E. M. Burbidge and G. R. Burbidge made a spectroscopic study of the rotation of NGC 5128, and deduced a total mass of roughly 200 billion Suns, on the supposition that the distance is 5 Mpc. They found evidence of internal velocities of up to 200 kilometers per second in the gas clouds of this galaxy. A study of radio radiation by B. F. C. Cooper, R. M. Price, and D. J. Cole later showed two main sources 25′ apart and numerous minor sources spread over a large area around the galaxy.

Sidney van den Bergh of David Dunlap Observatory wrote in 1977: "The origin of the gas and dust which is so abundantly present in NGC 5128 remains a mystery. The existence of strong emission lines shows that the gas in this galaxy was heavily contaminated by material ejected from evolving stars. Either the gas and dust that we see was derived from evolving stars in NGC 5128 itself, or from a spiral galaxy that was sucked into NGC 5128 by dynamical friction."

NGC 5090

13ʰ18ᵐ3, −43°28′

Ga, 12ᵐ9, 1′5 × 1′5
type: E

NGC 5128

13ʰ22ᵐ4, −42°45′

Ga, 7ᵐ2, 11′2 × 8′7
type: E0p

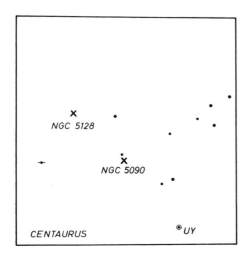

NGC 5128

NGC 5090

CENTAURUS ⊙ UY

13ʰ 25ᵐ   13ʰ 20ᵐ   13ʰ 15ᵐ   13ʰ 10ᵐ

−42°

−43°

−44°

An excellent amateur photograph of Omega Centauri taken by K. Rihm. (Newtonian reflector, f = 120 cm.)

NGC 5139 = ω Centauri

The two largest globular star clusters in the whole sky are NGC 104 = 47 Tucanae (page 25) and the cluster shown here, NGC 5139 = Omega Centauri. Their apparent diameters are about equal to that of the full Moon. Nevertheless, when seen with the naked eye, the two objects differ little from stars of magnitude 5. This explains why the two clusters initially received a number and a Greek letter, respectively. In 1837 J. Herschel observed ω Centauri from South Africa and described it thus: "The densest part of this most beautiful of all globular clusters completely filled the field of my 18¾-inch telescope with thousands of stars." In

Europe this wonderful object can only be seen from Gibraltar, Sicily, and Crete, but in the U.S.A one can observe it from all the southern states.

The astronomers of the Royal Greenwich Observatory have made a comprehensive investigation of ω Centauri with telescopes in South Africa. From the 130 RR Lyrae type variable stars known in this cluster, it has been possible to determine its distance with high accuracy as 5.5 kpc or 18,000 light-years.

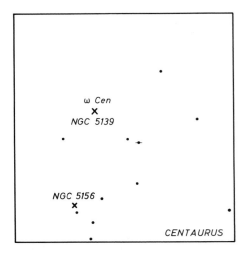

NGC 5139

(ω Cen)

13ʰ23ᵐ8, −47°03′

Gl, 4ᵐ2, F7
φ = 65′, type: VIII

NGC 5156

13ʰ25ᵐ7, −48°39′

Ga, 12ᵐ9, 1′.5 × 1′.5
type: S

M51,
the Whirlpool galaxy, with NGC 5195. The spiral arms are marked by bright young blue stars of stellar Population I. Between the spiral arms, and in the companion galaxy, older, yellower stars of Population II predominate. Thirty-minute exposure on chilled High Speed Ektachrome with the 40-inch f/3.8 Ritchey-Chrétien reflector of the U. S. Naval Observatory at Flagstaff, Arizona.

M51 = NGC 5194

M51 is one of the finest and most photographed objects in the sky. It has the most easily observed spiral structure of any galaxy; the two main arms winding in a counterclockwise direction (left-handed system) can be followed for one and a half turns.

Messier, who discovered this remarkable object in 1772, described it as a faint double nebula, whose components were touching one another. This description fits very well the appearance of M51 in a small telescope. To find the object, look one-third of the way from η Ursae Majoris to α Canum Venaticorum.

Just north of M51 one can recognize the "companion," NGC 5195. The above photograph shows that this galaxy is relatively structureless compared to M51. In fact, for a long time it was considered to be an irregular type of stellar system. E. M. Burbidge and G. R. Burbidge determined that the companion is of type S0 and is physically connected. It is not yet clear whether the northern spiral arm of M51 is projected on the companion or vice versa.

Although we are looking almost vertically onto the central plane of M51, E. M. Burbidge and G. R. Burbidge were able to establish spectroscopically a rotation curve and from this they derived a total mass of 60 billion solar masses, assuming the distance to be 4 Mpc. M51 is a radio source.

My photograph, taken before dawn, shows the trails of two Russian rockets: Cosmos 103 (interrupted trail) and Cosmos 106 (continuous trail). A detailed description of satellite movements during the 75 minutes of this exposure begins on page 228. On the left side of the picture a meteor has inscribed its path.

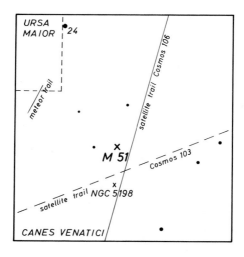

NGC 5198

13h28m2, +46°56'

Ga, 12m9, 0'6 × 0'5
type: E2

M51   NGC 5194

Whirlpool galaxy

13h27m8, +47°27'

Ga, 8m9, 10'7 × 7'0
type: Sc

NGC 5195

13h27m9, +47°31'

Ga, 10m5, 2'0 × 1'5
type: Irr

M83. In this striking three-color composite photograph, processes of stellar birth and evolution that were painstakingly pieced together by astronomers before the advent of color astrophotography come dramatically to life.

The inner edges of the spiral arms are lined with dark clouds of gas and dust, which redden (or brown) the light of stars shining through. In many of these clouds, bright pink emission nebulae appear, where clusters of hot, newly formed stars have condensed out of the dark material and excite the gas to glow by their ultraviolet light. Eventually their radiation disperses the nebular matter, leaving bright associations of young blue stars. These are seen here just outside the regions of star formation. In the center of the galaxy dust and gas are generally absent, and older, yellower stars provide most of the light.

Photograph made from three plates taken with the 4-meter telescope at the Cerro Tololo Inter-American Observatory. Copyright 1980, Association of Universities for Research in Astronomy, Inc.

M83 = NGC 5236

One of the ten largest galaxies in the whole sky, and indeed one of the most beautiful in the Southern Hemisphere, is NGC 5236 = M83. Lacaille discovered this object in 1751 or 1752, and Messier saw this "nebula without stars" quite by accident on March 18, 1781, while searching for comets. He described it as structureless and wrote that it could only be seen with the greatest difficulty. J. Herschel found M83 "a very remarkable object" and noted its bright center. The enlargement above shows the characteristic details of an S-type galaxy in the de Vaucouleurs classification system (see page 90): a relatively small central bulge from which two prominent spiral arms emerge in the shape of an S. Many star clouds and extensive patches of absorbing matter are easily recognizable.

According to de Vaucouleurs, M83 is about eight million light-years away from us. With an absolute magnitude of −19^{m}5, it is about equal in luminosity to our Milky Way or the Andromeda nebula (page 17). According to R. Hanbury Brown and C. Hazard, M83 is an intense radio source. Four supernovae have been observed in this galaxy, in 1923, 1950, 1958, and 1968.

The brightest of the several faint galaxies in this field is NGC 5253, within the constellation Centaurus. Older classifications place it among the elliptical galaxies, but de Vaucouleurs finds that it is an irregular barred galaxy.

HYDRA

•

•   •

•   x
    M 83

- - - - - - - - - - - - - - - - - -

NGC
  x
5253   CENTAURUS

M83   NGC 5236
13ʰ34ᵐ3, − 29°37′

Ga, 8ᵐ0, 10ʹ5 × 9ʹ3
type: Sc

NGC 5253
13ʰ37ᵐ1, − 31°24′

Ga, 10ᵐ8, 3ʹ5 × 1ʹ4
type: 1Bp(Vau)

-29°

-30°

-31°

13ʰ|40m   13ʰ|35m   13ʰ|30m

M3
photographed at Lick Observatory
on Mount Hamilton.

M3 = NGC 5272

Next to M13 in Hercules (page 167), M3 is the most magnificent globular star cluster in the northern sky. Even with binoculars, one can find the cluster easily by centering the field of view ½° north of the star β Comae (4ᵐ3) and sweeping about 7° eastward. In a telescope of 10-cm aperture, one can make out some individual stars near the edges, but even with the largest telescopes it is not possible to resolve fully the central area.

M3 has long been and still is the subject of ardent research. One reason for this is the position of the cluster far away from the Milky Way in a region exceptionally free of interstellar absorption. Many astronomers have studied the more than 200 variable stars, mostly of the RR Lyrae type, which have been found in M3, and by means of the period-luminosity relation, have tried to assess its distance. On 10 exposures taken with the 200-inch Hale telescope, H. L. Johnson and A. R. Sandage counted 44,500 stars, exclusive of the unresolved central regions. From this they derived a total mass of about 245,000 suns. Their work also included the compilation of a color-magnitude diagram, which shows all the typical signs of a globular cluster: the thin horizontal giant branch and the much broader main sequence, which ends with the yellow dwarf stars because the still-fainter red dwarfs are not visible at such a great distance.

W. Lohmann determined the distances of M3 and 66 other globular clusters, taking into consideration the effect of interstellar absorption on the total brightness. For the absolute magnitude of the cluster's RR Lyrae stars, he adopted 0ᵐ7 instead of 0ᵐ0. This resulted in a new distance of 9.6 kpc for M3 as compared with the older value of 13 kpc. Studying the brightness distributions from the center to the edge of 16 globular clusters, Lohmann deduced central densities of up to 10,000 solar masses per cubic parsec; for M3 the figure was 5,000 solar masses. In 1973 G. Alcaino found an improved distance of 10.7 kpc. N. J. Woolf has estimated the age of M3 as 10 billion years.

CANES VENATICI

×
M 3
.

.

BOOTES

CO
MA

M3 NGC 5272
13ʰ39ᵐ9, +28°38′

Gl, 7ᵐ2, Sp: F7
φ = 18′.6, type: VI

+30°

+29°

+28°

+27°

13ʰ 45ᵐ   13ʰ 40ᵐ   13ʰ 35ᵐ

M101 from an exposure taken with the 200-inch Hale telescope.

M101 = NGC 5457

When I am taking photographic exposures in higher declinations, the camera does not require much guiding, which allows me enough time to observe the main object through binoculars. Often this is easier than with a medium size telescope, provided one knows the object's position relative to some nearby stars. To do this an ordinary atlas will not suffice, as very often the neighboring stars are fainter than 8^m0.

During such a visual exploration I saw M101 through 10 x 50 binoculars, though it is said to be as faint as visual magnitude 9.6. I could make out an unmistakable pale but well-defined spot. On the other hand, this object, which spreads over an area of several hundred square minutes, was suspected rather than seen in a 15-cm telescope.

Messier saw M101 on March 27, 1781, after Méchain had discovered this object earlier in the same year. In the mid-

dle of the last century Lord Rosse recognized the object as a spiral nebula. Even my small-scale photograph shows a great deal of detail in this classic Sc spiral, but a giant telescope is needed to reveal the intricate fine structure in the well-resolved spiral arms, as seen above. Near the small but very bright central lens is a large area of interlaced slender dark lanes which more or less follow the course of the spiral arms.

The American radio astronomer N. H. Dieter measured the profile of the 21-cm line of neutral hydrogen at many points in the galaxy. From her data E. E. Epstein later deduced a mass of 180 billion suns for M101. According to A. Sandage and G. Tammann (1974), M101 is 1.2 Mpc distant; other estimates have placed it at about 4 Mpc.

The Earth satellite which drew the faint trail in the lower right part of the photograph could not be identified.

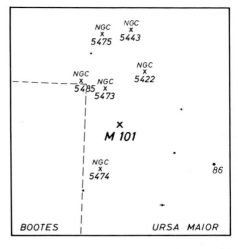

Ga, 9m0, 24'.5 × 23'.4
type: Sc

NGC	α	δ	m_p	Dim:	Type:
5422	13h59m0	+ 55°24'	13m0	3'.0 × 0'.6	Sa
5443	14 00.4	+ 56 03	13.7	2.2 × 0.8	S?
5473	14 03.0	+ 55 08	12.4	1.7 × 1.1	E
5474	14 03.2	+ 53 54	11.7	4.0 × 3.8	Sc
5475	14 03.5	+ 55 59	13.4	2.7 × 0.5	S
5485	14 05.4	+ 55 16	12.6	1.5 × 1.5	E

NGC 5907
U. S. Naval Observatory
photograph.

NGC 5866
Lick Observatory photograph with
the 120-inch Shane reflector.

NGC 5866 (M102)

The galaxy M102 is not among the objects Messier took into his catalogue or supplements. Although the lens-shaped system was discovered by Méchain and reported by him to Messier, the latter never checked it, probably due to his old age. O. Gingerich has put this object in place of Messier's original M102, which proved to be identical with M101.

Whereas M102 looks rather insignificant on the facing picture, due to the small scale, the lower photograph on this page reveals several noteworthy details, such as the bright central bulge with an elliptical halo, girdled by a very narrow disk, which appears as a dark line in front of the central bulge but a bright one in front of the halo. According to a study by E. M. Burbidge and G. R. Burbidge, the absorption zone is inclined 2° to the plane of symmetry of the system.

Among the faint galaxies in this field in Draco, NGC 5907 shows up prominently as an edgewise spiral system. It resembles NGC 4565 (page 123) but has a smaller central bulge, which is partly covered up by dusty matter.

DRACO

NGC 5879
x

NGC
x
5907

x
M 102

NGC NGC
x x 5905
5908

BOOTES

NGC 5908
15ʰ15ᵐ4, +55°36'

Ga, 13ᵐ0, 2'.8 × 0'.7
type: S

NGC 5905
15ʰ14ᵐ1, +55°42'

Ga, 13ᵐ1, 3'.6 × 2'.6
type: Sb

M102   NGC 5866
15ʰ05ᵐ1, +55°57'

Ga, 11ᵐ5, 2'.4 × 1'.3
type: Sa

NGC 5907
15ʰ14ᵐ6, +56°31'

Ga, 11ᵐ8, 11'.8 × 1'.3
type: Sc

NGC 5879
15ʰ08ᵐ4, +57°12'

Ga, 12ᵐ1, 4'.3 × 1'.3
type: Sb

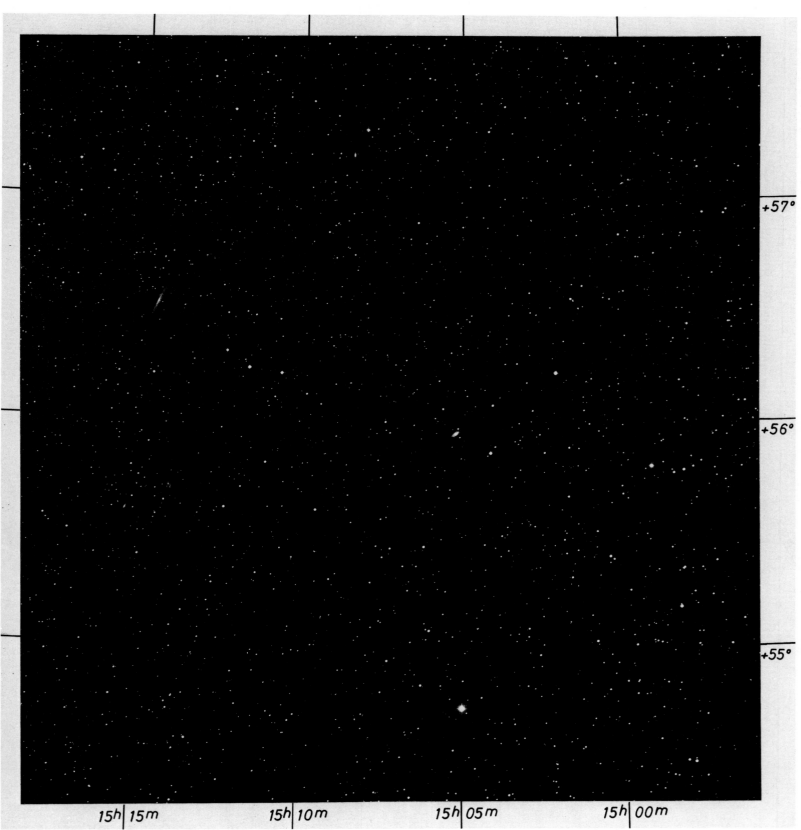

+57°

+56°

+55°

15ʰ 15ᵐ   15ʰ 10ᵐ   15ʰ 05ᵐ   15ʰ 00ᵐ

Planetary nebulae (Pl)

Among the nebulae that spectroscopic observations reveal as being gaseous, some have well-defined circular or elliptical disks, which when viewed in a telescope often resemble planetary disks. We therefore call these objects planetary nebulae, though they have nothing in common with planets. The most obvious difference between them and the chaotic nebulae is their symmetric structure. One finds among them circular disks of uniform brightness (NGC 246, page 19), well-shaped rings (M57, page 199), and overlapping incomplete rings. The largest planetary nebulae have apparent diameters of up to 15 minutes of arc (NGC 7293, page 235). About a dozen have diameters of just over one minute, but the great majority are only a few seconds of arc in size and are thus rather difficult to distinguish from stars. From the few reliable distance estimates, the true dimensions of planetary nebulae vary between 0.02 and 5 pc. Well over 1,000 planetary nebulae have been catalogued. For the planetary nebulae in this book, the following data are given: name and position, apparent photographic magnitudes of the nebula (m_p) and of the central star, longest and shortest angular dimension (Dim), and type.

The distribution of planetary nebulae over the sky shows a concentration toward the central line of the Milky Way, especially in the case of the smaller (often more distant) nebulae. A few brighter ones can, however, be found in higher galactic latitudes. Furthermore, there seems to be a concentration toward the galactic center. Clearly, the planetary nebulae are members of our galaxy and have a space distribution typical of Population I stars. According to current theory, every star that is not too massive goes through a planetary-nebula stage late in its life. At the center of each planetary nebula is a usually dim but always very hot star, which as a rule is up to seven magnitudes fainter than the total light of the nebula. For the larger planetaries, spectroscopic evidence confirms that the gaseous shell is expanding outward from the central star. This ejection is much less violent than the outburst of a nova or a supernova (compare Crab nebula, M1, page 63).

The planetary nebulae without exception have emission-line spectra, sometimes with some indication of a continuum. The nebulae are induced to shine by the ultraviolet radiation of the central star.

Continued

M5 = NGC 5904

The bright globular star cluster M5 was discovered as early as 1702 by G. Kirch. It is very close to the star 5 Serpentis (5^m2), somewhat outside the band of the Milky Way. M5 stands out well in a field that is sparse in stars. It is clearly visible in binoculars, and under extremely favorable conditions can even be detected with the naked eye. When seen in a large amateur telescope, this splendid cluster is most impressive, as the number of relatively bright stars (12^m0 to 14^m0) is quite large.

H. C. Arp is among the many astronomers who have investigated this cluster. His color-magnitude diagram for more than 1,000 stars to as faint as 22^m0 was compiled from photometric measurements with the 200-inch Hale tele-

scope. This diagram shows a great similarity to that of M3 (page 153). M5 is 8 kpc away from us. It is one of the oldest globular clusters known; Arp in 1962 calculated an age of 13 billion years. In our photograph the cluster's diameter is only 12', but large telescopes show it to be as much as 20' across.

The two stars 5 and 6 Serpentis are visual doubles. The Aitken Catalogue lists them, respectively, as ADS 9584 with components A = 5^m2 and B = 9^m2 at a distance of $27''2$ (component C of 9th magnitude is $127''$ distant in the same direction as B), and ADS 9596 with A = 5^m5 and B = 10^m1 at a distance of $3''1$.

M5   NGC 5904

15ʰ16ᵐ0, +2°16′

GI, 7ᵐ0, F5
φ = 19′.9, type: V

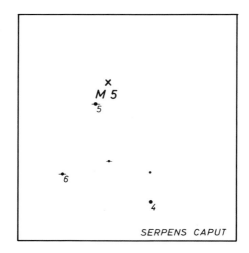

SERPENS CAPUT

+3°
+2°
+1°

15ʰ 20ᵐ   15ʰ 15ᵐ   15ʰ 10ᵐ

The classification of planetary nebulae that has been adopted for this book indicates their outward appearance:

I   = stellar
IIa = oval, uniformly bright, concentrated
IIb = oval, uniformly bright, without concentration
IIIa = oval, unevenly bright
IIIb = oval, unevenly bright, with brighter edges
IV = annular
V   = irregular
VI = anomalous

Other objects

The text accompanying the photographs often mentions neighboring bright stars that are helpful in locating the clusters, galaxies, and nebulae. Visual magnitudes on the Harvard system are given for these reference stars.

Also, a number of prominent double stars that are easily resolved in small telescopes have been included, if they are in the same field of view as the principal object. These doubles are identified by their number in the Aitken Catalogue (ADS). For each double, apparent magnitude and angular separations are given. A few variable stars are described.

M80 = NGC 6093

This chart photograph should be viewed with the one following, because these fields in the constellation Scorpius partly overlap. The alert reader will notice that some stars shown on both pictures are different in appearance. The reason is that the facing photograph was exposed on an orthochromatic film and the following one on a somewhat coarser-grained panchromatic emulsion. The second picture shows rather better the outer parts of the reflection nebulae, whose data are given on page 163. Almost the entire field, with the exception of the upper right corner, is covered with dark clouds of interstellar dust, completely blotting out some of the background stars.

A small but very concentrated globular cluster, M80, is situated on the western border of one of these dark clouds. This cluster was discovered by Méchain in 1781. In May 1860, a nova (T Scorpii) appeared in the cluster, quickly brightening to magnitude 6.8, but fading to invisibility by June 16th. Five variable stars are known in this cluster, whose distance from us is 7.8 kpc.

The second known case of a nova in a globular cluster was observed in M14.

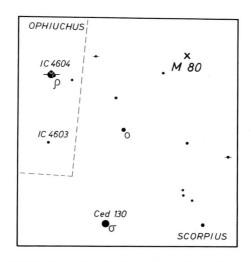

IC 4603 – 4
16ʰ22ᵐ3, − 23°20′

N, m⋆ = 4.76
φ = 145′ × 70′, type: c

M80   NGC 6093
16ʰ14ᵐ1, − 22°52′

Gl, 8ᵐ4, Sp: F4
φ = 5′.1, type: II

Ced 130
16ʰ18ᵐ2, − 25°28′

N, m⋆ = 3.08
φ = 85′ × 40′, type: c

The Milky Way in the Scorpius-Sagittarius region. The northern part of this photograph overlaps the one on page 184.

All of Scorpius is visible here. Antares, at upper right center, is seen surrounded by the red reflection nebula IC 4606 and accompanied by the globular cluster M4 (see page 163). Visible above ζ Scorpii are the clusters NGC 6231 and H12, topped by the reddish nebula IC 4628 (see page 171). The globular clusters M19 and M62 (page 173) can be found in this photo with the aid of a good star atlas as faint "stars" in the region east of Antares.

Northwest of the two tail stars of Scorpius, λ and ν, the two nebulae NGC 6334 and 6357 lie in the Milky Way's Great Rift (page 179). The bright open clusters M6 and M7 (page 183) are prominent a little farther east and north. The Lagoon nebula (M8) is the bright red glow at upper left. Above it can be seen the Trifid nebula (M20) and the cluster M21 (see page 187).

The three "spout" stars of the Teapot asterism in Sagittarius are near the left edge. A bright star cloud of the Milky Way seems to emerge northwestward from the spout like a puff of steam.

Photograph by the author.

M4 = NGC 6121

The photograph at right shows a remarkable area of the sky, the region northwest of Scorpius' main star, Antares (1^{m}2). If an observer points his or her telescope at Antares and moves it slightly westward, the magnificent globular cluster M4 will come into vision. P. L. de Chéseaux discovered this object in 1746, but it was Messier who recognized M4 as a cluster in 1764. In contrast to most other globular clusters, M4 is fairly open, and when viewed through a telescope of only 6-10-cm aperture, even gives the impression of being an open cluster. This may be partly due to its comparatively small distance of only 1.8 kpc, according to G. Alcaino (1975).

Another much smaller globular cluster is NGC 6144, about ½° northwest of Antares. It was first seen by W. Herschel in 1784. The trail of a meteor is seen in the middle of the picture, making a kind of celestial exclamation mark.

Most of the field is covered by clouds of interstellar gas and dust. Absorption by the dust completely blots out the stars in the background. In the neighborhood of bright stars, these cosmic dust clouds reflect starlight. One example of such a reflection nebula appears at top center: IC 4604 near the double star ρ Ophiuchi (ADS 10049, A = 5^{m}9, B = 5^{m}2, distance 3″5). Almost one degree below it is another: IC 4603, near the star CD −24° 12684 (8^{m}3). Also nearby are IC 4605 near 22 Scorpii (4^{m}9), IC 4606 north of Antares, and the nebula Cederblad 130 near σ Scorpii (3^{m}1).

Antares is a double star (ADS 10074), having a companion of magnitude 6.5 at a distance of 2″9; J. Hopmann calculated a period of 853 years, but this is extremely uncertain.

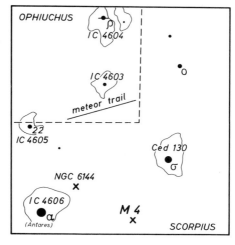

M4 NGC 6121
16ʰ20ᵐ6, −26°24′

Gl, 7ᵐ4, Sp: F
φ = 22′.8, type: IX

NGC 6144
16ʰ24ᵐ2, −25°56′

Gl, 10ᵐ8, Sp: ?
φ = 6′.2, type: XI

Nebula	α	δ	Dim:	Sp:
Ced 130	16ʰ17ᵐ8	−25°28′	130′ × 80′	c
IC 4603	16 22.1	−24 21	25 × 20	c
IC 4604	16 22.3	−23 20	124 × 124	c
IC 4606	16 26.4	−26 20	85 × 80	c
IC 4605	16 27.0	−25 03	30 × 30	c

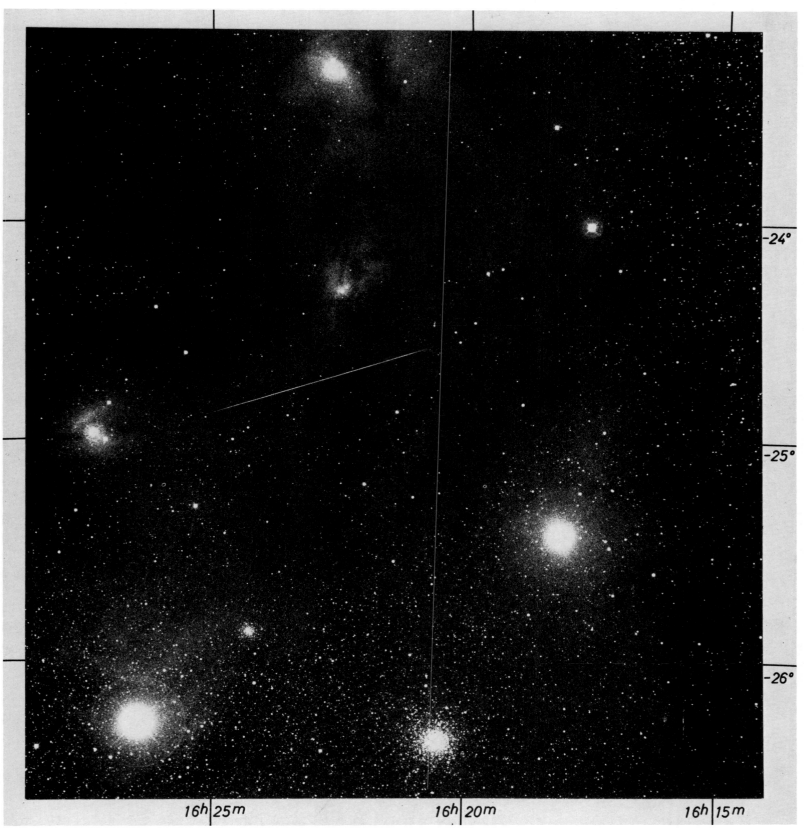

CHARLES MESSIER

Charles Messier and his catalogue

Messier's catalogue of nebulae and clusters, which is so widely used today, was not the outcome of a systematic search for these objects, as was the work of William Herschel, who used much larger instruments a short time later. Messier's interest centered on a completely different group of celestial bodies, namely comets. As a comet observer and discoverer, he achieved more success than any other astronomer before him. Messier found 21 new comets, 15 of them before they were observed by anyone else, and closely followed the orbital movements of nearly 50 others.

In 1751, when Messier was 21 and his parents had just died, he left his home in Badonvillier, Lorraine, and moved to Paris as an assistant to the astronomer J. N. Delisle (1685-1768). At first Messier was employed only as a copyist, but later he was allowed to do some observing. From the year 1754 he did all the observation work at Delisle's observatory, which was then situated in the attic of an eight-sided tower belonging to the Hotel de Cluny in Paris.

His first effort to find a comet ended in failure. Delisle had made a chart showing the anticipated path Halley's comet would take during its 1758-59 return, and he gave this to Messier as a guide. For 18 months Messier systematically probed the area in which the comet was expected, but without success; the orbit Delisle used was incorrect. Thus on Christmas of 1758, Johann Georg Palitzsch, a farmer from Prohlitz near Dresden in Saxony, found the comet before Messier. Due to bad communications in those days, made even worse by the Seven Years' War then raging, news of the discovery took three months to reach Paris. In the meantime Messier had become skeptical of the chart and found the comet on January 21, 1759, just one month after Palitzsch. Thereafter Messier followed the comet on every clear night.

Continued on page 168

M107 = NGC 6171

M107 is a small, loose globular cluster in Ophiuchus. It is one of the seven objects discovered by Méchain and later confirmed by Messier that did not receive M numbers until 1954, when O. Gingerich at Harvard Observatory evaluated the original Messier notes.

Photometric research on M107 began only as late as 1961.

Three-color measurements of 293 stars in the cluster have been made by A. Sandage and B. Katem, who compiled a color-magnitude diagram. The cluster's stars show signs of relatively high metal content, unlike stars in other globulars. Due to the sparsity of stars near the cluster's edge, the apparent diameter of M107 may be an underestimate; a value of 10'.0 has recently been suggested.

M107 NGC 6171

16ʰ29ᵐ7, − 12°57′

Gl, 10ᵐ1, Sp: G2
φ = 7ʹ.8, type: X

OPHIUCHUS

ζ

ν

×
M 107

16ʰ 35ᵐ   16ʰ 30ᵐ   16ʰ 25ᵐ

−11°

−12°

−13°

M13
Hale Observatories photograph.

M13 = NGC 6205

M13 is one of the most beautiful objects in the northern sky. With an apparent diameter of 23′, it is the largest globular cluster north of the celestial equator. Halley saw the cluster as early as 1714, and when Messier observed it some 50 years later he described it as a nebula without stars, round and bright, and fainter toward the edge. W. Herschel was the first to recognize it as a cluster and estimated that it contained 14,000 stars. Modern estimates give 500,000 stars.

It is an instructive experience to observe M13 first with the naked eye, then in binoculars, in a 6-cm telescope, and finally with a large aperture. The increase in resolution will be vividly brought home. This same effect can be produced photographically with a large instrument by giving a longer exposure time to each successive picture. The beginner can easily identify this cluster in binoculars; once seen, its appearance and its characteristic position between two 8th-magnitude stars cannot be forgotten.

Of the many scientific studies of M13, that by H. C. Arp and H. L. Johnson is one of the most significant. Their very accurate color-magnitude diagram of a large number of M13 stars shows particularly clearly how the spectral distribution of these stars differs from that in open clusters. In 1963, S. I. Kadla announced that he had measured the proper motion of M13, using the galaxy NGC 6207 as a standard of rest. My photograph shows this galaxy about ½° above and to the left of M13. Only 10 variable stars have been discovered in this rich cluster.

M13   NGC 6205
16ʰ39ᵐ9, +36°33′

Gl, 6ᵐ8, Sp: F5
φ = 23′.2, type: V

NGC 6207
16ʰ41ᵐ3, +36°56′

Ga, 12ᵐ3, 2′.7 × 1′.2
type: Sb

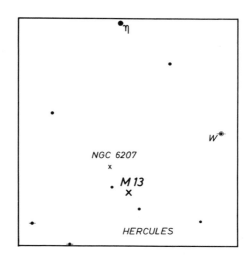

But Delisle had become a gouty, stubborn old man, and refused to give Messier permission to publicize his discovery. Eventually, as the comet approached the Sun's vicinity, it was lost from view. When, at last, news of Palitzsch's discovery reached France, it was too late for further observations.

Other astronomers, angered by Delisle's stubbornness, refused to recognize Messier's observations as authentic. On the other hand, Delisle was not inclined to accept the discovery of a farmer from Saxony.

Fortunately, Messier did not let himself be put off by these circumstances. Delisle soon retired and Messier took his place. In 1759 he found his second comet, and for the next 15 years nearly all new discoveries were his. He came to consider this particular domain his very own, and King Louis XV even gave him the nickname "Comet Ferret."

Moreover, Messier was an ardent observer of occultations and eclipses, and his notebooks contain extensive data on sunspots and meteorology. However, the development of his famous catalogue, containing deep-sky objects between declination 70° north and 35° south, was quite slow, being a by-product of his comet observations. The main reason for drafting the catalogue was to help comet observers avoid being misled by objects of similar appearance. This resemblance is most noticeable in spherical and elliptical galaxies, as well as in the central regions of others. With binoculars or the naked eye, open clusters of the Milky Way appear diffuse, hazy, and cometlike; the same effect is present for globular clusters viewed with a small telescope.

Messier used several small instruments, which were quite adequate for his work of locating comets. In his early days he particularly favored a Gregorian reflector with an aperture of 19 cm and a length of 80 cm. In light-gathering power it was comparable to a modern instrument of only about 9-cm aperture, due to the poor quality of its metal mirrors. Likewise, the 20-cm Newtonian telescope belonging to Delisle, which apparently was the main instrument at the Marine Observatory, also had a slow f-ratio. Later, Messier used several achromatic lenses from Dollond, all with a 9-cm aperture and a 110-cm focal length. Hence, all the instruments at his disposal can be duplicated by any enthusiast today.

Messier's catalogue is not arranged by right ascension but roughly in order of discovery. Its first object is the Crab nebula in Taurus, which he found on September 12, 1758, while watching a comet he had detected 14 days before. Messier marked its exact position on the chart he had been using for following the comet, a

Continued

M10 = NGC 6254, M12 = NGC 6218

Within this field of evenly distributed faint stars in the constellation Ophiuchus are two globular star clusters: M10 and M12. They are not only alike in brightness and apparent diameter, but also in concentration, and both are about 5 kpc distant from us. Messier discovered them on two consecutive nights in May, 1764.

As already mentioned, the apparent diameter of a globular cluster depends on the size of the telescope. Visually, it is influenced by the observer's eyesight; photographically, the exposure time and sensitivity of the emulsion are decisive. It is not surprising that published figures of the same cluster grow larger and larger as time progresses. The sequence for M12 runs: 8'.0 in 1929, 9'.3 in 1937, 12'.2 in 1946, and 14'.5 in 1977.

H. C. Arp, who studied M10, found that the color-magnitude diagram he plotted for 256 member stars showed a marked resemblance to those of M2 and M92.

M10   NGC 6254
16ʰ54ᵐ5, − 4°02′

Gl, 7ᵐ6, Sp: G0
φ = 12′.2, type: VII

M12   NGC 6218
16ʰ44ᵐ6, − 1°52′

Gl, 8ᵐ0, Sp: F7
φ = 12′.2, type: IX

×
M 12

×
M 10

OPHIUCHUS

−2°

−3°

−4°

16ʰ 55ᵐ   16ʰ 50ᵐ   16ʰ 45ᵐ

procedure he employed for all subsequent discoveries. M2, a globular cluster in Aquarius, is shown on a chart for Halley's comet. In 1764 Messier began searching with more zeal, and in the following months added 38 "nebulae" to his collection. He then made a special search for some of the nebulae discovered by Hevelius with the naked eye some 200 years previously. Most of these turned out to be only loose groups of faint stars, and Messier listed them as nonexistent. But in the case of M40 he had some doubts, and included it, though only two faint stars without nebulosity were visible. M40 has since been omitted from the Messier catalogue.

In January 1765 he accidentally found the cluster south of Sirius (M41), and in March certified the positions of three previously known objects, the Orion nebula (M42 and M43), Praesepe (M44), and the Pleiades (M45). Although Messier discovered most of the objects in his catalogue, many of them, as in the case of M1, were known before, a fact which he did not try to hide upon publication.

In his first list of 45 objects, presented to the French Academy in 1771 and published in 1774, a number of southern objects are missing, though they had already been reported by Lacaille in 1755. These were added later.

Three nights after handing over the list, Messier recorded the positions of four additional objects, two of which could not be found again, even though their alleged positions were in relatively sparse areas near good comparison stars.

Further numbers were added during the next year. In 1777 he observed the cluster M55, which Lacaille had already detected. It had been listed as an uncertain nebula, because Messier was unable to find it in 1764. Then in 1779, while following a comet, he quickly detected nine nebulae, one after the other, most of them lying in the Coma-Virgo region. For the 1781 edition of the French astronomical yearbook Connaissance des Temps, he was able to supply a supplementary list of 23 numbers, through M68.

Continued

IC 4628, NGC 6231, 6242, 6268

The facing photograph represents part of the Scorpion's tail. The picture is dominated by three galactic clusters, NGC 6231, NGC 6242, and NGC 6268. NGC 6231, half a degree north of ζ^1 and ζ^2 (not a binary), is the richest in bright stars.

Above the center a cloud of ionized hydrogen can be seen with a detached small component northeast of it. The correct position of IC 4628, found by E. E. Barnard in the year 1893, is given in J. L. E. Dreyer's New General Catalogue and Index Catalogue, whereas the well-known Atlas Coeli and catalogue by A. Becvar give an incorrect position at

R.A. = 16^h49^m3, Dec. = $-40°18'$ for 1950.0. Obviously in this position there is no nebulosity.

In and south of IC 4628 a noticeable association of about 200 stars, known as H 12, seems to be physically connected.

On the left-hand side are some remarkable elongated dark clouds. On the right-hand, star chains, both straight and curved, attract our attention. The general consensus of astronomers is that such chains are merely accidental groupings on the sky.

IC 4628
16ʰ53ᵐ3, −40°18′

N, 34′ × 16′

H12
16ʰ52ᵐ7, −40°38′

Cl + N, 8ᵐ5, 200 ★
ϕ = 40′, type: c

NGC 6231
16ʰ50ᵐ7, −41°43′

Cl, 8ᵐ5, 120 ★
ϕ = 15′, type: e

NGC 6268
16ʰ58ᵐ6, −39°39′

Cl, 9ᵐ5, 30 ★
ϕ = 10′, type: f

NGC 6242
16ʰ52ᵐ2, −39°25′

Cl, 8ᵐ1, 40 ★
ϕ = 10′, type: f

Soon after 1780 another successful comet discoverer, Pierre Méchain (1744-1805), came onto the scene. He had been introduced to astronomy by Lalande and, through his excellent theoretical work, had distinguished himself from Messier, who was purely an observer.

Méchain found two new comets in 1781. During his probing of the heavens in 1780-1781, he discovered about 30 nebulous objects that were previously unknown. But there was no jealousy between these enthusiastic observers. Méchain always informed his older colleague of new findings, and Messier in turn checked their positions while making his own observations. Finally, the objects were numbered and included in the catalogue. Méchain seems to have paid particular attention to the numerous faint nebulae in the Coma-Virgo area. Following Méchain, on March 18, 1781, Messier himself discovered nine nebulae in this area. One of these, M91, is among the missing Messier objects.

In 1781 Messier completed the second supplement to his catalogue. It included 27 objects discovered by Méchain and brought the catalogue numbers up to 103. Unfortunately, Messier did not check on two nebulae reported by Mechain in Ursa Major and included them as M101 and M102. Later M102 proved identical with M101, the well-known and beautiful galaxy near Eta Ursae Majoris. On the other hand, the last entry, M103, is an unimportant cluster in Cassiopeia. This list was published in the 1784 edition of the Connaissance des Temps, with the positions of M102 and M103 omitted. Bode's Berlin Astronomical Yearbook of 1786 listed M46 to M100, and his Uranographia of 1801 included the Messier catalogue from M1 to M100.

In November, 1781, Messier's work was interrupted by an unfortunate accident. While walking in the park of Manceau, he hastily stepped through an open doorway and plunged about 25 feet into an ice cellar. Luckily he was soon found and, with the aid of ropes and ladders, was hauled to the top, where it was discovered that he had multiple fractures.

But a year after his accident Messier was back in the observatory preparing for a Mercury transit. With feverish zeal, he dedicated himself to observing many objects, including comets and Herschel's newly discovered planet Uranus, as well as occultations and eclipses.

From Messier's notes it can be seen that he periodically checked and rechecked the positions of various nebulae, as well as some new ones that Méchain had brought to his attention. He gathered this information for a revised and improved edition of his catalogue to be published in 1790, but due to the confusion of the 1789 revolution and the ensuing inflation, the publication was canceled. Messier's salary as a member of the Academy ceased, and even the overhead expenses for the observatory were stopped. Although he possessed some capital, this did not last very long in the inflation period. Occasionally he was forced to borrow oil from Lalande for his observing lamp. Despite everything, he continued with his observations and in September, 1793, discovered a new comet. To work out the comet's orbit he sent his findings to Bochard de Saron, former president of the French Assembly and an able mathematician, who was at the time in prison (and soon afterward executed).

Continued on page 176

M19 = NGC 6273, M62 = NGC 6266

Not far east of Antares (α Scorpii) lie two very pretty globular star clusters, M19 and M62. These differ almost exactly 4° in declination and have practically the same right ascension. In order that both clusters could be shown together, our picture has been turned 45° to place north at upper right. The clusters resemble each other in their angular diameter and apparent brightness. In each, the brightest stars are of magnitude 14 to 15. As can be surmised from their M numbers, Messier discovered them at very different times, in fact 15 years apart (1764 and 1779).

The two clusters belong to a group seemingly concentrated around the galactic center (see also page 132). They lie amid the rich star clouds of the Sagittarius Milky Way, where dark matter is also seen. This makes it difficult to determine the true sizes of these clusters, since they are dimmed by interstellar absorption and blend with the faint stars of the Milky Way, which are foreground objects. W. Lohmann, who made a statistical study of 67 globular clusters, came to the conclusion that interstellar absorption strongly diminishes the apparent diameters of M19 and M62.

M19 NGC 6273
16ʰ59ᵐ5, −26°11'

Gl, 8ᵐ3, Sp: F3
$\phi = 5'.3$, type: VIII

M62 NGC 6266
16ʰ58ᵐ1, −30°03'

Gl, 8ᵐ2, Sp: F8
$\phi = 6'.3$, type: IV

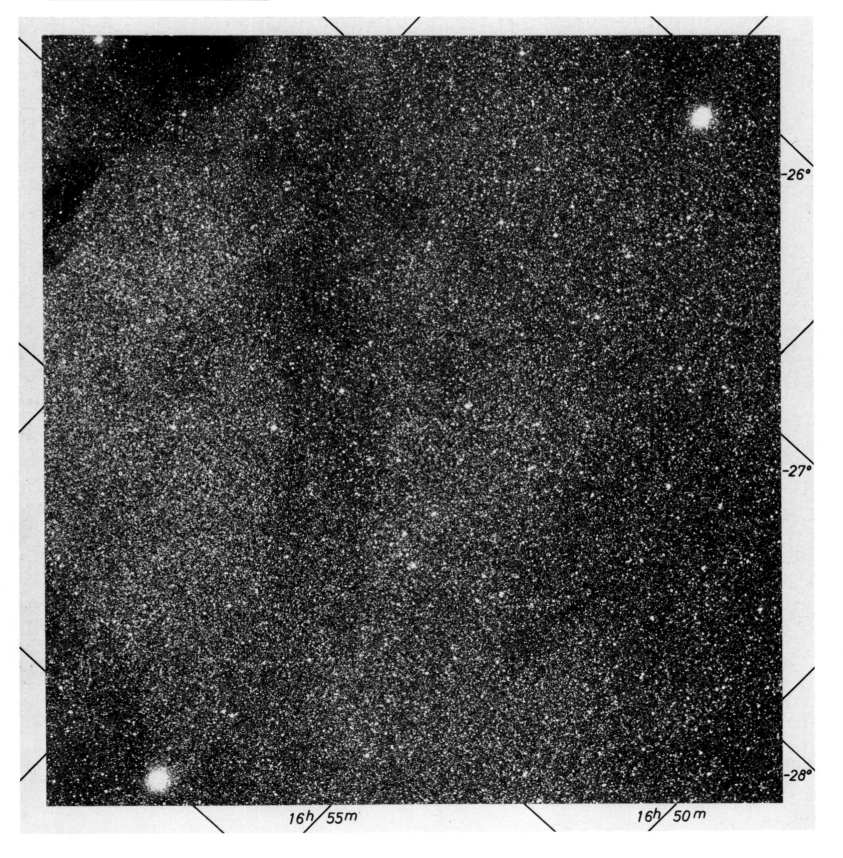

M 19

M 62

OPHIUCHUS

−26°

−27°

−28°

16ʰ 55m

16ʰ 50m

M92. Lick Observatory photograph with the 120-inch Shane reflector.

M92 = NGC 6341

The globular star cluster M92 in the constellation Hercules is less conspicuous and only half as large in angular diameter as its famous neighbor M13 (page 167). All the same, it is possible to resolve its outer regions into stars with a telescope of only 10-cm aperture. Messier observed M92 on March 18, 1781, and compared its appearance to that of the head of a comet. The object had already been discovered by J. E. Bode in 1777.

In an important study of M92, A. Sandage and M. F. Walker compiled a detailed color-magnitude diagram of over 200 stars, all fairly bright and of low metal content. The total mass of M92 is about 340,000 solar masses, according to G. Alcaino, who gives the distance as 8.1 kpc.

M92 NGC 6341

$17^h15^m6, +43°12'$

Gl, 7^m3, Sp: F2
$\phi = 12'2$, type: IV

M 92

HERCULES

+44°

+43°

+42°

+41°

17^h 20^m   17^h 15^m   17^h 10^m

Méchain, who between 1791 and 1797 worked on geodesy to establish the new unit of length (1 m = 1 ten-millionth of the distance from the Earth's equator to its pole), also lost all his possessions and money. However, after political conditions improved, both astronomers were reinstated as members of the Academy of Science and the Bureau des Longitudes, and Méchain was made director of the Observatory in Paris. Messier died on April 12, 1817, at the age of 86.

Apparently Messier intended to bring out a revised and extended edition of his catalogue after 1800, arranged in order of right ascension. But, probably through pressure of work and of old age (he was already 70 at the turn of the century), this project was never realized.

Around 1801 he comprehensively voiced his views on the purpose of his catalogue in the Connaissance des Temps:

"What caused me to undertake the catalogue was the nebula I discovered above the southern horn of Taurus on September 12, 1758, while observing the comet of that year. . . . This nebula had such a resemblance to a comet, in its form and brightness, that I endeavored to find others, so that astronomers would not confuse these same nebulae with comets just beginning to shine. I observed further with the proper refractors for the search of comets, and this is the purpose I had in forming the catalogue. After me, the celebrated Herschel published a catalogue of 2,000 objects which he had observed. This unveiling of the sky, made with instruments of great aperture, does not help in a perusal of the sky for faint comets. Thus my object is different from his, as I only need nebulae visible in a telescope of two feet [length]. Since the publication of my catalogue I have observed still others; I will publish them in the future, according to the order of right ascension, for the purpose of making them easier to recognize, and to reduce the uncertainty for those searching for comets."

Most of the above account was taken from descriptive notes by Owen Gingerich (Harvard Observatory) in Sky & Telescope. He was instrumental in extending Messier's catalogue from M103 to M109. The addition of these numbers seemed justified, as the objects were discovered by Méchain and their existence was confirmed by Messier. The proof of this was found in Messier's handwritten notes in his personal copy of the original catalogue, as well as a letter published in the Berlin Astronomical Yearbook.

The missing objects in Messier's catalogue

What explanation is there for the absence of Messier numbers 40, 47, 48, 91 and 102? M40 and M102 have been accounted for previously. The remaining three cases are a little more complicated.

Some time ago, Owen Gingerich of Harvard Observatory made a probable identification of these objects, from a careful study of all the available observing notes, sketches, and original publications of Messier.

The Connaissance des Temps of 1783 gave the following description of M46, M47, and M48 (positions reduced to 1950.0):

M46 = 7^{h}39^{m}6, − 14°42′
Cluster of very faint stars, between the head of the Great Dog and the two hind feet of the Unicorn, located by comparing this cluster with the 6th-magnitude star 2 Navis (according to Flamsteed); these stars can be seen only with a good refractor; the cluster contains a little nebulosity.

M9 = NGC 6333

Within a Milky Way field in Ophiuchus less than 3 square degrees in size, we find three globular star clusters: M9 = NGC 6333, NGC 6342, and NGC 6356. The largest of these, M9, was discovered by Messier on May 28, 1764. It is situated near the border of a prominent dark cloud. When viewed in a small telescope, these three clusters, not far from η Ophiuchi, do not look very different from stars.

The magnitudes and colors of stars in M9 have been measured by A. Sandage and G. Wallerstein. These astronomers find that the cluster's stars are comparatively metal-rich. M9 and NGC 6342, whose distances are given as 9.1 and 9.8 kpc respectively, lie close to the center of our galaxy, while NGC 6356, at 18 kpc, belongs to the galactic halo on the far side of the galactic center.

NGC
x
6356

x
M 9

NGC
x
6342

OPHIUCHUS

NGC 6356
17ʰ20ᵐ7, − 17°46′

Gl, 9ᵐ7, Sp: G5
φ = 3′.5, type: II

M9　NGC 6333
17ʰ16ᵐ2, − 18°28′

Gl, 8ᵐ9, Sp: F2
φ = 5′.5, type: VIII

NGC 6342
17ʰ18ᵐ2, − 19°32′

Gl, 11ᵐ4, Sp: ?
φ = 1′.3, type: IV

−18°

−19°

−20°

17ʰ 20ᵐ　　17ʰ 15ᵐ

M47 = 7^h52^m7, − 15°13'
> *Cluster of stars a short distance from the preceding; the stars are brighter; the middle of the cluster was compared with the same star, 2 Navis. The cluster contains no nebulosity.*

M48 = 8^h11^m0, − 1°46'
> *Cluster of very faint stars, without nebulosity; this cluster is a short distance from the three stars that form the beginning of the Unicorn's tail.*

From the description of M47, it can be seen that Messier had observed a prominent object in the vicinity of M46, but nothing can be found in the given position. Messier established the positions of his objects by comparison with a reference star whose coordinates were known. In the case of M46 and M47 he used the same star, 2 Navis (now 2 Puppis). Thus, Messier recorded that the position of M47 minus that of 2 Puppis = R.A. + 9^m5, Dec. − 0°6. If one reverses the signs, the following position is obtained for M47: 7^h33^m7, − 14°00', which is almost the exact position of NGC 2422 (7^h34^m3, − 14°22'). Messier's description — near preceding cluster, brighter stars than M46 — also fits, and therefore it can be assumed that he had actually observed this prominent cluster and called it M47. Either when he recorded his observation or later when he copied it, he made an error in the signs.

The explanation for M48 is slightly more difficult, in that Messier did not name a reference star. At the given position no cluster can be found, but about 5° south and at the same right ascension we find NGC 2548, whose appearance tallies with the description of M48: very faint stars (for Messier's small instruments), and near the three stars 27, 28, and 29 Monocerotis. If Messier had used 27 Mon as his reference star, the discrepancy in declination could again be explained by an erroneous sign, for NGC 2548 lies about 2° south of the star rather than 2° north of it, as indicated by Messier's position. Moreover, since this is the only object in this area matching Messier's description, one can safely assume that M48 and NGC 2548 are identical.

The last remaining puzzle, M91, is listed as a nebula at a position in Coma Berenices. In 1779 Messier discovered three such "nebulae" in Virgo: M58, M59, and M60. On March 18, 1781, he found nine more near the border between Coma and Virgo, which were registered as numbers 84-91 and 94. One month later, on April 13th, he observed another three in this region. They are now known as M98-M100. In each of these three groups the numbers increase with right ascension. All his "nebulae" are bright objects, though with the instruments at Messier's disposal, they were difficult to detect. However, in the position he gives for M91, there is no object he could have seen.

The description of M91 shows some similarity with that of nearby M90: nebula without stars in Virgo, above the previous No. 90. Oddly, the positions given by Messier are in Coma and not in Virgo and in the upside-down image of the refractor, below and not above M90. There is in fact a galaxy within the range of Messier's instruments that, when seen through a refractor, lies slightly above M90 in Virgo. This is M58, discovered two years before and situated 0^m8 in R.A. east and 1°3 south of M90. Messier's position for M91 tallies in R.A. with M58, but the declination is 2° farther north. Thus, Owen Gingerich has suggested that M91 is actually a duplicate observation of M58. Another possible identity for M91 has been pointed out by W. C. Williams of Fort Worth, Texas, who believes Messier actually viewed the spiral galaxy NGC 4548 in Coma Berenices and, because of an observing error, incorrectly determined its position. In recent years there has been increasing acceptance of NGC 4548 as M91.

NGC 6334, NGC 6357

This exciting color photograph shows two little-known emission nebulae northwest of λ Scorpii. NGC 6334 and NGC 6357 are two complex H-II regions in the southern Milky Way, apparently projected onto a dark cloud (see photograph on page 184). From new investigations by T. Neckel, made at the Gamsberg, Namibia, station of the Max Planck Institute of Astronomy, it appears that the dark cloud is a foreground object and is not associated with the H-II region, as was supposed in prior studies. Most of the early-type stars, which seem to be the brightest members of a young open cluster, are considerably reddened. The internal extinction in these clusters reaches up to 2 magnitudes. Both objects are located in the Sagittarius arm of our galaxy, whereas earlier investigations placed them in the interarm region. Some radio sources are found in both objects.

The bright bluish star beneath the small galactic cluster H 16 is υ Sco (B3), a young hot star of magnitude 2.80. λ Sco is situated not far from it to the east.

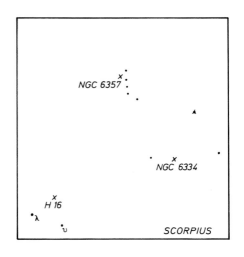

SCORPIUS

H16
17h27m4, −36°49′

Cl, 20 ★
φ = 15′, type: e

NGC 6334
17h17m2, −36°01′

N, ★ = A0 8m0
20′ × 20′, type: c

NGC 6357
17h21m3, −34°07′

N, m★ = 10
57′ × 44′, type: e

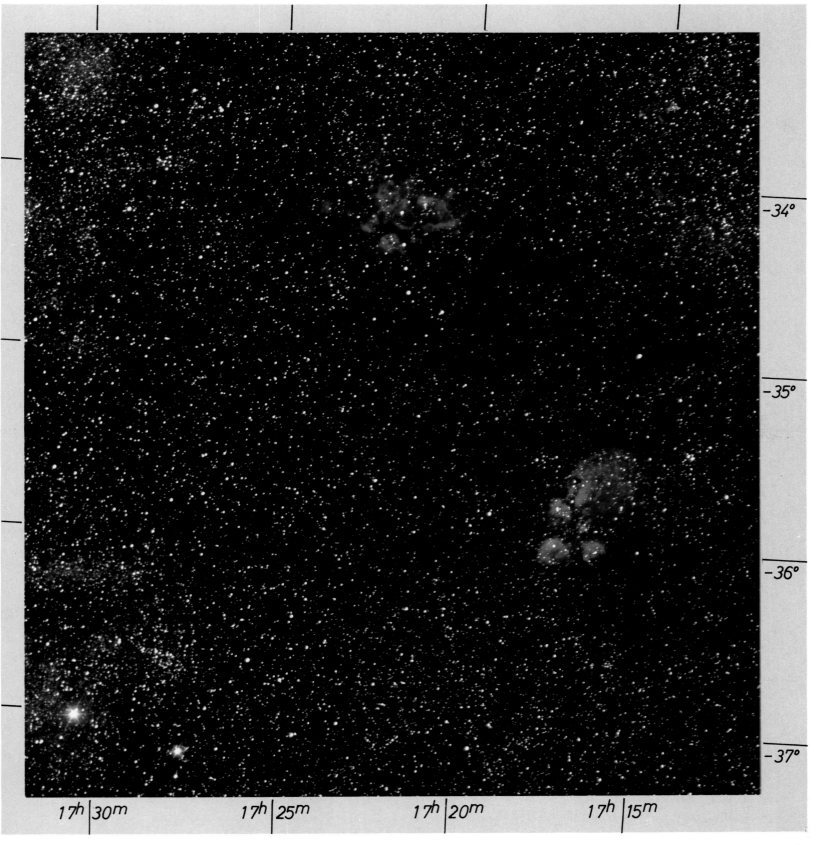

Lacaille and his catalogue of southern objects

Of the many successful French astronomers in the 18th century, Abbé Nicolas Louis de Lacaille is now largely forgotten. This is surprising, for his pupil Lalande said of him, "During Lacaille's relatively short life (1713-1762), he made more discoveries and calculations than all other astronomers together." Possibly this is somewhat exaggerated, but it is a fact that during his two-year stay at the Cape of Good Hope, Lacaille measured the positions of almost ten thousand stars of the Southern Hemisphere.

Continued on page 192

M14 = NGC 6402

The globular star cluster M14 in Ophiuchus is neither particularly bright nor very large, and its brightest stars are only of magnitude 15. This cluster, situated between the stars τ and 41 Ophiuchi, was discovered by Messier in 1764. J. Herschel described M14 as "a most beautiful and delicate cluster; not very bright, but of the finest stardust." In 1964, the Canadian globular cluster expert H. B. Sawyer Hogg and her colleague A. Wehlau discovered that a nova had been photographed in the cluster in 1938. There are only two other possible novae believed associated with globular clusters. One is T Scorpii, which was seen visually in M80 (page 161) in 1860, and the other is a 1943 outburst photographed at the edge of NGC 6553 in Sagittarius.

About one minute east of 47 Ophiuchi (4^{m}6), in the lower right corner of our photograph, is the cluster NGC 6366. For a long time, its claim to be a globular cluster was disputed because of its loose structure, but in 1977 G. Alcaino included it in his catalogue of 132 globulars. Its distance is approximately 8.5 kpc, placing it close to the center of our galaxy.

M14 NGC 6402
17h35m0, −3°13′

GI, 9m4, Sp: G0
φ = 6′.7, type: VIII

NGC 6366
17h25m1, −5°02′

GI, 12m1, Sp: ?
φ = 5′.8, type: XI

OPHIUCHUS

M 14

NGC 6366 47

M7
photographed by K. Rihm with a Newtonian reflector of 180-cm focal length.

M6 = NGC 6405, M7 = NGC 6475

In this striking picture of the Milky Way in Scorpius, there are no less than five open star clusters and one globular cluster. Messier's instruments were only able to reach the two most conspicuous: M6 and M7. The latter is the southernmost object listed by Messier. He entered the two bright clusters in his catalogue during the spring of 1764. However, the discovery of M6 is credited to P. L. de Chéseaux in 1764, and that of M7 goes all the way back to Ptolemy, about A.D. 138.

M6 has a great many relatively bright stars between 8^{m}0 and 12^{m}0 and is a beautiful sight in even the smallest telescope. M7 is more outstanding yet, having many stars of magnitudes 6.5 to 8.0. To the naked eye it looks like a misty spot. On our photograph the cluster is partly masked by having a rich star cloud as a background (see photograph on page 162).

M6 has been studied by K. Rohlfs, K. W. Schrick, and J. Stock. They find that its stellar contents resemble those of the Pleiades (page 51). An age of 100 million years was derived. From several studies, it appears that the distance of M6 is in the neighborhood of 500 pc. M7 is nearer to us, about 240 pc.

NGC 6416, a very loose galactic cluster, is hardly visible against the background of stars, whereas NGC 6404, the most distant of the open clusters reproduced here, shows a distinct nucleus. The globular cluster NGC 6453 is veiled by faint foreground stars. It was once thought to belong to the halo of the Milky Way system, on the far side of the galactic center, but the latest distance estimate places it just this side of the center, at 7.8 kpc.

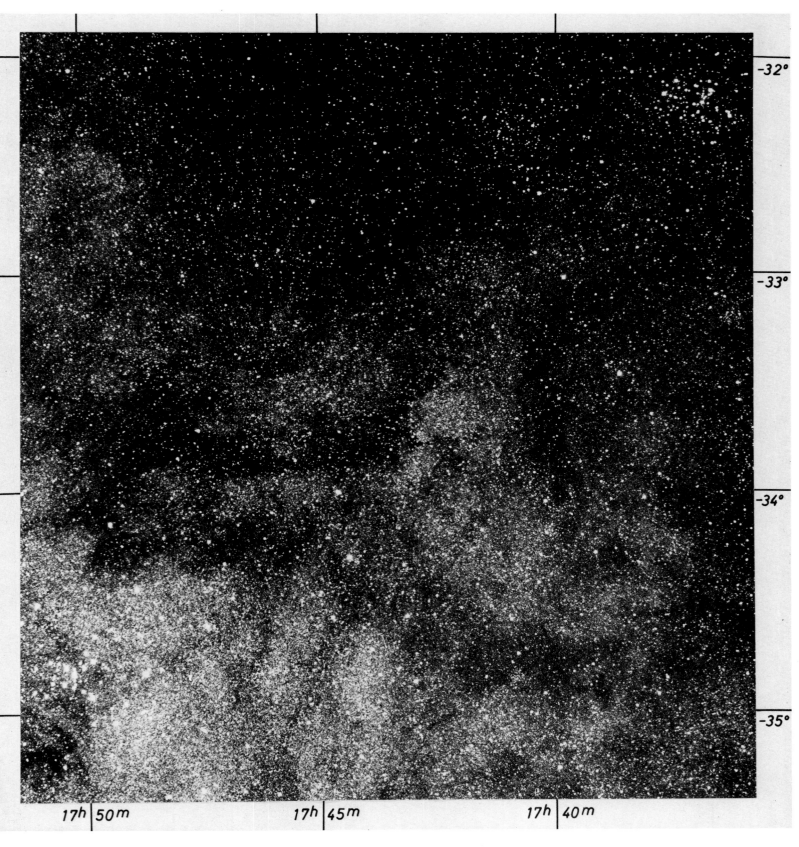

NGC 6453
17ʰ48ᵐ0, − 34°37′

Gl, 11ᵐ4, Sp: G5
φ = 3ʹ.6, type: IV

NGC 6404
17ʰ36ᵐ3, − 33°13′

Cl, 10ᵐ6, 35 ★
φ = 5′, type: g

M6   NGC 6405
17ʰ36ᵐ8, − 32°11′

Cl, 4ᵐ6, 132 ★
φ = 26′, type: e

NGC 6416
17ʰ41ᵐ0, − 32°20′

Cl, 8ᵐ7, 30 ★
φ = 22′, type: e

M7   NGC 6475
17ʰ50ᵐ7, − 34°48′

Cl, 3ᵐ3, 130 ★
φ = 50′, type: e

SCORPIUS

The Scutum-Sagittarius Milky Way. North is slightly to the right of up. The southern part of this photograph over-laps the one on page 162.

The largest pink object is the Lagoon nebula, M8. Just to its north, the much smaller Trifid nebula M20 and the open cluster M21 can be seen (see page 187). The large cluster M23 lies about 4° farther north, on the back-ground of a dark nebula (see page 185). Much larger is the star cloud M24 to its east, at right center, on the Great Rift that runs down the middle of the Milky Way. M25 (page 191) lies still farther east.

The globular clusters M22 and M28 (page 193) appear almost stellar near λ Sagittarii east of M8. They can be identified here with the aid of a star atlas, as can the globulars M9 and NGC 6356 in southern Ophiuchus (page 177). Above the M24 star cloud are the two pink nebulae M17 and M16 (page 189). At top, the open clusters M11 and M26 (page 197) appear almost bluish. Just east of α Scuti, the cluster NGC 6664 is visible as a faint smudge. A star atlas will aid in finding many other objects.

One-hour exposure by David F. Malin with an f/4 Hasselblad 6 x 6 cm format camera, on High Speed Ekta-chrome pushed to ASA 400. Photo copyright 1981, Anglo-Australian Telescope Board.

M23 = NGC 6494

In front of a remarkable dark cloud that projects blunt arms into the bright Milky Way, we find the splendid open star cluster M23. Its angular size almost matches that of the Moon, and it contains numerous fairly bright stars. In binoc-ulars this object is an entrancing sight. Messier discovered M23 on June 20, 1764, a night when he discovered several other objects.

H. L. Johnson measured the colors and brightnesses of stars in this cluster and found its distance to be about 650 pc. It is difficult to specify the apparent diameter of this star grouping with its poorly defined boundaries. Figures between 25′ and 51′ have been published, while estimates of the total number of member stars range from 100 to 250.

M23 *NGC 6494*
17ʰ54ᵐ0, − 19°01′

Cl, 5ᵐ9, 120 ★
φ = 27′, type: e

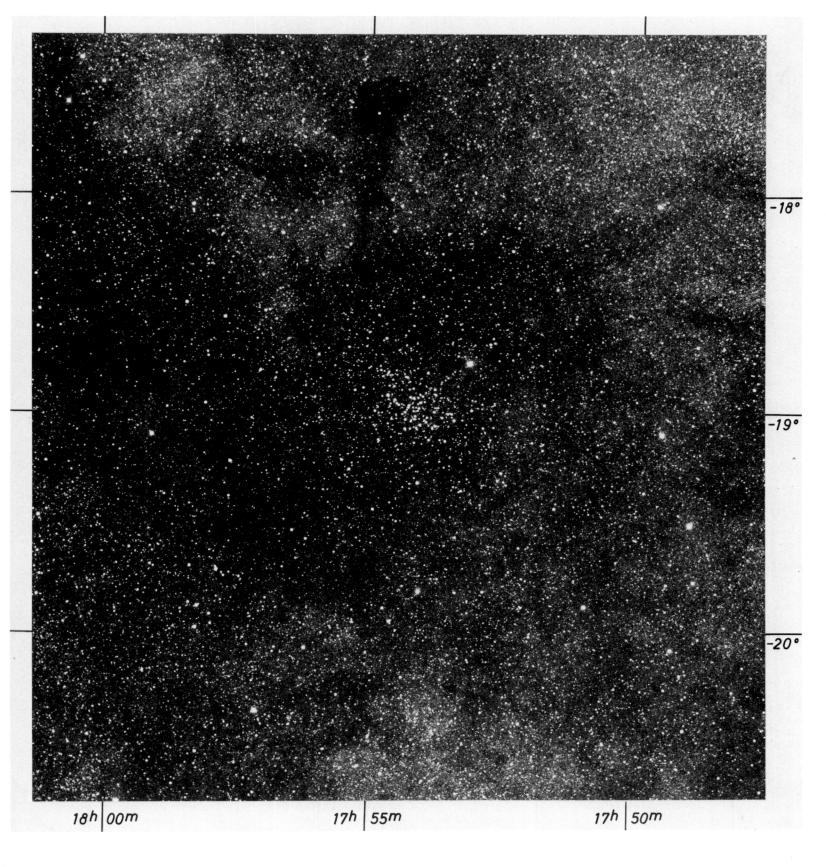

SAGITTARIUS

M8, the Lagoon nebula. This three-color composite print was prepared from three plates exposed with the 1.2-meter United Kingdom Schmidt camera at Siding Spring, Australia. It was printed with the unsharp masking technique to bring out detail in both the bright center and faint outer edges. Dust lanes and globules can be seen throughout. Photo copyright 1981, The Royal Observatory, Edinburgh.

M8 = NGC 6523 (Lagoon nebula), M20 = NGC 6514 (Trifid nebula), M 21 = NGC 6531

This chaotic field is near the galactic center (located at $\alpha =$ 17^h42^m4, $\delta = -28°55'$ for epoch 1950.0), and is partly interlaced by tubelike dark clouds. In it we find two gaseous nebulae. Like the Orion nebula (page 65), these shine because of ultraviolet radiation from nearby hot stars.

M20, the nebula in the upper part of the photograph opposite, is called the Trifid nebula because of its triple division. The blue region in its northern part is a reflection nebula. M8, the Lagoon nebula, is crossed by a broad absorbing lane from which its name derives (however, others have likened this feature to more of a channel). The feature is clearly visible in the photograph above. Messier listed M20 on June 5, 1764, and M8 on May 23, 1764. The discovery of M20 was made by Le Gentil before 1750 and that of M8 by Flamsteed around 1680. While observing M20, Messier discovered the open cluster M21 nearby. The sight of both objects through a wide-field comet seeker is just as imposing as that of the Orion nebula. However, the considerable southern declination permits observers in north temperate latitudes to see this group of nebulae to advantage only on particularly dark and clear summer nights.

The Russian astronomer M. A. Kasarian studied M20 and M8 in the light of the hydrogen $H\alpha$ line. He deduced the masses of their hydrogen to be 70 and 1,690 solar masses, respectively. Both nebulae lie at approximately the same distance from us, 700 to 800 pc. When observing the two nebulae visually, one recognizes some open star clusters among them. In M20, the cluster NGC 6514 is made up of about 45 stars, while in M8, next to the central cluster NGC 6523 (40 stars) there is the cluster NGC 6530 (60 stars), which can be partly seen on the above enlargement.

On the left of the facing star field two further emission nebulae can be seen, IC 1274-75 and NGC 6559. The group of stars within and between the two nebulae is listed in catalogues as the open cluster Cr 367. In addition, this remarkable field is graced with the open cluster M21 and the globular cluster NGC 6544.

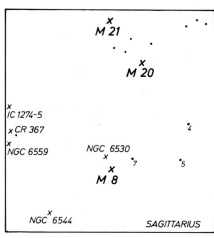

NGC 6559
18ʰ06ᵐ8, − 24°08′

N, 8′ × 6′, Sp: e

NGC 6544
18ʰ04ᵐ3, − 25°01′

Gl, 11ᵐ0, Sp: G1
φ = 1′, type: IX

M21   NGC 6531
18ʰ01ᵐ8, − 22°30′

Cl, 7ᵐ2, 50 ★
φ = 12′, type: d

M8   NGC 6523
Lagoon nebula
18ʰ01ᵐ6, − 24°20′

N, 60′ × 35′, Sp: e

IC 1274 − 75
18ʰ06ᵐ7, − 23°46′

N, 12′ × 8′, Sp: e

Cr 367
18ʰ06ᵐ6, − 24°00′

Cl, 6ᵐ5, 45 ★
φ = 48′, type: e

NGC 6530
18ʰ01ᵐ7, − 24°20′

Cl, 7ᵐ7, 60 ★
φ = 14′, type: e

M20   NGC 6514
Trifid nebula
17ʰ58ᵐ9, − 23°02′

N, 29′ × 27′, Sp: e

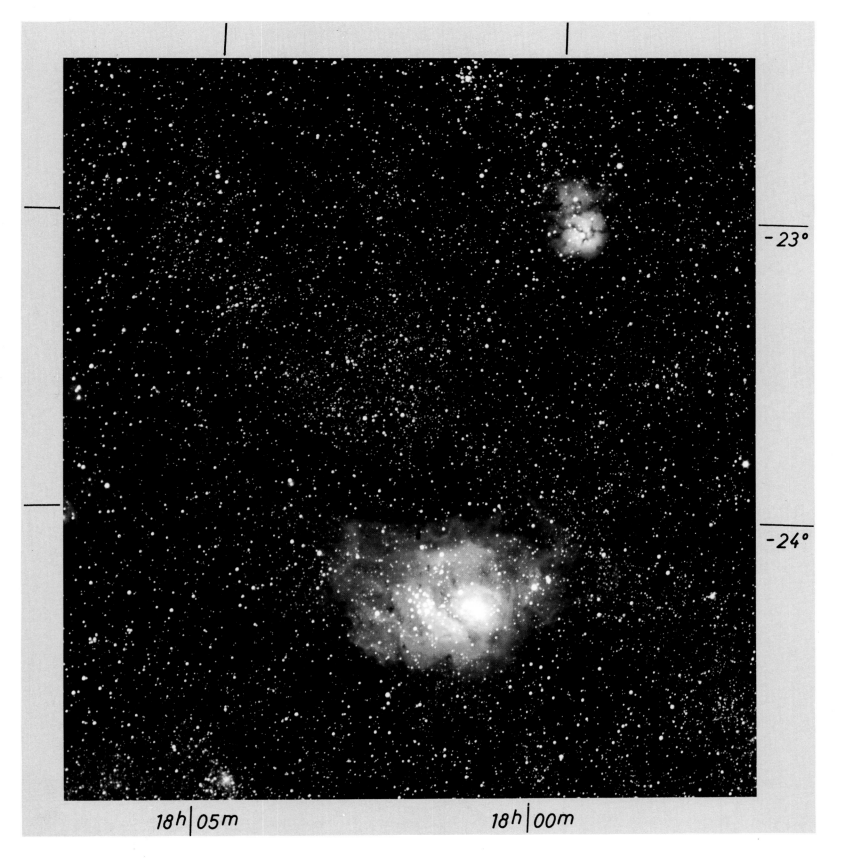

M17, the Omega nebula. Three-color composite photograph by E. Alt, E. Brodkorb, K. Rihm, and J. Rusche.

M16 = NGC 6611, M17 = NGC 6618 (Omega nebula)

In this very star-rich region between the constellations Scutum and Sagittarius are two open star clusters wreathed in bright nebulosity: M16 = NGC 6611, and the Omega nebula M17 = NGC 6618.

Messier saw M16 on June 3, 1764, and described it as "a cluster of small stars enmeshed in a faint glow." He estimated the diameter at 8', which is far too small; presumably he saw only the cluster. According to Cederblad, the nebula alone is four times as large. Like the Rosette nebula (page 75), the large-scale view on page 190 shows "elephant trunks" and hints of the tiny black markings called globules, which are believed to be the first stage of stellar evolution. C. R. O'Dell and his associates have studied the distribution of ionized hydrogen in M16.

Messier recorded M17 on the same night as M16. He described this object as a starless band of light, 5' to 6' long,

shaped like the Andromeda nebula, but very faint. J. Herschel called M17 a "magnificent object, very large and very bright." The name "Omega nebula" was given to M17 because of a fanciful resemblance to the Greek capital letter Omega (seen here upside down, with a large, bright extension to its left). In English literature M17 is often called the Horseshoe nebula. M16 and M17 were discovered by P. L. de Chéseaux in 1746.

Russian astronomers, in particular, have studied the Omega nebula. B. P. Artamonov and R. E. Gerschberg reported variations in brightness in the nebula's center, which may be related to strong turbulent motions (radial velocities between −54 to +40 km/sec). R. E. Gerschberg determined the nebula's distance to be 3 kpc.

Northwest of M16 is the small open cluster H19 = Tr32.

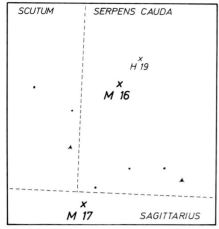

M17 NGC 6618
Omega nebula
18ʰ18ᵐ0, − 16°12′

Cl + N, 6ᵐ9, 50 ★
$\phi_{Cl} = 20′$, *Dim_N: 46′ × 37′*
type_Cl: c, type_N: e

M16 NGC 6611
18ʰ16ᵐ0, − 13°48′

Cl + N, 6ᵐ6, 60 ★
$\phi_{Cl} = 8′$, *Dim_N: 35′ × 28′*
type_Cl: c, type_N: e

H19 = Tr 32
18ʰ14ᵐ5, − 13°18′

Cl, 12ᵐ2, 20 ★
$\phi = 5.5$, *type: g*

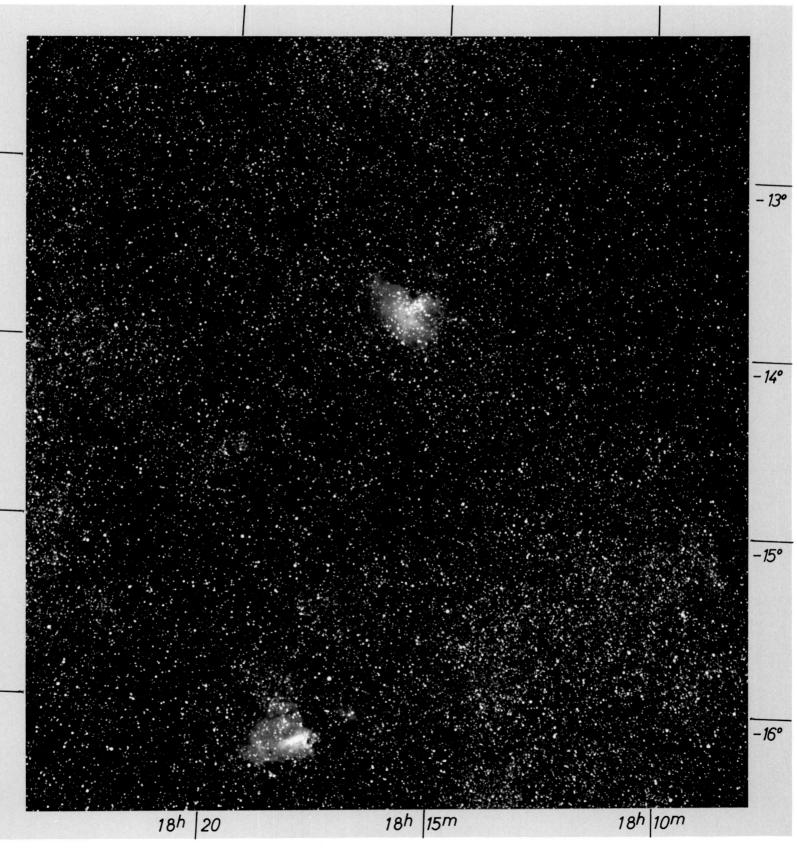

M16 (see previous page). Three-color composite photograph by E. Alt, E. Brodkorb, K. Rihm, and J. Rusche.

M18 = NGC 6613, M24, M25 = IC 4725

Amid the star clouds of the Sagittarius Milky Way, dappled here and there with dark nebulae, are found three open star clusters: M18 above, M24 on the right edge of the chart photo, and M25 below on the left. In order to get all three objects onto one page, the picture had to be rotated 30°.

Messier reported M24 as a very large cluster, which suggests that he was observing the whole star cloud nearly two degrees in diameter. In fact, M24 is not a star cluster but a detached portion of the Milky Way, in which the galactic star cluster NGC 6603 is embedded as a small and very dense stellar system. M24 and NGC 6603 are not identical, though some catalogues list them as the same object.

M25 has a number of bright stars, but so widely scattered that doubts arise as to whether these are in fact cluster members. The cluster was discovered by de Chéseaux in 1746 and listed by Messier on June 20, 1764. A. U. Landolt measured magnitudes and colors of 1,401 stars in and around the cluster and found its distance to be between 600 and 800 pc. The brightest star in the cluster is U Sagittarii ($6^m4 - 7^m0$), a classical δ Cephei star with a period of 6.74 days. From its apparent brightness and the period-luminosity relation, A. Sandage derived a distance of 550 pc.

The star cluster M18 resembles M25 in that it is comprised of only a few bright stars. However, they are not so widely scattered. M18 was discovered by Messier on June 3, 1764.

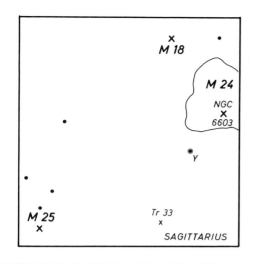

Tr 33
18ʰ21ᵐ8, −19°43′

Cl, 8ᵐ8, 25 ★
φ = 5′5, type: d

M25   IC 4725
18ʰ28ᵐ8, −19°17′

Cl, 6ᵐ2, 80 ★
φ = 35′, type: d

M18   NGC 6613
18ʰ17ᵐ0, −17°09′

Cl, 8ᵐ0, 18 ★
φ = 7′, type: d

NGC 6603
18ʰ15ᵐ5, −18°27′

Cl, 11ᵐ4, 50 ★
φ = 4′5, type: g

M24
18ʰ13ᵐ0, −18°30′

Star cloud, 4ᵐ5
Dim: 120′ × 40′

Credit must also be given to Lacaille for giving names to 14 southern constellations, including Sculptor, For-nax, Pyxis, Pictor, Antlia, Norma, Caelum, and Mensa. As he filled in the last blank areas in the southern skies, he frequently named new star groups after his instruments: Telescopium, Circinus, Octans, Reticulum, Horologium, and Microscopium.

Originally Lacaille studied theology, but no record can be found that he ever performed any duties of a priest. He devoted his time to mathematics and astronomy. While Jacques Cassini (son of the celebrated Giovanni Cassini) was director of Paris Observatory, Lacaille was actively engaged in several geodetic tasks, mainly the remeasurement of the great meridian of France.

In the middle of the eighteenth century, several decades before Messier's discoveries, the lack of astronomical observations from the Southern Hemisphere was hampering measurements of the true shape of the Earth. Besides, there was need for a reliable catalogue of southern stars for navigation.

The Abbe-Lacaille was chosen by the French Academy of Sciences to solve these problems, and after a voyage of some months he arrived at the Cape of Good Hope equipped with several telescopes, one being only of one-half-inch aperture and 28-inches focal length. After his return in 1753 he dispatched to the French Academy a list of 42 nebulae, which appeared in the Connaissance des Temps *in 1755.*

His list was in three sections: nebulae, nebulous star clusters, and stars with nebulosity. Each of the three sections contains 14 objects, which perhaps is not accidental but an indication of selection. As a whole, Lacaille's list is very incomplete, though it does include such well-known objects as η Carinae, ω Centauri, and 47 Tucanae, as well as eight southern Messier objects.

In Lacaille's list, which follows, nine objects are nonexistent. Twelve of the remaining 32 are reproduced in this book.

Continued

The Milky Way region in Sagittarius reproduced here is very rich in stars and is traversed by slender bands of dark matter. Furthermore, we find an extraordinary accumulation of globular star clusters.

M28 on our photograph presents an image like the star λ Sagittarii (2^{m}9). This is due to the faint background stars around the edge of the bright star's image. The cluster's apparent diameter has been cited from 5′ to 15′, an understandable uncertainty because of the denseness of the star cloud in which the cluster is embedded. Messier discovered M28 on July 27, 1764, and described the object as a "nebula without stars."

NGC 6638, about 3^m east of λ Sagittarii, is a very small and compact globular cluster. At a distance of 11 kpc, it is probably beyond the galactic center.

M22 = NGC 6656, M28 = NGC 6626

On our picture NGC 6642 resembles NGC 6638, but in size and brightness it has been described by some authorities as a highly concentrated galactic cluster. H. B. Sawyer Hogg considers it to be a globular cluster.

The most prominent globular cluster in this picture is NGC 6656 = M22, discovered as early as 1665 by A. Ihle while engaged in an observation of Saturn. Later, in 1747, it was seen by Le Gentil, who recognized it as a cluster. Messier entered M22 into his observation book on June 5, 1764. H. C. Arp and W. G. Melbourne have studied 400 of the cluster's stars down to 15^{m}0 and found a resemblance with the stars in M13 (page 167). G. Alcaino derived a distance of 3.1 kpc.

Two small planetary nebulae, NGC 6629 near the upper right corner of our picture and NGC 6644, about 3^m northeast of NGC 6638, can hardly be identified among the close-packed faint stars of the Milky Way.

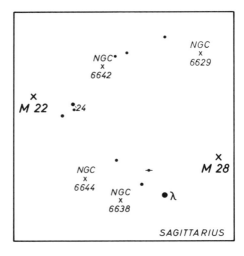

NGC 6642
18ʰ28ᵐ8, −23°31′

Gl, 10ᵐ3, Sp: ?
φ = 0′.8, type: IV

NGC 6629
18ʰ22ᵐ7, −23°14′

Pl, 10ᵐ6, m⋆ = 13.6
16″ × 14″, type: IIa

M22   NGC 6656
18ʰ33ᵐ3, −23°58′

Gl, 6ᵐ5, Sp: F6
φ = 17′.0, type: VII

NGC 6644
18ʰ29ᵐ5, −25°11′

Pl, 12ᵐ2, m⋆ = 11.5
2″ × 2″, type: II

NGC 6638
18ʰ27ᵐ9, −25°32′

Gl, 10ᵐ2, Sp: G2
φ = 2′.2, type: VI

M28   NGC 6626
18ʰ21ᵐ5, −24°54′

Gl, 8ᵐ5, Sp: F9
φ = 15′.0, type: IV

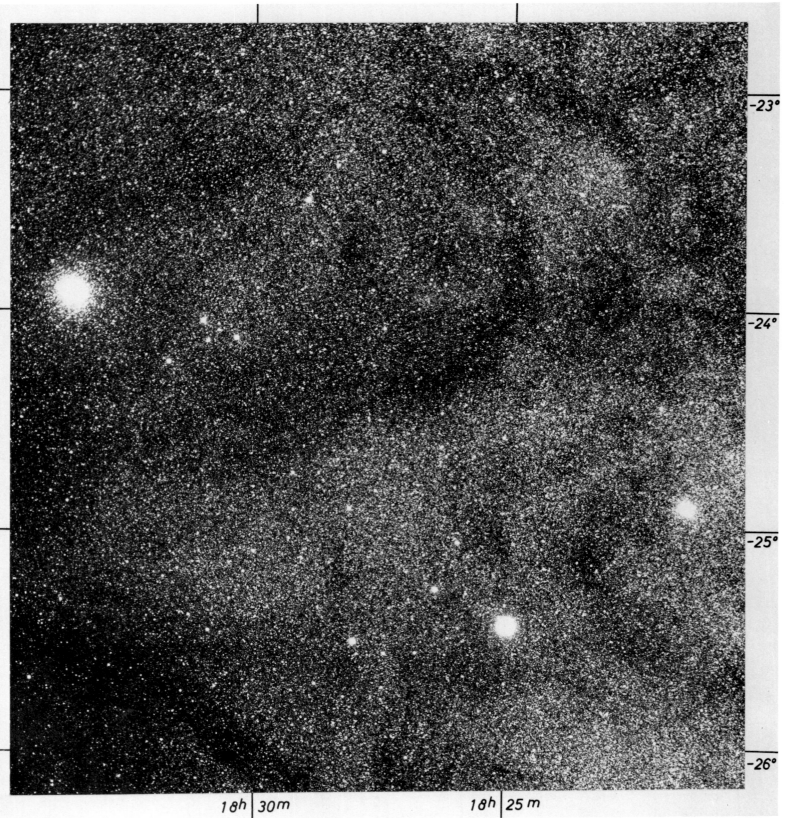

Lacaille Group I: Nebulae

Lac I	NGC	α	1950.0 δ	type	name	page
1	104	00ʰ21ᵐ9	− 72°21′	Gl	47 Tuc	25
2	2070	05 39.9	− 69 04	N	30 Dor	61
3	2477	07 50.5	− 38 25	Cl		
4	4833	12 56.0	− 70 36	Gl		
5	5139	13 23.8	− 47 03	Gl	ω Cen	147
6	5236	13 34.3	− 29 37	Ga	M83	151
7	5281	13 43.1	− 62 39	Cl		
8	6124	16 22.2	− 40 35	Cl		
9	6121	16 20.6	− 26 24	Gl	M4	163
10	6242	16 52.2	− 39 25	Cl		
11	6637	18 28.1	− 32 23	Gl	M69	195
12	6656	18 33.3	− 23 58	Gl	M22	193
13	6777	19 21.4	− 71 39	—		
14	6809	19 36.9	− 31 03	Gl	M55	205

Lacaille Group II: Nebulous star clusters

Lac II	NGC	α	1950.0 δ	type	name	page
1	—	04ʰ02ᵐ1	− 44°35′	—		
2	—	07 24.4	− 34 02	—		
3	2516	07 59.7	− 60 44	Cl		
4	2546	08 10.6	− 37 29	Cl		
5	IC 2391	08 38.8	− 52 53	Cl	o Vel	
6	—	08 44.8	− 42 23	—		
7	3228	10 19.7	− 51 28	Cl		
8	3293	10 31.5	− 57 56	Cl + N		103
9	IC 2602	10 41.0	− 64 08	Cl		
10	3532	11 03.4	− 58 24	Cl		
11	—	11 20.7	− 58 03	—		
12	4755	12 50.6	− 60 05	Cl	ϰ Cru	135
13	6231	16 50.7	− 41 43	Cl		
14	6475	17 50.7	− 34 48	Cl	M7	183

Continued

M69 = NGC 6637, M70 = NGC 6681

In the constellation Sagittarius, this extraordinarily rich and uniform star field contains three globular clusters of small apparent size. On this photograph they look much the same as some of the bright stars. M69 was discovered by Lacaille in 1751-52. Messier saw M70 for the first time on August 31, 1780, and he listed M69 on the same night. Presumably as a result of its small diameter, NGC 6652 was not noticed by Messier.

None of these southern clusters rise even as high as 10° above the horizon of Paris, where Messier observed.

All three of these globular clusters appear to lie on the far side of the center of our galaxy. Recent distance determinations that make due allowance for interstellar absorption of light give 11.6 pc for M69, 10.8 for M70, and 14.1 for NGC 6652.

NGC 6652
18ʰ32ᵐ5, −33°02′

Gl, 9ᵐ8, Sp: G2
ϕ = 2′.3, type: VI

M69   <small>NGC 6637</small>
18ʰ28ᵐ1, −32°23′

Gl, 8ᵐ9, Sp: G5
ϕ = 3′.8, type: V

M70   <small>NGC 6681</small>
18ʰ40ᵐ0, −32°21′

Gl, 9ᵐ0, Sp: G2
ϕ = 4′.1, type: V

SAGITTARIUS

−31°

−32°

−33°

18ʰ 40ᵐ   18ʰ 35ᵐ   18ʰ 30ᵐ

Lacaille Group III: Stars with nebulosity

Lac III	NGC	α 1950.0	δ	type	name	page
1	—	05^h02^m0	−49°33′	—		
2	2547	08 08.9	−49 07	Cl		
3	—	08 40.6	−47 53	Cl		
4	IC 2488	09 25.7	−56 45	Cl		
5	3372	10 43.1	−59 25	N	η Car	103
6	3372	10 43.1	−59 25	N	η Car	103
7	3766	11 34.2	−61 19	Cl		
8	5662	14 31.5	−56 21	Cl		
9	—	15 18.6	−59 01	—		
10	6025	15 59.4	−60 22	Cl		
11	6397	17 36.8	−53 39	Gl		
12	6405	17 36.8	−32 11	Cl	M6	183
13	6523	18 01.6	−24 20	N	M8	187
14	—	21 27.7	−58 48	—		

Describing his list, Lacaille said: "In the Southern Hemisphere I found many more nebulae of these three types, but I do not profess to have included them all, particularly as those of the first and third group were only visible on dark moonless nights. All the same, I hope that the list I have compiled includes the most noteworthy objects in these three groups and is fairly complete."

Continued on page 200

M11 = NGC 6705, M26 = NGC 6694

Within the bright Scutum cloud we find the two open star clusters M11 and M26, in areas which are not too overcrowded with stars. M11 contains at least 200 stars, some sources even saying as many as 600, of 15^{m}0 and brighter. One glance at our picture explains why the question of whether M11 is a globular or a galactic cluster remained unanswered for so long. A telescope of 6-cm aperture is adequate to resolve the border into stars, but with larger instruments one is able to see individual stars right into the center, so that Trumpler and Shapley quite rightly classified the object among the open clusters.

M11 was already known long before Messier, having been mentioned by Kirch in the year 1681. Admiral Smyth, a famous 19th-century English amateur, compared the cluster to a "flight of wild ducks." From photographic and photo-electric measurements of 400 stars in the three colors U (ultraviolet), B (blue), and V (yellow-green), H. L. Johnson, A. R. Sandage, and H. D. Wahlquist plotted a color-magnitude diagram. This enabled them to deduce that this cluster is intermediate in age between the Praesepe and the Pleiades.

M26, with about 50 stars down to 15^{m}0, is not as rich as M11 but is still very concentrated for an open cluster. Messier saw M11 on May 30, 1764; it had previously been seen by Le Gentil in 1749. W. Becker and J. Stock compiled a color-magnitude diagram from which a distance of 1,670 pc was derived for M11. In 1967, C. Grubissich found 1,550 pc, almost the same distance, for M26.

The small globular cluster NGC 6712 is at a distance of 7 kpc and is thus in the vicinity of the galactic center.

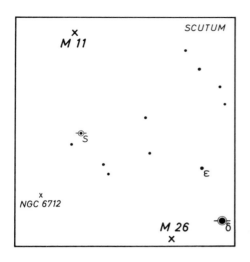

SCUTUM

M 11

S

ε

NGC 6712

M 26

M26   NGC 6694
18ʰ42ᵐ5, −9°27′

Cl, 9ᵐ3, 50 ★
$\phi = 9'$, type: f

M11   NGC 6705
18ʰ48ᵐ4, −6°20′

Cl, 6ᵐ3, 400 ★
$\phi = 12'.5$, type: g

NGC 6712
18ʰ50ᵐ3, −8°47′

Gl, 10ᵐ5, Sp: G2
$\phi = 4'.2$, type: IX

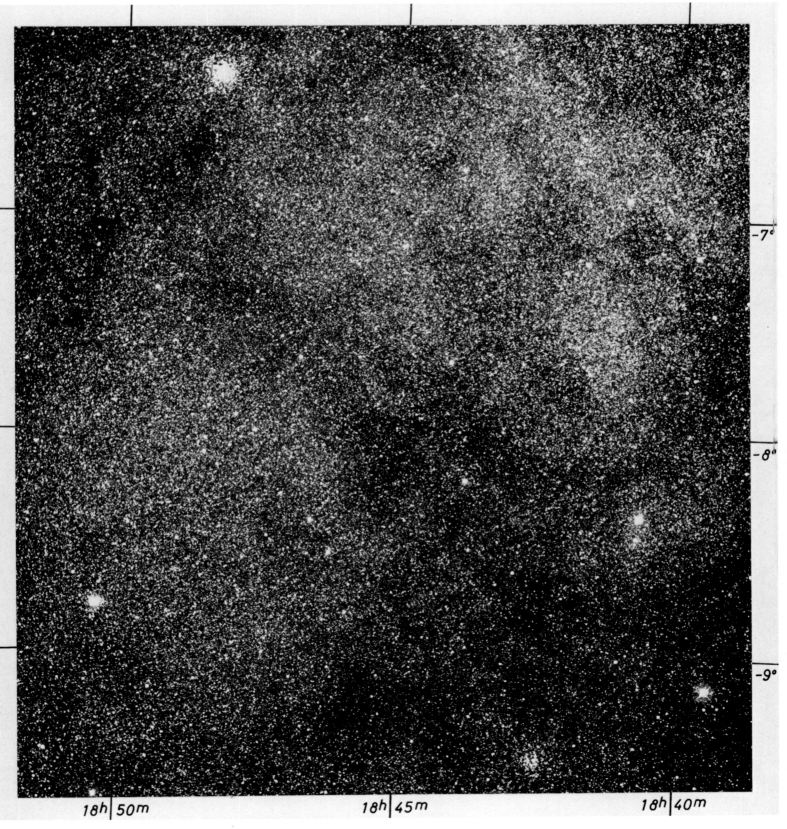

−7°

−8°

−9°

18ʰ 50m   18ʰ 45m   18ʰ 40m

M57, the Ring nebula. Lick Observatory photograph with the 120-inch Shane reflector.

M57 = NGC 6720 (Ring nebula)

With M57 = NGC 6720, the famous Ring nebula in Lyra, the sequence of our pictures in order of right ascension brings us back once more to the northern sky, after having remained south of the equator from pages 161 until 197, where objects in Scorpius, Sagittarius, Ophiuchus and Scutum have been depicted (see the general reference chart on this book's endpapers). M57 was first seen in the same year (1779) by Messier and A. Darquier.

The Ring nebula in Lyra is the best known planetary, though its small size makes it less prominent than some others. It is easily found with a telescope of 6- or 8-cm aperture as a pale disk between the stars β Lyrae (3^{m}4 — 4^{m}3) and γ Lyrae (3^{m}3), slightly nearer to the former. Apertures of 20 cm and upward are needed to reveal the oval shape of the ring and the fainter features at its ends. The central star

(about 15^m) can only be seen in very large instruments or in photos like the one above. Our facing picture was given an exposure time of only five minutes in order not to lose the dark interior of the ring. In spite of this, the central star is clearly visible on the negative, proof again of the efficiency of the Schmidt camera.

What we see as a ring around the central star is the projection of a roughly spherical, expanding gaseous shell, which is excited to shine by the ultraviolet radiation of this extremely hot star. According to L. H. Aller and M. F. Walker, the spectrum of the gas shows all the typical lines of emission nebulae, "forbidden" lines of singly and doubly ionized oxygen and nitrogen, as well as the lines of the Balmer series of hydrogen. Recent distance determinations range from 620 to 780 pc.

M57 **NGC 6720**
Ring nebula
18ʰ51ᵐ7, +32°58′

Pl, 9ᵐ3, m★ = 14.7
1ʹ4 × 1ʹ0, type: IV

LYRA

The long-continued popularity of Messier's list, despite its unsystematic character, is partly due to its convenient numbering system, which provides simple and easily remembered names for prominent objects. But Lacaille's list with its three groups, each starting from the number 1, is inconvenient and somewhat confusing. One must bear in mind that Lacaille used a smaller telescope for his measurements of star positions than did Messier in comet hunting. The threshold magnitude for his objects is about 8.0, and it is not surprising that his list includes only one galaxy, M83. On the other hand, Lacaille included some minor groupings of stars, which in his small telescope were mistaken for clusters.

More about the historical background of Lacaille's and other early astronomers' investigations in the Southern Hemisphere can be read in The Astronomy of Southern Africa by Patrick Moore and Pete Collins (Howard Timmins, Cape Town, 1977).

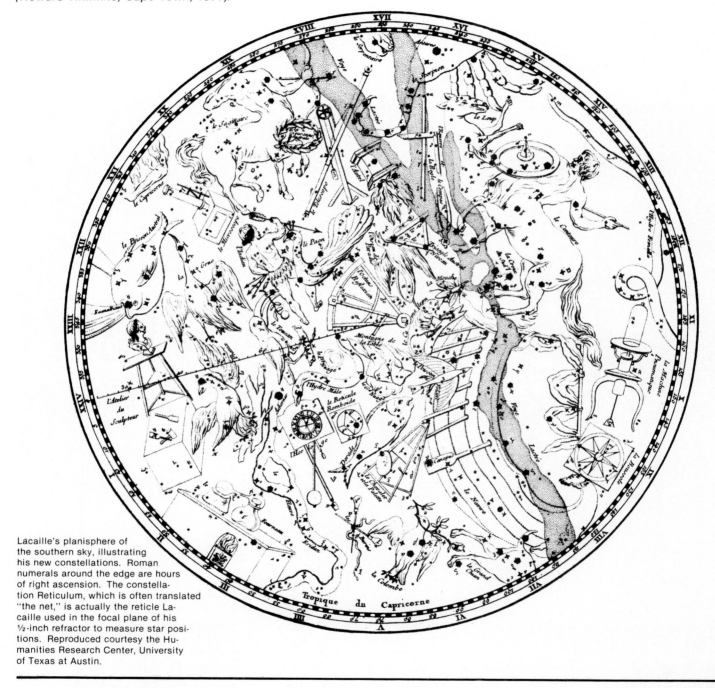

Lacaille's planisphere of the southern sky, illustrating his new constellations. Roman numerals around the edge are hours of right ascension. The constellation Reticulum, which is often translated "the net," is actually the reticle Lacaille used in the focal plane of his ½-inch refractor to measure star positions. Reproduced courtesy the Humanities Research Center, University of Texas at Austin.

M54 = NGC 6715

The small globular star cluster M54, near the edge of the star cloud within the constellation Sagittarius, was first described by Messier on July 24, 1778, as a faint nebula with a bright center. Its brightest stars are of magnitude 14 and the center is so concentrated that even large amateur instruments fail to resolve it.

L. Rosino and F. Nobili carried out a photographic study of the cluster and discovered 54 of the 77 variable stars now known in it, of which 62 are RR Lyrae stars. Its distance is 20.4 kpc, according to W. E. Harris (1976).

M54 NGC 6715
$18^h52^m0, -30°32'$

Gl, 8^m7, Sp: F7
$\phi = 5'.5$, type: III

ξ
×
M 54

SAGITTARIUS

-30°

-31°

-32°

$19^h 00^m$ $18^h 55^m$ $18^h 50^m$

Bernhard Schmidt and his camera

Having presented the two celebrated astronomers, Charles Messier and Nicolas de Lacaille, each of whom began his career as a nonprofessional, I wish to tell the story of another extraordinary man, Bernhard Schmidt.

Fritz Zwicky, who used Schmidt cameras with such great success, said this gifted optician's invention was as important to astronomy as the telescope itself. This remark seems a little exaggerated to me. Zwicky was an astronomer whose main discoveries were made with the celebrated 48-inch Palomar Schmidt camera. (He once told me, however, that his favorite instrument was the old 18-inch Palomar Schmidt camera). A more realistic appraisal is that Schmidt's camera brought to the modern exploration of the universe an advance comparable to the progress realized when W. Herschel's 20-foot telescope supplanted the small instruments of his 18th-century contemporaries.

I feel strongly that this book would have been impossible to produce without Schmidt's ingenious invention.

Schmidt had an unusual life. He was born in 1879 on the Estonian island of Nargen, the son of a German father and a Swedish mother. As a youngster, instead of going to church one Sunday morning, he experimented with gunpowder, and the resulting explosion cost him his right forearm.

He enrolled as a student in the Institute of Technology at Göteborg, Sweden, where he specialized in optics. At the start of the 20th century we find Schmidt at Mittweida, a small, drowsy town in Thuringia, not far from the Zeiss optical works at Jena. Here he supported himself by grinding and polishing telescope mirrors, and soon he became known for their excellent quality. Schmidt was unusually successful in other optical and astronomical undertakings. He built a 31-cm coelostat of 30-m focal length, and took exposures of the Sun's granulation that could compete with the best Yerkes Observatory photographs. Another of his experiments was a water-driven guiding system, which enabled him to hold one of Jupiter's moons bisected on his crosswires for several minutes without any guiding corrections.

Continued

M56 = NGC 6779

Roughly midway between γ Lyrae (3^{m}3) and β Cygni (3^{m}2 + 5^{m}4) is the highly concentrated globular cluster NGC 6779 = M56. On our picture it resembles the star 2 Cygni (4^{m}9). Messier discovered it on January 23, 1779, and described the object as a "nebula without stars."

M56 is a globular cluster of the galactic halo in a very rich field. R. Barbon in 1965 carried out a study of the brightnesses and colors of 340 stars in the region of this cluster. From this and the periods of a Cepheid and an RR Lyrae star within it, he derived a distance of 11.5 kpc. In 1973 G. Alcaino revised this to 10.0 kpc.

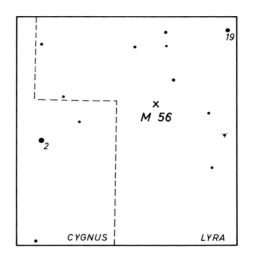

CYGNUS   LYRA

M56   **NGC 6779**
19ʰ14ᵐ6, +30°05′

Gl, 9ᵐ6, Sp: F5
φ = 5′.0, type: X

19ʰ 20m   19ʰ 15m   19ʰ 10m

+31°
+30°
+29°

In 1905, Schmidt sent a parabolic mirror of 40-cm aperture and only 90-cm focal length to Potsdam Observatory for examination. Clearly, Schmidt was already interested in fast optical systems of great light-gathering power. Doubtlessly the examination was very satisfying, and this was the beginning of Schmidt's cooperation with German observatories and well-known optical firms.

Some years after the first world war, R. Schorr, then director of Hamburg-Bergedorf Observatory, encouraged Schmidt to design a fast photographic system with a wide field that would be as free as possible of coma. In those days not only Hamburg, but all major observatories and the most qualified opticians were searching for more efficient systems for astrophotography, in particular a fast, wide-field camera. The off-axis optical aberrations of existing lenses and mirrors of low focal ratio diminished the coma-free field to only a few minutes of arc.

Schmidt found a relatively simple solution by introducing a thin, deformed corrector plate, placed at the center of curvature of a spherical mirror. Today, when looking back, it seems incredible that even optical works such as Zeiss, with large staffs of able opticians, attempted to deform mirrors or use corrector lenses, which introduced chromatic aberration, in fruitless efforts to solve this problem.

Schmidt himself was an introverted man who published next to nothing about his new optical system. He preferred to sit in his optical shop, which Schorr had installed for him at Hamburg-Bergedorf Observatory, sometimes smoking excellent cigars, sipping cognac, and reflecting on optical laws, and sometimes working day and night at grinding and polishing to realize new ideas.

The idea for his coma-free reflecting system came to him while he was sailing with Walter Baade to an eclipse in the Philippines. A very short description of the new system by Schmidt himself can be read in Zentralzeitung für Optik und Mechanik, *published in 1931. There Schmidt writes:*

"If the light losses of a mirror and of a lens system are compared, for the same aperture ratio the mirror shows a smaller loss of light than the lens system. A freshly silvered mirror reflects at least 90 percent of the incident light, while a two-lens system transmits at most 80 percent, and a three-lens system at most 70 percent. In the cases of large lenses, the situation is still more unfavorable because of the stronger absorption of short wavelengths by the glass.

"In large telescopes, the parabolic mirror thus would be more advantageous in general than a lens system, but unfortunately with large aperture ratios the usual field of view is very limited by coma. . . . Coma increases in direct proportion to the field diameter, astigmatism proportional to its square."

Continued

M55 = NGC 6809

The splendid globular star cluster M55 belongs, with M69 and M70 (page 195), and M54 (page 201), among the most southern of the 28 globular clusters that Messier listed in his catalogue. This cluster was first discovered by Lacaille in 1751-52 and seen again by Messier on July 24, 1778. As far as its apparent magnitude (about 7^m) and distance (5 kpc) are concerned, M55 is similar to the well-known Hercules cluster M13 (page 167), but it is barely half as large and its stars are much less concentrated. Due to its southern position, observers in more northern latitudes can see it in the evening only for a period during summer, and then only when conditions are right.

T. D. Kinman made a major study of southern globular clusters, including M55, paying particular attention to their motions and spectroscopic peculiarities. Among other things, he found evidence for very high space velocities. At such great distances from the galactic center, this can only be explained by the assumption that the globular clusters move in extremely elongated orbits around the center of our galaxy, somewhat like long-period comets in the solar system.

M55 NGC 6809
19ʰ36ᵐ9, −31°03′

Gl, 7ᵐ1, Sp: ?
φ = 14′.8, type: XI

Schmidt then explains that a spherical mirror of f/8 or f/10 with an aperture stop at its center of curvature is free of coma and astigmatism. The one small disadvantage is longitudinal aberration: in other words, the image surface lies on a sphere equal in radius to the focal length, with its convex side turned to the mirror. (Because light entering a Schmidt camera makes only a single reflection from the mirror before reaching the film, the images are reversed and the resulting negatives must be placed in an enlarger with their emulsion side up.) Schmidt then continues:

"If the aperture ratio is greatly increased, however, the spherical aberration becomes very large since it increases at the third power of the aperture ratio. With a focal length of 1 meter, the effect for paraxial rays then would be 1.2mm for an 1:3 aperture ratio, and 4mm for 1:2, giving for the smallest possible confusion disk 0.3mm and 1mm respectively. In this case, therefore, a spherical mirror no longer would be useful.

"I shall now show how completely sharp images can be obtained with a spherical mirror of large aperture ratio. A concentric curved glass plate can be placed immediately in front of the spherical mirror, and one of its surfaces deformed. This plate can be optically sagged to such an extent that one side becomes plane again while the other has a pure deformation curve. A suitably shaped cover plate of this kind for a spherical mirror also has the practical advantage that the silver coat of the mirror is well protected. However, owing to the passage of light twice through the glass plate, about 20 percent of the light is lost.

"If the correcting plate is instead brought to the center of curvature, then the light goes through the plate only once. The same relationship holds as in the case of the spherical mirror with an aperture stop at the center of curvature, but with the difference that the spherical aberration is now abolished over the whole field. Thus, it is possible to use aperture ratios of 1:3 or 1:2 and to obtain freedom from coma, astigmatism, and spherical aberration.

"If the mirror has the same diameter as the correcting plate, then the incident cylinder of rays for outer images falls eccentrically on the mirror and is partly masked, so that the outer portions of the plate receive somewhat less light. To avoid this, the mirror should have a greater diameter than the clear aperture and be about twice the plate diameter.

"The rapid coma-free mirror system offers great advantages in regard to light-gathering power and aberration-free imagery. It is assumed, however, that how to make the correction plate is completely understood."

Schmidt's publication finished with this last, somewhat mysterious sentence. He said nothing about how the thin corrector plate could receive its small deformation. But this was the salient point! To attempt it with grinding tools would be a disappointing job and would surely produce a plate full of zone defects. For a long time Schmidt kept secret how he had solved the problem and told only a few friends, including Walter Baade, about his technique.

The method was as simple as it was elegant. Schmidt fitted the glass plate to the carefully ground edge of a heavy metal pan, a bit smaller than the plate's diameter; then, with a hand pump, exhausted air from the pan until a manometer indicated that the calculated negative pressure was obtained. The vacuum warped the plate slightly, and while it was warped Schmidt ground the upper surface plane again. After releasing the vacuum, the plate's bottom was once more plane, whereas the upper surface had the desired figure.

Continued

NGC 6820, NGC 6823, NGC 6830

NGC 6823 in Vulpecula is a small galactic star cluster, surrounded by the inconspicuous emission nebula NGC 6820. While the cluster was first observed by W. Herschel, the nebula was found by Marth at Malta with Lassell's 4-foot reflector. He described it as "faint, small, round, brighter in the middle."

One theory about such combinations of a star cluster and a nebula is that the emission nebula was bigger in early times and has contracted, and that most of its matter has been consumed during formation of the cluster's stars. NGC 6820 resembles a smaller image of the Rosette nebula (see page 75).

Below the galactic cluster NGC 6830, on the left-hand edge of the photograph, is the bright star 12 Vul.

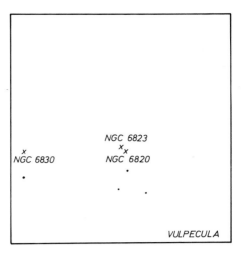

NGC 6823
x
NGC 6830
x x
NGC 6820

VULPECULA

NGC 6830
19ʰ48ᵐ9, +22°58′

Cl, 9ᵐ0, 20 ★
φ = 10′, type: d

NGC 6820
19ʰ40ᵐ5, +22°58′

N, 13ᵐ3, 26′ × 22′

NGC 6823
19ʰ41ᵐ1, +23°12′

Cl, 9ᵐ8, 30 ★
φ = 5′, type: d

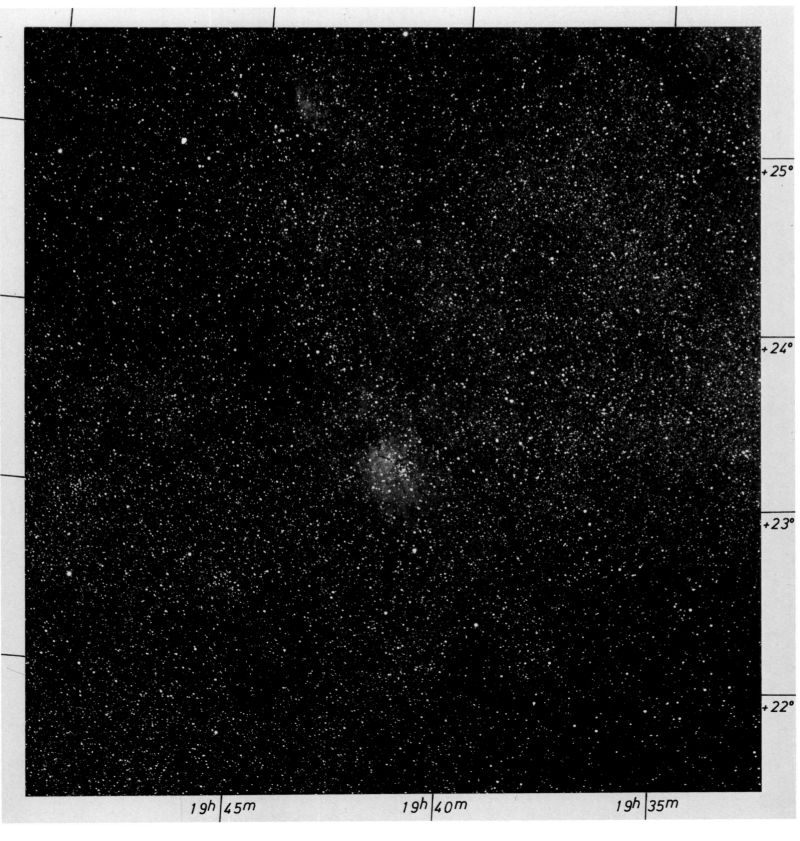

+25°

+24°

+23°

+22°

19ʰ 45m   19ʰ 40m   19ʰ 35m

Schmidt lived simply and was uninterested in money; therefore, he refused to have his inventions patented. He died in 1935, worried that his camera would be used in the anticipated World War II. It should never be forgotten that all his excellent optical and mechanical work was done with the handicap of a missing right hand, perhaps the reason that Bernhard Schmidt became an ardent pacifist.

Working with a Schmidt camera is by no means a complicated venture. After some practical experience, this type of astrocamera is quite easy to use. My second Schmidt camera (the first one of 45-cm focal length is now mounted near Cape Town) was assembled by myself after buying the optical parts from Lichtenknecker Optics, presently at Hasselt, Belgium. Its focal length is 100 cm, mirror diameter 45 cm, and corrector plate diameter 30 cm; the starfields are round and eight degrees in diameter. Nearly half of the chart photographs in this book are enlarged from exposures taken with this camera.

Considering the shadowing by the filmholder, the aperture ratio is about f/3.5. For exposing color photographs of faint nebulae, which has been my main endeavor since 1973, this aperture ratio was too slow. Such exposures need at least f/2 when commercial color emulsions are used. Moreover, it was a disadvantage not to have the filmholder supported by invar bars, which would have avoided out-of-focus images from changes in the length of the tube caused by temperature variations.

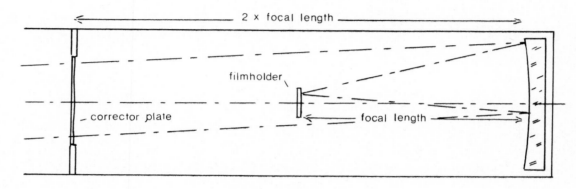

Schmidt Camera

Continued

NGC 6822

In the Milky Way of eastern Sagittarius is the irregular galaxy NGC 6822, large but faint, and somewhat resembling the Magellanic Clouds. Discovered visually in 1884 by E. E. Barnard, it was photographed for the first time by M. Wolf in Heidelberg. Many years ago E. Hubble extensively studied NGC 6822 on photographs taken with the 100-inch Hooker reflector at Mount Wilson Observatory. He not only resolved this galaxy into stars right to the center but was able to prove the presence of clusters, nebulae, and some δ Cephei stars. Due to its low surface brightness the galaxy is a difficult object to observe visually. E. Hubble commented that NGC 6822 appears "fairly conspicuous" when viewed through a 4-inch telescope with low magnification, whereas when observed through the 100-inch telescope, the object is "barely discernible."

NGC 6822 belongs to the local group of galaxies, which includes our Milky Way, the Andromeda galaxy with its two companions, the Magellanic Clouds, the Triangulum galaxy and at least a dozen other fainter galaxies. S. E. Kayser established from 13 δ Cephei variables in NGC 6822 a distance of 560 kpc and a mass of 1.7 billion solar masses.

The wide double star 54 Sagittarii is also known as ADS 12767. Its components A = 5^m4 and B = 8^m9 are separated by 46″.

NGC 6822

$19^h42^m1, -14°53'$

Ga, 11^m0, $16'.6 \times 13'.0$
type: I

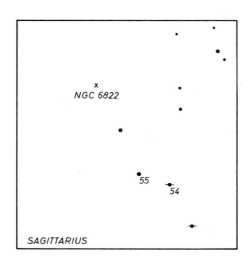

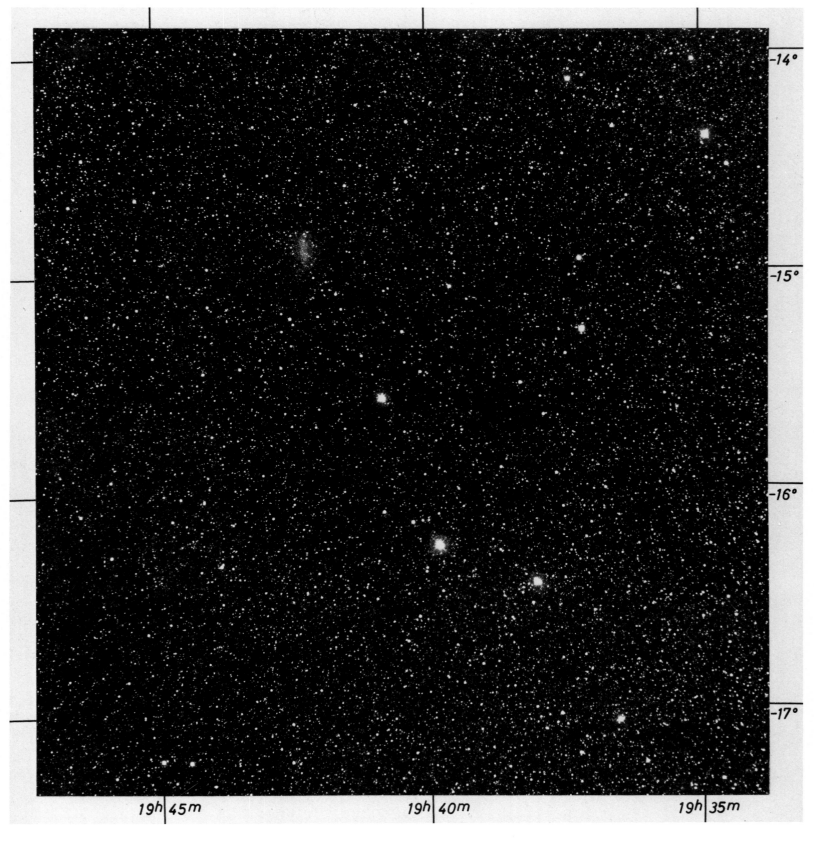

In 1975 I installed a Celestron 14-inch Schmidt camera with an aperture ratio of f/1.7 but a lesser focal length of 60 cm. This is, in fact, a very fast camera, allowing far-reaching exposures in a few minutes. Such short exposure times are particularly advantageous because moisture in the air tends to warp the film during extended exposures, resulting in blurred pictures.

Photographs taken with Schmidt cameras sometimes contain "ghosts," which are symmetrically placed false images on the negatives, caused by reflection from the back side of the corrector plate. Fortunately, only very bright stars give a bright enough reflection to produce an image on the emulsion. The size of the ghosts is different for each Schmidt camera and changes whenever adjustments are made. Relative to the plate center, the ghost is situated opposite the bright star's image at an equal distance. A ghost image has so characteristic an appearance that there is no danger of mistaking it for stars or celestial objects. For example, in this book ghosts can be seen on pages 29, 51, and 55.

The 300/450/1000 Schmidt camera (corrector plate diameter, mirror diameter, and focal length respectively, all in millimeters) was supported on an older Zeiss IV mounting with an axis 60 mm in diameter. This typical German mounting surely is not the ideal support for such a camera. Yet it has enough room to carry further instruments and can carry a total of several hundred pounds easily, without shuddering whenever the observer accidentally knocks against it.

Continued on page 214

M71 = NGC 6838

The star cluster M71, probably seen for the first time by de Chéseaux in 1746, is halfway between γ and δ Sagittae. Messier described the cluster on October 4, 1780, as a nebula without stars. It was left to W. Herschel to recognize this object as being a cluster, resolving it into individual stars.

Oddly enough, in numerous studies, M71 has been called a galactic cluster about as often as a globular. A glance at our photograph shows it as a compact, not quite round collection of stars. Its appearance, its nearness to the galactic equator (galactic latitude 5°.5 south), and its lack of RR Lyrae stars suggest that it is a very rich and remote galactic cluster. On the other hand, its high radial velocity of −80 km/sec, its great distance of 5 kpc, and the results of detailed studies by W. Becker and more recently by J. Cuffey, make one think that it is a globular cluster. For instance, its color-magnitude diagram shows the typical giant branch of a globular cluster, but also the absence of blue stars on the horizontal branch.

Less than half a degree south of M71 is the small star cluster H20, which hardly stands out from its background stars.

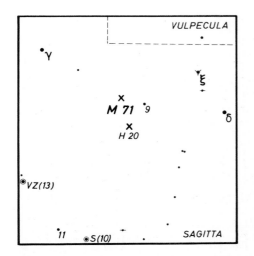

VULPECULA

• γ

ξ

× M 71 • 9

× H 20

⊙ VZ (13)

• 11 ⊙ S (10) SAGITTA

M71 *NGC 6838*

19ʰ51ᵐ5, +18°39′

Cl? Gl?, 8ᵐ3, Sp: G5
$\phi = 6'.1$, type: ?

H20

19ʰ50ᵐ9, +18°13′

Cl, 9ᵐ6, 30 ★
$\phi = 7'.8$, type: d

+19°

+18°

+17°

19ʰ 55m   19ʰ 50m   19ʰ 45m

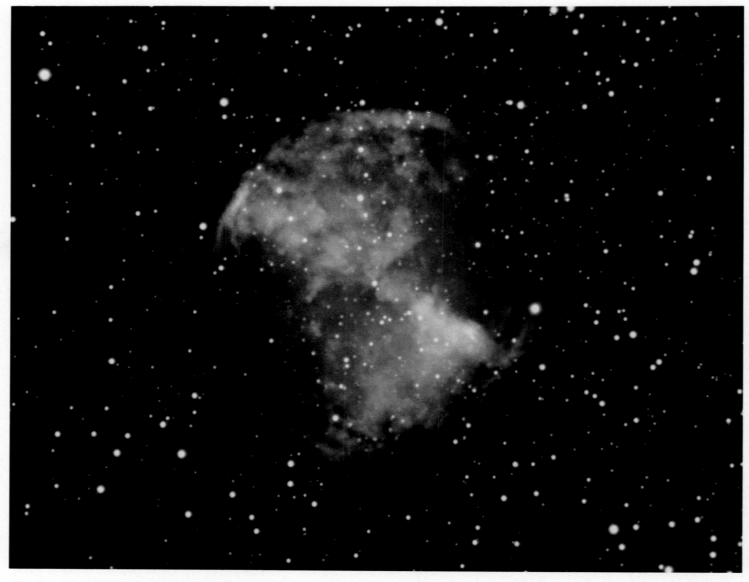

M27. Even in small telescopes this nebula can appear distinctly greenish, making it one of the few deep-sky objects to show color visually. Forty-five minute exposure on chilled High Speed Ektachrome with the 40-inch f/6.8 Ritchey-Chrétien reflector of the U. S. Naval Observatory at Flagstaff, Arizona.

M27 = NGC 6853 (Dumbbell nebula)

The small constellation Vulpecula contains the brightest planetary nebula of the northern sky, M27. Messier discovered this "nebula without star" on July 12, 1764. Lord Rosse compared the object as seen through his large telescope to a weightlifter's dumbbell, and ever since, M27 has been familiarly known as the Dumbbell nebula. Its true shape can be seen on photographs taken with powerful telescopes, as in the picture above. The oval nebula shows two opposite dark segments, and elsewhere bright, well-defined edges that superficially resemble shock waves. The flocculent internal structure indicates turbulences. The very hot central star (13^{m}4) is masked in the facing picture by overexposed bright nebulosity.

M27 is a rewarding telescopic object for beginning observers, even under the unfavorable conditions near the glow of city lights. To find it, start at α Aquilae (Altair) and go 10° north to γ Sagittae (3^{m}7). From there another 3°.5 north brings one to the star 14 Vulpeculae (5^{m}7). M27 is just south

of the latter star. In a small telescope it looks like a pale spot, clearly different from a star. The Soviet astronomer O. N. Chudovicheva, of Pulkovo Observatory near Leningrad, measured the motion of the emission knots in M27 by comparing pairs of photographs taken 25 years apart. She found that the nebula is expanding at a rate of 0".068 per year. If M27 has expanded steadily at this rate, it would have been born just 3,000 to 4,000 years ago. Other astrometric measurements of the expansion have found a rate of 0".005 in radius per year, resulting in an estimated age of about 45,000 years. Chudovicheva derived a distance of 150 pc for the nebula; other estimates range up to 300 pc. Either way, it is one of the nearest such objects to Earth.

On the western edge of our field we find the inconspicuous open star cluster NGC 6830, a group of 20 to 30 widely scattered stars. A. Landolt compiled a color-magnitude diagram of this cluster, which indicates a distance of 700 pc.

M27   NGC 6853
Dumbbell nebula
$19^h57^m4, +22°35'$

Pl, 7^m6, $m_\star = 13.4$
$8' \times 7'$, type: IIIa

NGC 6830
$19^h48^m9, +22°58'$

Cl, 9^m0, 20 $\star$
$\phi = 10'$, type: d

Some of the adjustments of a Schmidt camera are far more critical than others: (1) the distance of the film surface to the mirror (the focus); (2) the matching of the filmholder axis to the optical axis of the system, which is to say the surface of the filmholder must be perpendicular to the mirror axis; (3) the mirror axis passing through the optical center of the correcting plate. Less critical adjustments are the distance from the corrector plate to mirror and filmholder, and the perpendicularity of the corrector plate to the optical axis.

In front of the corrector plate there is a dewcap, fitted on the inside with absorbing felt. However, the corrector plate is so large and relatively thin that the cap does not always prevent dew during damp nights. Therefore on both sides around the plate I placed heating wires taken from an electric blanket, rated as less than 20 watts. The arrangement works perfectly, stopping formation of dew yet warming the glass plate so little that definition is not impaired. The heat remains turned on during the whole exposure time. On extremely damp nights, the corrector plate is defogged between exposures with the help of a hair dryer.

In spite of the great care given to photo reproduction in this book, these pictures give only a slight idea of the rich detail on the negatives. Some details are inevitably lost in copying and reproducing, and unfortunately this is particularly true of the color pictures. Nevertheless, I do hope that the reproductions make my love for the Schmidt camera understandable.

The 14-inch Celestron Schmidt camera of 60-cm focal length and f/1.7, here on the Gamsberg, a remote table mountain in Namibia with excellent observing conditions and far from any artificial lights. The mounting, made by Zeiss, belongs to the Max Planck Institute at Heidelberg. While the camera is much younger than the first one, pictured on page 210, the author is 15 years older.

M75 = NGC 6864

Just inside the constellation Capricornus, near its boundary with Sagittarius, we find the small globular cluster M75. It lies in an area completely devoid of bright stars. This object was discovered by Méchain on August 27, 1780. Messier recorded that M75 is "composed of very small stars," and this was confirmed by W. Herschel with his larger telescopes. It is strange that Messier believed he could detect individual stars in one of the most compact globular clusters, for he often described more easily resolvable globulars as "nebulae without stars." In good binoculars M75 is quite easy to see, due to its great integrated brightness of 8^{m}0 and apparent diameter of only 4'.6.

According to G. Alcaino, the distance to M75 is 18 kpc, which would place it on the far side of our galaxy. This cluster contains a dozen known variable stars.

215

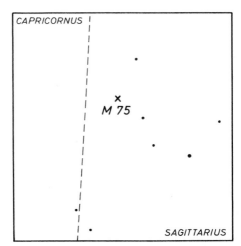

M 75   NGC 6864
$20^h03^m2, -22°04'$

GI, 9^m5, Sp: G1
$\phi = 4'.6$, type: I

Color photo by the author of the same region as on the facing page. The brilliant star at center is γ Cygni; the brightest star near bottom is P Cygni. Southwest of P is the small cluster IC 4996.

M29, Nebulae around γ Cygni.

It is not yet known which early-type star causes the nebulae around γ Cygni to shine. With a spectral type of *F*8, the bright star is too cool to be the powerhouse. The great size and gross filamentary structure set this nebula apart from other H II regions. It also has high internal motion and is a source of strong radio emissions.

M29 is a rather unpretentious galactic cluster, a loose accumulation of about 20 stars. Messier, who first saw it on July 29, 1764, described it as a "cluster of 7 to 8 very small stars," slightly above γ Cygni (as seen in a refractor giving inverted images). W. Becker and J. Stock carried out a photometric study of M29 from which a color-magnitude

diagram was compiled. The distance is 1,700 pc, according to H. L. Johnson.

The star P = 34 Cygni is a novalike variable of high intrinsic luminosity. C. S. Beals showed that the star is in a continuous state of eruption and expels gaseous shells. P Cygni was unknown until 1600, when it brightened to 3^m, afterward fading to 6^m in 1620. In 1655 it again rose to 3^{m}5, but since 1715 has varied only slightly from an average of 5^{m}2.

Compare these views with that on page 220.

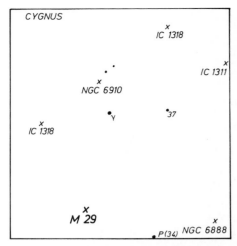

IC 1318
20ʰ14ᵐ7, +41°39′

N, 24′ × 17′

20ʰ26ᵐ7, +39°47′

N, 70′ × 20′

NGC 6910
20ʰ21ᵐ3, +40°37′

Cl, 6ᵐ7, 40 ★
φ = 8′, type: d

M29   NGC 6913
20ʰ22ᵐ2, +38°21′

Cl, 9ᵐ0, 20 ★
φ = 7′, type: d

IC 1311
20ʰ09ᵐ1, +41°02′

Cl, 13ᵐ1, 30 ★
φ = 5′, type: e

NGC 6888
20ʰ10ᵐ7, +38°16′

N, 18′ × 12′, type: e

+42°

+41°

+40°

+39°

+38°

20ʰ |25ᵐ   20ʰ |20ᵐ   20ʰ |15ᵐ   20ʰ |10ᵐ

The brightest portion of the Veil nebula is the northeast part of NGC 6992 — 5, shown here. This region may be detected as a small, very dim reddish glow in the Milky Way photograph on page 220. It has been reported seen in 7 x 50 binoculars under ideal conditions. Some of the fine, filamentary structure is visible in large amateur telescopes. U. S. Naval Observatory photograph.

NGC 6960, NGC 6979, NGC 6992 — 95 (Veil nebula)

Armed with a comet seeker on a dark, clear night, the amateur can observe in the southern part of Cygnus, near the star 52 Cygni (3^{m}2), several faint nebulae 2° apart and running in a north-south direction. These objects are the emission nebulae NGC 6960 and NGC 6992 — 95 which, together with the fainter nebula NGC 6979 between and north of them, are known as the Veil nebula. Our photograph (and especially the above large-scale picture) shows that the nebulosity is an intricate mass of luminous filaments, reminding one of the filaments in the Crab nebula.

The Veil nebula was discovered by W. Herschel in 1784. That the pieces form parts of a single gigantic loop (hence the name Loop nebula) became generally recognized only after R. Minkowski took a photograph on a red plate with the 48-inch Schmidt camera at Palomar Observatory. It shows a vast circular ring, open toward the south, with a diameter of 2°.7 and thin filaments in its interior. E. Hubble compared photographs of the nebulae taken 27 years apart and found a radial expansion of 6″ per century. This was later confirmed by W. G. Fessenkov and his associates.

If, as is believed today, these filaments are the remnants of a supernova outburst, this event must have occurred about 160,000 years ago, if the speed of expansion has remained constant. According to unpublished radial velocity measurements by M. L. Humason, the present expansion rate is about 45 km/sec; combined with the angular rate (0″.06 per year), this indicates a distance of roughly 400 pc for the Veil nebula. If one accepts the theory of F. Zwicky and J. H. Oort that the original speed of expansion was 1,000 km/sec and has decreased to the present 45 km/sec through the resistance of interstellar clouds, then the explosion would have taken place some 30,000 years ago. The existence of dark clouds outside the loop can be clearly seen by the scarcity of faint stars west of NGC 6960.

The supernova theory is also supported by the strong radio radiation that has been measured by several astronomers, among them D. S. Mathewson and his associates. The radio emission comes mainly from the edge of the loop. Up to now, no hot central star has been found that could be either the stimulant for the nebula's luminosity or the former supernova itself.

NGC 6992 − 5
Cirrus (or Veil) nebula
20ʰ54ᵐ3, +31°30'

N, 78' × 8', type: e

NGC 6960
Cirrus (or Veil) nebula
20ʰ43ᵐ6, +30°32'

N, 70' × 6', type: e

NGC 6979
Cirrus (or Veil) nebula
20ʰ48ᵐ9, +31°56'

N, 40' × 20', type: e

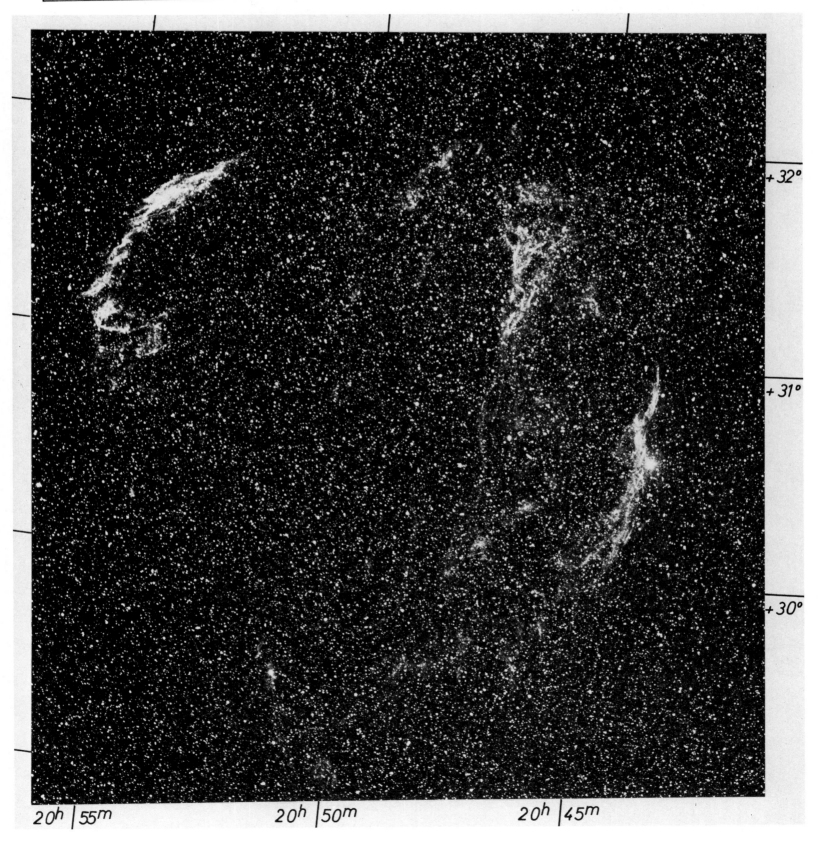

CYGNUS

NGC 6992   NGC 6979
NGC 6995
6960 • 52

+32°
+31°
+30°

20ʰ 55ᵐ   20ʰ 50ᵐ   20ʰ 45ᵐ

The Cygnus star cloud of the Milky Way. The entire Northern Cross is visible here, from bright Deneb at top left to Albireo at lower right. The scale of this photo is almost exactly the same as that of the Tirion deluxe *Sky Atlas 2000.0* and the Becvar deluxe *Atlas of the Heavens,* either of which can be used to identify dozens of the stars and deep-sky objects recorded here.

The North America nebula glows dimly east of Deneb; compare it with the views on pages 222 and 223. Nebulae are also visible around γ Cygni; compare with pages 216 and 217. M29 near γ appears starlike. The field of the Veil nebulae (page 219) can be found near 52 Cygni at lower left; these nebulae, especially NGC 6992-5, may be barely detectable in this reproduction. The globular cluster M56 (page 203) appears as a very faint "star" not far from Albireo.

Locating difficult objects in photos such as this is good indoor practice for finding them under the more trying conditions at the telescope. Ten minute exposure by Dennis di Cicco with a 50-mm f/2.8 lens on Fujichrome R-100.

M72 = NGC 6981, M73 = NGC 6994

Slightly more than halfway from ϑ Capricorni (4ᵐ2) to ε Aquarii (3ᵐ8), we find the small and inconspicuous globular star cluster M72, discovered by Mechain in 1780. When viewed in a small telescope, this cluster is a nebulous spot resembling a comet without a tail. A 20-cm telescope and high magnification are needed to resolve the border into stars.

L. Rosino discovered photographically all but six of the 40 variable stars now known in M72; of these 35 are of RR Lyrae type. The patience and diligence necessary to determine the light curves and periods of these variables are suggested by the fact that they are as faint as magnitude 17.

East of M72 by 1°3 is a clump of four stars which Dreyer listed in his catalogue as NGC 6994. This "cluster" does not deserve the name; it is no more prominent than the uncatalogued group at the bottom edge of our photograph, and similar ones can be found in any part of the sky. Nevertheless, Messier listed this object as M73 in his catalogue. Although some have questioned whether these stars are really what Messier intended as the entry in his list, his own description of the objects makes this clear. He wrote, "Cluster of three or four small stars, which resembles a nebula at first glance, containing very little nebulosity; this cluster is located on the parallel [of declination] of the preceding nebulosity [M72]."

M72 NGC 6981
$20^h 50^m 7$, $-12°44'$

GI, $10^m 2$, Sp: G2
$\phi = 5'.1$, type: IX

M73 NGC 6994
$20^h 56^m 4$, $-12°50'$

CI? $8^m 9$, 4 ★
$\phi = 2'.8$, type: ?

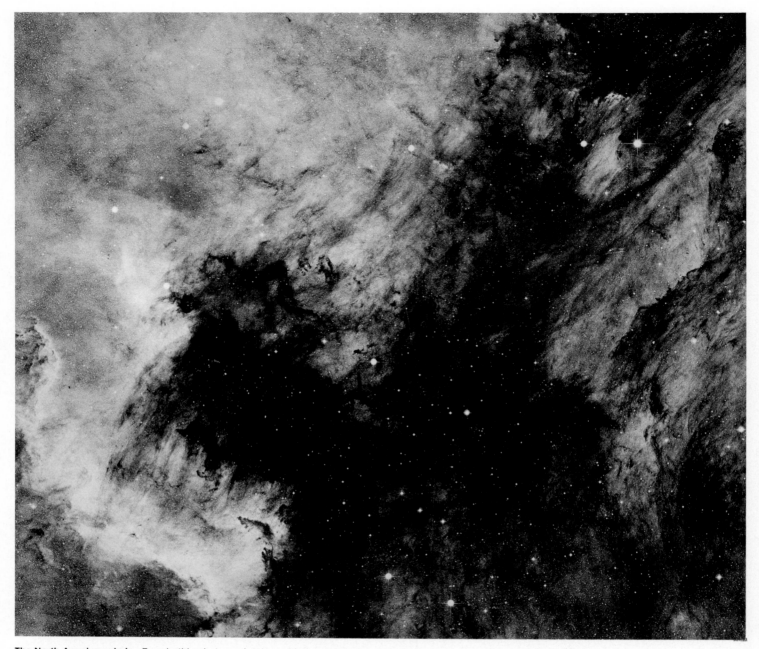

The North America nebula. Even in this photograph taken with the world's largest Schmidt camera, the nebula shows detail down to the limit of resolution. Ninety minute exposure with the 1.34-meter Schmidt at Karl Schwarzschild Observatory, Tautenberg, East Germany. Kodak 103a-E film, RG1I filter.

NGC 7000 = North America nebula

On December 12, 1890, Max Wolf in Heidelberg photographed for the first time NGC 7000, a nebula that W. Herschel had discovered in 1786 between ξ Cygni (3^{m}9) and 57 Cygni (4^{m}7). From its shape, Wolf gave it the name "North America nebula." On dark, clear nights, the central parts of the nebula can be seen with binoculars, but the abundance of stars in this area makes recognition difficult. The best way to find the object is to be guided by the two bright stars mentioned above.

The spectrum of NGC 7000 shows both continuous and line emissions. Originally it was thought that Deneb (1^{m}3), the brightest star in Cygnus, of spectral type A2, excited the nebula to shine. Later investigations revealed that the ultraviolet radiation from this star would be too weak to power the nebula. For a number of years HD 199579 (the 6^{m}0, spectral type O6 star just below "Hudson Bay") was thought to be the nebula's source of energy. However, if NGC 7000 were really as far away as this star (about 1 kpc) then it

would have to be exceptionally large to appear the size it does. Too large, in fact, to be excited by HD 199579 alone. Recent work by T. Neckel, A. Harris, and C. Eiroa indicates a star greatly dimmed by dark material near the "Atlantic coast" to be a likely candidate to power the nebula. If this is the case, then the nebula may be only 100-200 pc away and of a size more consistent with other H II regions in our galaxy.

Near the right-hand edge of the picture can be seen other faint nebulosities that are parts of IC 5067-5070, the "Pelican nebula." These nebulosities belong physically to the North America nebula and are separated only by a broad band of absorbing dark clouds.

The facing photograph was taken with the three-color composite technique: where three exposures on 103a-O (blue), 103a-G (green), and 103a-E (red) emulsions were dyed before assembling into the final print.

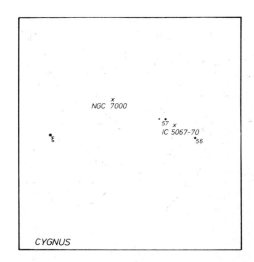

CYGNUS

NGC 7000
North America nebula
20ʰ57ᵐ0, +44°08'

N, 120' × 100'
type: c, e

IC 5067 – 70
Pelican nebula
20ʰ46ᵐ9, +44°11'

N, 85' × 75'
type: c, e

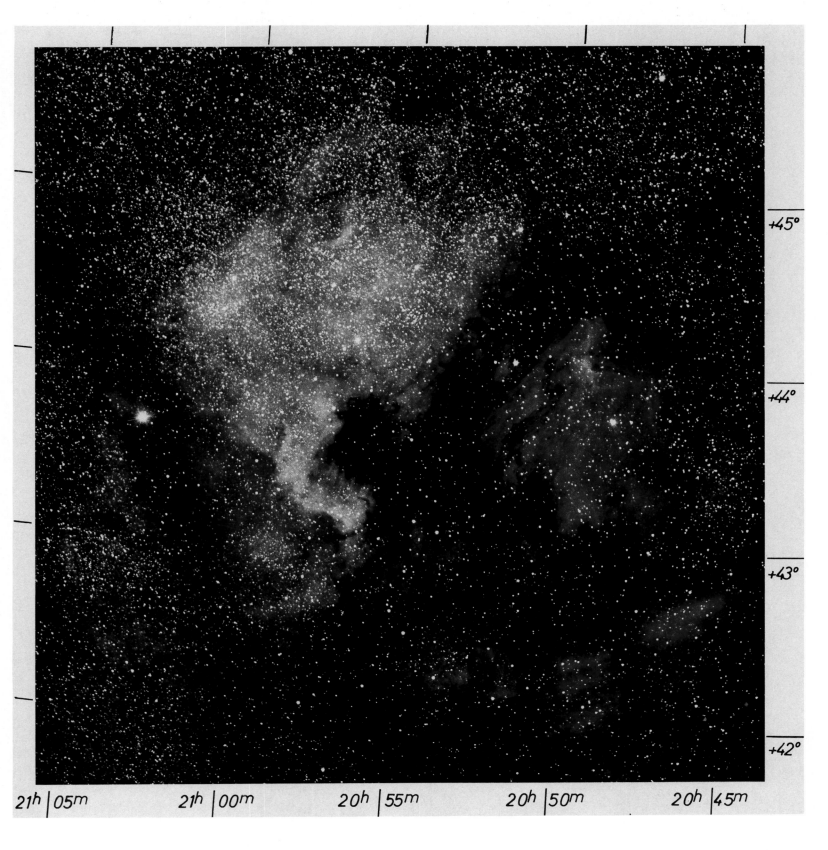

An extremely sharp color photograph of M15. The smallest star images are approximately 0".7 in diameter. The lack of striking color is due to each star image being overexposed in its center and dropping off sharply to black sky. This is a truer representation of how globular clusters look than most color photographs, in which a strong yellow or green cast results from the film's response to fuzzy outer edges of star images. Close inspection, however, shows that many of the brighter stars here have an orange hue; as in all globular clusters, the brightest stars are late-type giants.

Twenty-five minute exposure during excellent seeing by Laird A. Thompson on hypersensitized Ektachrome ASA 400 film with the 3.6-meter f/4.2 Canada-France-Hawaii telescope at Mauna Kea. Photograph from the Institute for Astronomy, University of Hawaii. North is to the upper left.

M15 = NGC 7078

The globular star cluster M15 in Pegasus is the farthest east of the four great globulars of the Northern Hemisphere's summer sky, the others being M3, M13, and M92. J. D. Maraldi discovered M15 in 1745 and described it as a rather bright nebula with a few stars, between ε Pegasi and β Equulei. Nineteen years later Messier saw M15 as a nebula without stars and a diameter of 3'.

Standing out distinctly in a star-poor field, M15 can be easily seen with small telescopes, but its center cannot be resolved into stars. The average magnitude of its 25 brightest stars is 14ᵐ5.

Inspection of the abundant astronomical literature about M15 reveals a noticeable increase in apparent diameter over the years: Melotte (1915) D = 6', Wirtz (1923) D = 4', Shapley (1930) D = 7'.4, Mowbray (1946) D = 12'.3. More recently I. King made star counts and photometric measurements of M15 that revealed some members as far as 15' away from the center.

About 1° south of M15 is the binary ADS 15007, whose components A = 7ᵐ4 and B = 7ᵐ4 are separated by about 1".5. It can be resolved by medium-size amateur instruments.

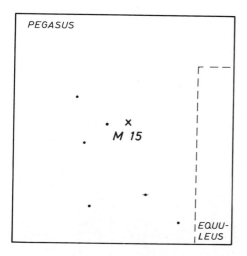

M15 NGC 7078
21^h27^m6, $+11°57'$

Gl, 7^m3, Sp: F3
$\phi = 12'3$, type: IV

+13°

+12°

+11°

21h 30m   21h 25m

Satellite trails on sky photographs

Whenever a bright artificial satellite crosses a field that is being photographed, it leaves behind a visible trail that shows all its light peculiarities. Because of some satellites' rotation, especially the tumbling action of long booster rockets, variable reflection of sunlight can often be seen. Hence it is feasible to derive the tumbling period, the time interval (from one maximum to the next one), and roughly the amplitude of light fluctuation, provided the angular speed with which the satellite crosses the field of view is known, possibly from a prediction. Alternatively, the observer can fit a very fast shutter device to the camera, which is connected to a clock mechanism, and close the lens for a brief moment every second. The trail will then show regularly spaced interruptions from which the angular velocity and the satellite's position relative to the stars in the field can be ascertained.

By this method many hundreds of photographs are taken every day all over the world. The ensuing data provide predictions for further observations, without which the quickly changing orbits of the satellites would soon be lost track of. This gigantic task is carried out by large electronic computing centers, at the Goddard Space Flight Center in Greenbelt, Maryland (USA), the Smithsonian Observatory's world network of Baker-Nunn cameras, the Moscow Cosmos Center (USSR), the Satellite Research Centre in Slough (England), and by American and Soviet radar surveillance. In this way a check is held on the orbits of more than 4,000 objects. The 400 observation stations scattered all over the globe receive from these centers detailed predictions of all satellites in space — currently a bundle of 200 pages of closely printed figures every week. In this way a constant check is made of the numerous satellites, their launching rockets, and other cast-off parts.

Recently the U. S. Air Force began constructing powerful electronic cameras to scan the skies and automatically calculate the motions of all satellites that enter their fields of view. These systems, instituted for military purposes, can detect fainter objects and analyze orbital maneuvers by powered satellites in minutes, whereas photographic techniques require a minimum of an hour and a half.

Quite unintentionally the "trails of the space age" have left their marks on some of the photographs in this book, and the reader is thus able to see a tiny fraction of what is monitored daily by the large control centers. For this book I took nearly 400 exposures, and 60 of these have the trail of a satellite imprinted on them; some even show two and three trails.

Continued

IC 1396

The huge emission nebula IC 1396 has an area of nearly six square degrees. It was observed by E. E. Barnard with his 6-inch refractor at Nashville, Tennessee. J. L. E. Dreyer described this object merely as "a nebulous part of the Milky Way," but in fact this complex nebula shows an abundance of details.

So far, no single central star has been found that excites IC 1396 to shine. The O6 star HD 20267, close to the center of the nebula, is probably not the source of illumination, but ½° northwest of the center a galactic cluster of 30 OB stars possibly could be responsible. The bright star on the northern tip of IC 1396, Mu Cephei, a very red semiregular variable of spectral type M2, $3^m6 — 5^m1$, is out of the question; it is too cool to provide sufficient ultraviolet light.

No supernova remnant or pulsar has been found in IC 1396. Conspicuously silhouetted against its luminous portions are the deep black patches known as globules, which are contracting dust clouds that will eventually become stars. In the western part, some so-called "elephant trunks" like those in the Rosette nebula can be identified.

IC 1396
21ʰ37ᵐ5, +57°14'

N + Cl, ★ = O6n 5ᵐ64
165' × 135', type: e

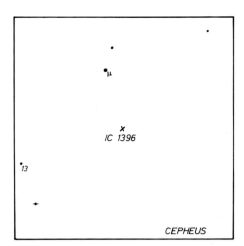

CEPHEUS

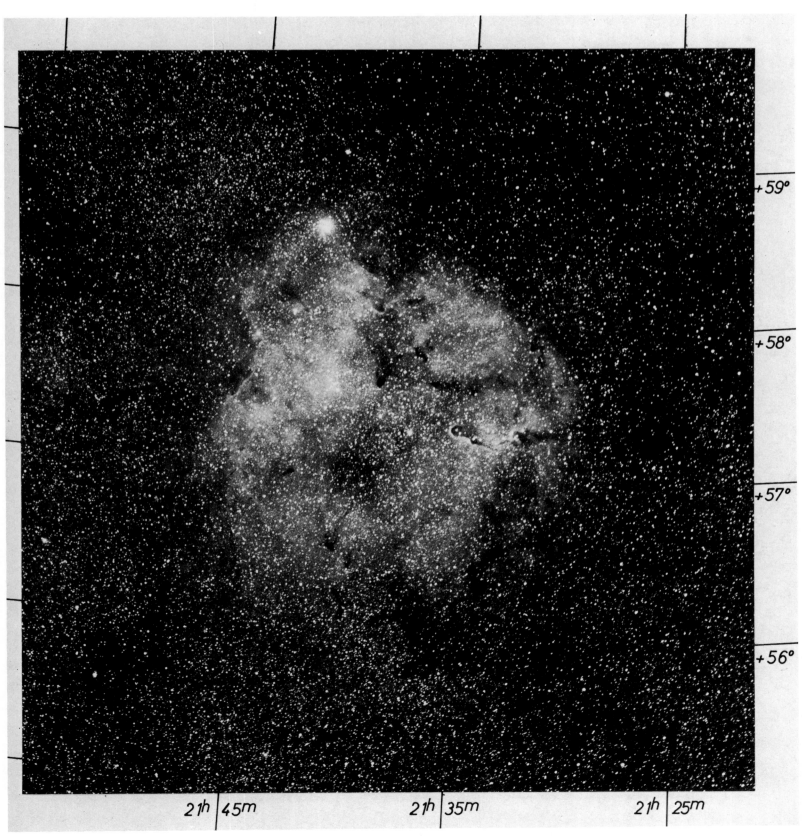

228

In the final stage of my project, an average of one in three photographs showed satellite trails. I was therefore forced to retake many exposures in order not to end up with an "Atlas of Satellite Trails." U. Guentzel-Lingner (Astronomisches Rechen-Institut, Heidelberg) calculated that at the time there were 120 Earth satellites bright enough and orbiting in such a way as to be within the range of my Schmidt camera at Falkau (diameter of field $7°.5$). All these satellites were brighter than $5^m.0$. Their angular velocity varied between $2°.5$ and $0°.8$ per second, depending on height and zenith distance. The sample included the three very bright balloons Echo 1, Echo 2, and Pageos 1, two smaller American balloons, and a number of U. S. launcher rockets. However, most were Russian booster rockets of the Cosmos satellite series, all tumbling very rapidly, resulting in light fluctuation periods between 0.4 and 3.5 seconds.

Photographs in this book showing trails of satellites can be seen on pages 19, 23, 137, 143, and 149, for example. The photographing of these trails was the result of pure chance. It had to be worked out afterward which satellites they were, and this often very difficult task was undertaken by U. Guentzel-Lingner and H. Koehnke of Stade, West Germany.

Perhaps the most unusual happening of this nature occurred while I was taking the exposure of M51 in the Hunting Dogs (page 149) on February 20, 1966, between 3:43 and 4:48 UT. Two bright Cosmos rockets crossed midfield at an interval of 34 minutes, one having a striking light fluctuation period of 0.4 seconds, and the other a slow brightness change whose period could not be ascertained exactly. A third, very weak trail of a Cosmos satellite, parallel to the second one, can be seen near the right edge.

This exposure can serve as an example of how the satellites are identified afterward. One prerequisite was availability of current predictions of all brighter satellites. We used those from the Goddard Space Flight Center, which gave the exact time and geographical longitude of the south-to-north equatorial passage of each satellite for each of its 14 to 17 orbits per day over a period of six to 14 days

Continued

M39 = NGC 7092, IC 5146 (Cocoon nebula)

The object that makes this Cygnus field so interesting is not the open star cluster M39 at the top right-hand corner of the photograph, but the unusual circular nebulous spot IC 5146 in the lower left corner, known as the Cocoon nebula. This formation, which has a certain similarity to the Trifid nebula (page 187) is situated at the end of a network of starless lanes. Star counts in the area have proved that these are interstellar dark clouds, such as are found in many places along the Milky Way.

IC 5146 was first mentioned by T. E. Espin in 1894. In the same year E. E. Barnard and M. Wolf took the first photographs of the object. More recent studies show that the nebula has a continuous spectrum identical with those of

the hot stars in it. M. F. Walker found from three-color photometry of 76 stars to as faint as $17^m.0$ inside the nebula that they form a very young cluster similar to NGC 2264 inside the S Monocerotis nebula (page 77). G. H. Herbig reports an unpublished finding by the late W. Baade that there are numerous faint red stars within IC 5146. It would appear that the Cocoon nebula can best be compared with the great Orion nebula (page 65).

The very open cluster M39 was examined by H. L. Johnson, who measured magnitudes and color indices of 28 of its stars. Their color-magnitude diagram shows some similarity with that of the Praesepe cluster (page 95). At a distance of 275 pc, M39 is rather near to us for a galactic cluster.

IC 5146
Cocoon nebula

$21^h51^m3, +47°02'$

$N + Cl, m_N = 9^m6$
$m_{Cl} = 8^m3$
$Dim_N = 12' \times 12'$
$Dim_{Cl} = 12'$
$type_{Cl}: c \qquad type_N: c$

M39 NGC 7092

$21^h30^m4, +48°13'$

$Cl, 5^m3, 30 \star$
$\phi = 32', type: e$

CYGNUS

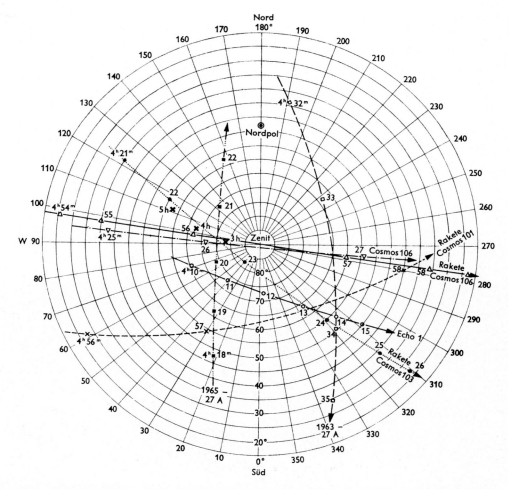

(depending on the height and stability of the orbit). From the equatorial passages, it was possible with the aid of a correction table to calculate when a satellite crossed some other parallel of latitude. In addition, the heights were given for the equator and different latitudes, which vary due to the orbital ellipticity. With this information at hand, it was possible without intricate calculations to plot the satellite's track projected on the surface of the Earth, or as in our case, on a suitable map of Europe. This sub-satellite path can be

Continued

M2 = NGC 7089

While J. D. Maraldi was searching for Chéseaux's comet in 1746, he discovered the globular star cluster M2 within the constellation Aquarius. In those days, hunting these transient and mysterious objects with tails was one of the foremost branches of astronomy, and cometlike objects encountered during a search would be plotted on a star chart to avoid any later confusion with comets. For this same reason, Messier entered his first objects on his published maps of the observed tracks of comets. Consequently, the M-numbers do not run in sequence of right ascension, a fact occasionally mentioned as a fault of Messier's catalogue. For example, M1 (Crab nebula, page 63) lies 16 hours in right ascension away from M2.

With a visual magnitude of 6^{m}3, M2 is an excellent object for observers with binoculars or small telescopes.

To find it easily, pinpoint β Aquarii (3^{m}1) and then move about 5° north and a little east; M2 will appear in the field of vision. Due to its great concentration, even large instruments resolve only the edge of the cluster into stars.

W. Lohmann, while carrying out a study of surface brightness in 16 globular clusters, found that M2 shows a particularly marked decrease in brightness from center to edge. The central square minute of arc contributes fully 37% of the total light, but at 5' from the center an equivalent area provides only 0.02% as much.

24 Aquarii (ADS 15176) is a close double star with the components A = 7^{m}4 and B = 7^{m}8, and a separation of 0."4 during the 1980's.

M2 **NGC 7089**
$21^h 30^m 9, -1°03'$

GI, $7^m 3$, Sp: F3
$\phi = 11'.7$, type: II

AQUARIUS

×
M 2

24

0°

-1°

-2°

21h 35m   21h 30m

divided into one-minute intervals from the predictions, showing over which part of the globe the satellite was flying at a specific moment. By then marking the place of observation on the map and having a sheet of tracing paper with an azimuthal grid drawn on it, it was possible to establish the directions (azimuths) and slant ranges to various points of the orbit. From the slant ranges and the predicted heights of the satellite, we could derive the zenith distances of these points with the aid of a nomogram.

By this method all the sub-satellite paths of the satellites that were above the horizon of Falkau during the exposure of M51 were plotted on a chart (see page 230). There were altogether nine passages in the 75-minute exposure time. The position of the center of the camera field was also converted into azimuth and zenith distance and marked as crosses on the map for 3:00, 4:00, and 5:00 UT. This position was changing relative to the fixed azimuthal coordinate system because of the Earth's rotation. Knowing the angular size of the camera field, we could immediately recognize which satellites passed through it.

This example shows that the astrophotographer who makes a long exposure must always expect to find one or more satellite trails on his or her negatives. During the long winter nights, the danger of such "adornments" is limited to about two hours in evening and morning twilight. But for observers in northern latitudes, the situation in spring and summer becomes much worse because the Sun never gets far enough below the horizon during the night so that satellites overhead will not be illuminated. Particularly during the bright summer nights, the present swarms of orbiting satellites make it almost impossible to avoid a satellite trail on a wide-field photograph taken with a powerful camera. Falkau is situated at 48° north latitude, and on June 21st the Sun is only 18.5 degrees below the horizon at midnight, which means that all satellites, rockets, and other objects orbiting at more than 360 km reflect sunlight, even in the zenith, which is the most favorable position for astrophotography.

Continued on page 236

M30 = NGC 7099

The globular star cluster M30 is one of those in high galactic latitudes and, with a visual brightness of 8^m4, is the most prominent cluster within the constellation Capricornus. The cluster can be easily recognized in binoculars. To do so, first locate the star 41 Capricorni (5^m3), which is only 20′ east of M30. A telescope of 10-cm aperture at a magnification of 160 can resolve the edges of M30 into individual stars. With larger instruments the very compact center still remains unresolved, but under good seeing conditions a few 12^m stars appear.

With the aid of the four RR Lyrae stars in M30, several distance calculations made between 1927 and 1954 led to a figure of 12 kpc. G. Alcaino's latest revision reduces the distance to only 8.3 kpc. L. Rosino has made a photographic study of the brightness of the stars in M30.

The double star 41 Capricorni is also known as ADS 15223, with components A = 5^m4 and B = 13^m5 separated $5″3$. The very large magnitude difference makes the companion quite difficult to see even with large telescopes.

M30 NGC 7099

21^h37^m5, $-23°25'$

Gl, 8^m6, Sp: F3

$\phi = 8'.9$, type: V

CAPRICORNUS

41 M 30

−23°

−24°

−25°

21^h 40m

21^h 35m

NGC 7293, the Helix nebula. Lick Observatory photograph with the 120-inch Shane reflector.

NGC 7293

The planetary nebula NGC 7293, sometimes called the "Helix" or "Sunflower" nebula, has an apparent diameter of 15′ (half that of the full Moon). Usually considered the nearest and largest of its kind, it is of such low surface brightness that even on dark and extremely clear nights it is barely distinguishable as a very faint patch. Nothing of the wonderful fine structure in the picture above can be seen visually in any telescope.

The 1,039 planetary nebulae that L. Perek and L. Kohoutek listed in their catalogue have long occupied the attention of astrophysicists because of the processes that cause the gas to shine. These spherical shells of extremely rarefied hydrogen, helium, oxygen, nitrogen, and other gases are about 1 pc in diameter on the average. Often a planetary is

stimulated to luminosity by a visually very faint central star. The high degree of ionization that characterizes the nebula's spectrum indicates that the central star emits chiefly ultraviolet radiation and must therefore be extremely hot indeed. In this way, it has been deduced that the central star of NGC 7293 has a surface temperature of 50,000° K. The central stars of some other planetaries have surface temperatures of 100,000°.

Observations show that all planetary nebulae are expanding at rates of from 10 to 50 km/sec. From this we must conclude that they are relatively young formations, cosmically speaking. L. P. Metik and R. E. Gerschberg have estimated the distance of NGC 7293 at 120 pc.

NGC 7293

$22^h27^m0, -21°06'$

Pl, 6^m5, $m_\star = 13.3$
$15' \times 12'$, type: IV

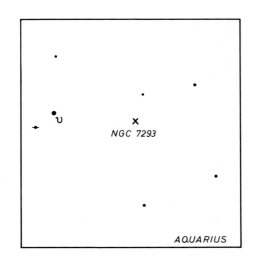

AQUARIUS

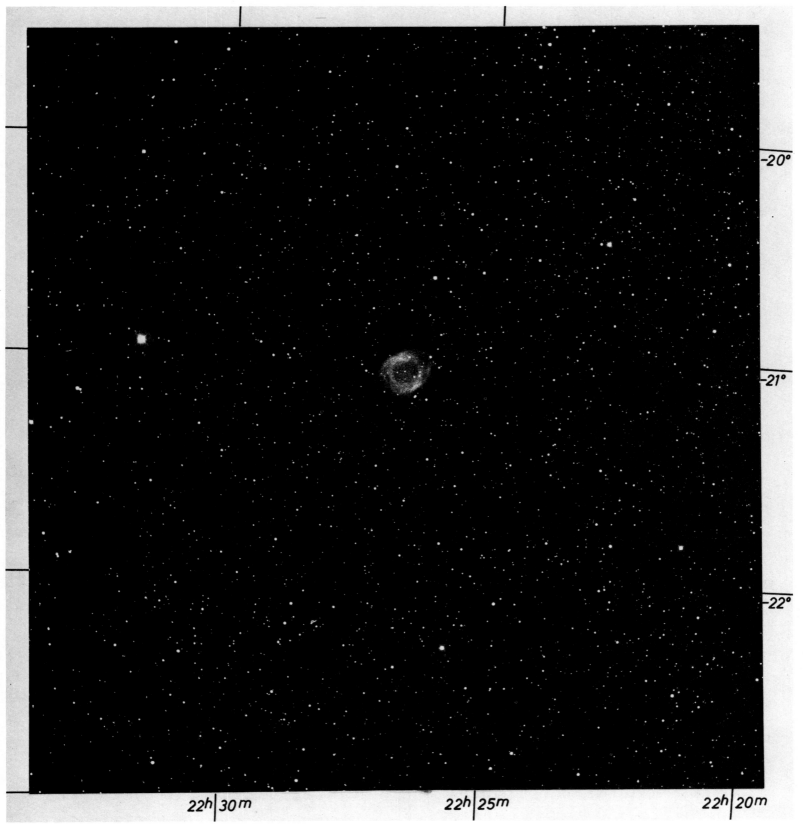

22ʰ|30m 22ʰ|25m 22ʰ|20m

During the period from May to June 1966, I took 15 photographs for this book, and all but two bore trails. The odd two were free of trails only because the fields were far south at midnight, where the Earth's shadow reaches higher up the sky.

In photographing a nebula or other extended object, it sometimes happens that the trail of a bright satellite cuts right through its center, thus making the photograph useless for photometric work. Anyone attempting to prepare a photographic star atlas today must anticipate considerable difficulties. At the present time, the completion of a project like the Palomar Observatory Sky Atlas without any satellite trails would be an almost impossible task, unless one worked to a strict satellite timetable, always interrupting the exposures whenever a brighter satellite threatened to come anywhere near the exposed field. Fortunately all the satellites, even the high-flying and geostationary ones like the Relay, Telstar and Syncom satellites, appear as trails and can be immediately recognized for what they are.

A study of the orbital inclinations of all the satellites flying in space today shows that the summer constellations in higher declinations (Ursa Major, Coma, Bootes, etc.) are especially liable to satellite trails for observers in northern latitudes. The danger could be diminished by using a smaller aperture which, however, would lengthen the exposure time; or else, as already mentioned, by carefully noting the geographical positions and times of brighter satellites from the predictions, and avoiding any areas through which they fly. However, this latter method entails a rather lengthy prediction on the part of the observer.

Up to now, astronomers from the large observatories have not lodged any serious protest regarding the disturbing influence of the Earth satellites. But the number of brighter satellites is increasing steadily from year to year, even though these bright ones are usually the low-flying type with short lifetimes. However, during the war in Vietnam, newspapers reported that the U. S military authorities were contemplating a reflector 600 meters across, to be put into a geostationary orbit 36,000 km high. It was intended to reflect sunlight to illuminate areas of up to 600 km in length with a light at least twice that of the full Moon. Since then, similar large mirror satellites have been proposed from time to time to provide illumination for both military and civilian purposes. With such prospects ahead of us, I wonder whether the days of astrophotography are not numbered. Perhaps, in the not so distant future, we shall be forced to depend entirely on our existing archives of plates.

M52 = NGC 7654

The last Messier object in order of right ascension is the open star cluster M52 in Cassiopeia, very impressive and rich in stars. Messier discovered this splendid cluster on September 7, 1774. At least 120 stars between magnitudes 9 and 13 are crowded together within a diameter of 13', many of them being early O- and B-type stars. Studies by H. L. Johnson and by P. Pesch indicate a distance of about 1,900 pc. W. Lohmann found for M52 a central density of 11.8 stars per cubic parsec, which is typical for clusters of normal density, even though our photograph suggests an unusually rich object. Two examples of very dense clusters are M7 (page 183) and M23 (page 185), which have 69 and 62 stars per cubic parsec, respectively. In contrast, the Coma star cluster (page 123) has a central density of only 0.33 stars per cubic parsec.

Another rather compact cluster is NGC 7510, with two companions, King 19 (31' east) and Markarian 50 (20' west), which, however, according to W. Becker, E. A. Müller, and U. Steinlin, have no physical connection with it. This group is considered to be the center of the association Cassiopeia II. C. Grubissich established the distance of the two companions at 1.4 kpc and 2.2 kpc, respectively.

Our field is further enriched with the diffuse nebulae NGC 7538 and NGC 7635. In older catalogues the latter was listed as a planetary nebula. In the *Catalogue of Galactic Planetary Nebulae* by L. Perek and L. Kohoutek, NGC 7635 has been omitted.

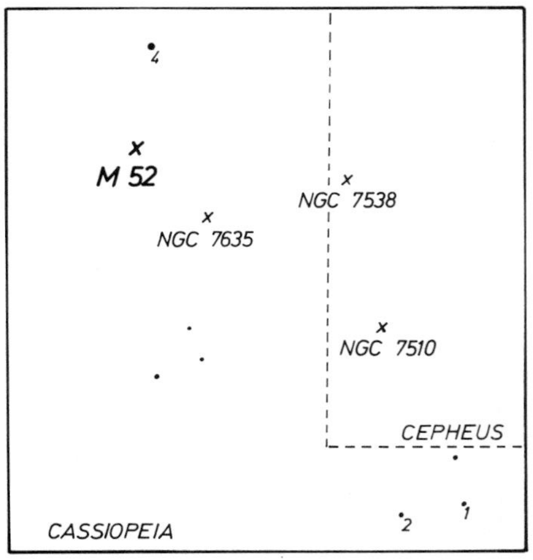

NGC 7538

23ʰ11ᵐ5, +61°14′

N, 10ᵐ0, 10′ × 5′
type: e

M52   NGC 7654

23ʰ22ᵐ0, +61°20′

CI, 8ᵐ2, 130★
φ = 13′, type: e

NGC 7635

23ʰ18ᵐ5, +60°54′

N, 8ᵐ5
3′.6 × 3′.0

NGC 7510

23ʰ09ᵐ2, +60°18′

CI, 9ᵐ3, 100★
φ = 3′, type: d

Index of Objects

and epoch 2000.0 positions. For index of Messier objects see endpapers.

NGC	R.A. (2000.0)	Dec.	Page	Notes
2437	7 41.9	− 14 49	87	Cluster: M46
2438	7 41.9	− 14 43	87	Planetary in M46
2447	7 44.5	− 23 52	89	Cluster: M93
2467	7 53.4	− 26 24	89	Nebula and cluster
2548	8 13.7	− 5 47	91	Cluster: M48
2632	8 40.4	+ 19 41	95	Cluster: M44, Praesepe or Beehive
2659	8 42.6	− 44 57	93	Cluster
2682	8 51.0	+ 11 49	97	Cluster: M67
2903	9 32.1	+ 21 31	99	Galaxy
2976	9 47.3	+ 67 54	101	Galaxy
3031	9 55.6	+ 69 04	101	Galaxy: M81
3034	9 56.0	+ 69 42	101	Galaxy: M82
3077	10 03.4	+ 68 43	101	Galaxy
3293	10 33.4	− 58 13	103	Cluster and nebula
3324	10 37.4	− 58 38	103	Nebula
3338	10 42.2	+ 13 44	105	Galaxy
3351	10 43.9	+ 11 42	105	Galaxy: M95
3367	10 46.7	+ 13 45	105	Galaxy
3368	10 46.8	+ 11 49	105	Galaxy: M96
3372	10 45.0	− 59 41	103	Nebula: Eta Carinae nebula
3379	10 47.8	+ 12 35	105	Galaxy: M105
3384	10 48.3	+ 12 38	105	Galaxy
3389	10 48.4	+ 12 32	105	Galaxy
3412	10 50.9	+ 13 25	105	Galaxy
3556	11 11.6	+ 55 41	107	Galaxy: M108
3587	11 14.9	+ 55 02	107	Planetary: M97, Owl nebula
3593	11 14.6	+ 12 50	109	Galaxy
3623	11 18.9	+ 13 07	109	Galaxy: M65
3627	11 20.2	+ 13 01	109	Galaxy: M66
3628	11 20.3	+ 13 37	109	Galaxy
3766	11 36.5	− 61 36	111	Cluster
3953	11 53.8	+ 52 20	113	Galaxy
3972	11 55.8	+ 55 18	113	Galaxy
3982	11 56.5	+ 55 07	113	Galaxy
3992	11 57.6	+ 53 22	113	Galaxy: M109
3998	11 57.9	+ 55 27	113	Galaxy
4096	12 06.0	+ 47 28	115	Galaxy
4144	12 10.0	+ 46 27	115	Galaxy
4168	12 12.3	+ 13 12	117	Galaxy
4189	12 13.7	+ 13 25	117	Galaxy
4192	12 13.8	+ 14 54	117	Galaxy: M98
4206	12 15.3	+ 13 03	117	Galaxy
4212	12 15.6	+ 13 54	117	Galaxy
4216	12 15.9	+ 13 08	117	Galaxy
4217	12 15.8	+ 47 05	115	Galaxy
4220	12 16.2	+ 47 53	115	Galaxy
4237	12 17.2	+ 15 19	117	Galaxy
4242	12 17.4	+ 45 37	115	Galaxy
4251	12 18.2	+ 28 10	123	Galaxy
4254	12 18.8	+ 14 25	117	Galaxy: M99
4258	12 19.0	+ 47 18	115	Galaxy: M106
4262	12 19.5	+ 14 52	117	Galaxy
4267	12 19.7	+ 12 46	117	Galaxy
4293	12 21.2	+ 18 23	119	Galaxy
4298	12 21.5	+ 14 36	117	Galaxy
4302	12 21.7	+ 14 36	117	Galaxy
4303	12 22.0	+ 4 28	121	Galaxy: M61
4312	12 22.5	+ 15 32	117	Galaxy
4321	12 22.9	+ 15 49	119	Galaxy: M100
4324	12 23.2	+ 5 14	121	Galaxy
4340	12 23.5	+ 16 43	119	Galaxy
4342	12 23.6	+ 7 05	121	Galaxy
4346	12 23.4	+ 46 59	115	Galaxy
4350	12 23.9	+ 16 41	119	Galaxy
4365	12 24.5	+ 7 19	121	Galaxy
4371	12 24.9	+ 11 42	125	Galaxy
4374	12 25.1	+ 12 53	127	Galaxy: M84
4377	12 25.2	+ 14 45	127	Galaxy
4378	12 25.4	+ 4 55	121	Galaxy
4379	12 25.3	+ 15 36	119	Galaxy
4380	12 25.4	+ 10 00	125	Galaxy
4382	12 25.3	+ 18 11	119	Galaxy: M85
4383	12 25.5	+ 16 28	119	Galaxy
4388	12 25.8	+ 12 39	125	Galaxy
4394	12 25.9	+ 18 12	119	Galaxy
4402	12 26.1	+ 13 07	125	Galaxy
4406	12 26.2	+ 12 56	125	Galaxy: M86
4417	12 26.8	+ 9 35	125	Galaxy
4419	12 26.9	+ 15 02	127	Galaxy
4424	12 27.1	+ 9 25	125	Galaxy
4429	12 27.4	+ 11 06	125	Galaxy
4435	12 27.7	+ 13 04	127	Galaxy
4438	12 27.8	+ 13 00	127	Galaxy
4442	12 28.1	+ 9 48	125	Galaxy
4448	12 28.3	+ 28 37	123	Galaxy
4450	12 28.4	+ 17 04	119	Galaxy
4459	12 29.0	+ 13 58	127	Galaxy
4461	12 29.1	+ 13 11	127	Galaxy
4472	12 29.8	+ 7 59	121	Galaxy: M49
4473	12 29.8	+ 13 25	127	Galaxy
4474	12 29.9	+ 14 04	127	Galaxy
4477	12 30.1	+ 13 38	127	Galaxy
4478	12 30.3	+ 12 19	125	Galaxy
4485	12 30.6	+ 41 41	137	Galaxy
4486	12 30.8	+ 12 23	125	Galaxy: M87
4490	12 30.7	+ 41 38	137	Galaxy
4494	12 31.4	+ 25 46	123	Galaxy
4498	12 31.7	+ 16 51	119	Galaxy
4501	12 32.0	+ 14 25	127	Galaxy: M88
4503	12 32.1	+ 11 10	125	Galaxy
4522	12 33.7	+ 9 10	125	Galaxy
4526	12 34.1	+ 7 41	121	Galaxy
4535	12 34.3	+ 8 11	121	Galaxy
4540	12 34.8	+ 15 33	127	Galaxy
4548	12 35.4	+ 14 29	127	Galaxy
4550	12 35.4	+ 12 13	125	Galaxy
4552	12 35.6	+ 12 33	125	Galaxy: M89
4559	12 36.0	+ 27 57	123	Galaxy
4564	12 36.5	+ 11 26	125	Galaxy
4565	12 36.4	+ 25 59	123	Galaxy
4567	12 36.5	+ 11 15	125	Galaxy
4568	12 36.6	+ 11 14	125	Galaxy
4569	12 36.8	+ 13 10	127	Galaxy: M90
4571	12 36.8	+ 14 12	127	Galaxy
4578	12 37.5	+ 9 29	125	Galaxy
4579	12 37.6	+ 11 49	125	Galaxy: M58

240

NGC	R.A. (2000.0)	Dec.	Page	Notes
4590	12 39.5	− 26 45	133	Globular cluster: M68
4594	12 39.9	− 11 37	131	Galaxy: M104, Sombrero galaxy
4608	12 41.2	+ 10 10	129	Galaxy
4618	12 41.6	+ 41 09	137	Galaxy
4621	12 42.0	+ 11 39	129	Galaxy: M59
4625	12 41.9	+ 41 17	137	Galaxy
4638	12 42.7	+ 11 27	129	Galaxy
4639	12 42.8	+ 13 15	129	Galaxy
4647	12 43.5	+ 11 35	129	Galaxy
4649	12 43.6	+ 11 33	129	Galaxy: M60
4654	12 43.9	+ 13 07	129	Galaxy
4660	12 44.5	+ 11 10	129	Galaxy
4694	12 48.2	+ 10 59	129	Galaxy
4736	12 51.0	+ 41 07	137	Galaxy: M94
4754	12 52.2	+ 11 19	129	Galaxy
4755	12 53.6	− 60 21	135	Cluster: Kappa Crucis cluster
4762	12 52.9	+ 11 15	129	Galaxy
4826	12 56.8	+ 21 31	139	Galaxy: M64
4852	13 00.1	− 59 36	135	Cluster
5024	13 12.9	+ 18 10	141	Globular cluster: M53
5053	13 16.3	+ 17 41	141	Globular cluster
5055	13 15.7	+ 42 01	143	Galaxy: M63
5090	13 21.2	− 43 44	145	Galaxy
5128	13 25.3	− 43 01	145	Galaxy
5139	13 26.8	− 47 29	147	Globular cluster: Omega Centauri
5156	13 28.7	− 48 55	147	Galaxy
5194	13 29.9	+ 47 12	149	Galaxy: M51, Whirlpool
5195	13 30.0	+ 47 16	149	Galaxy: companion of M51
5198	13 30.3	+ 46 41	149	Galaxy
5236	13 37.1	− 29 52	151	Galaxy: M83
5253	13 39.9	− 31 39	151	Galaxy
5272	13 42.2	+ 28 23	153	Globular cluster: M3
5422	14 00.8	+ 55 10	155	Galaxy
5443	14 02.1	+ 55 49	155	Galaxy
5457	14 03.2	+ 54 21	155	Galaxy: M101
5473	14 04.7	+ 54 54	155	Galaxy
5474	14 05.0	+ 53 40	155	Galaxy
5475	14 05.2	+ 55 45	155	Galaxy
5485	14 07.1	+ 55 02	155	Galaxy
5866	15 06.5	+ 55 45	157	Galaxy: M102
5879	15 09.7	+ 57 01	157	Galaxy
5904	15 18.5	+ 2 05	159	Globular cluster: M5
5905	15 15.4	+ 55 31	157	Galaxy
5907	15 15.9	+ 56 20	157	Galaxy
5908	15 16.7	+ 55 25	157	Galaxy
6093	16 17.1	− 22 59	161	Globular cluster: M80
6121	16 23.7	− 26 31	163	Globular cluster: M4
6144	16 27.3	− 26 03	163	Globular cluster
6171	16 32.5	− 13 03	165	Globular cluster: M107
6205	16 41.7	+ 36 27	167	Globular cluster: M13
6207	16 43.1	+ 36 50	167	Galaxy
6218	16 47.2	− 1 57	169	Globular cluster: M12
6231	16 54.2	− 41 48	171	Cluster
6242	16 55.6	− 39 30	171	Cluster
6254	16 57.1	− 4 07	169	Globular cluster: M10
6266	17 01.3	− 30 07	173	Globular cluster: M62
6268	17 02.1	− 39 43	171	Cluster
6273	17 02.6	− 26 15	173	Globular cluster: M19
6333	17 19.1	− 18 31	177	Globular cluster: M9
6334	17 20.6	− 36 04	179	Nebula
6341	17 17.1	+ 43 09	175	Globular cluster: M92
6342	17 21.2	− 19 35	177	Globular cluster
6356	17 23.6	− 17 49	177	Globular cluster
6357	17 24.6	− 34 10	179	Nebula
6366	17 27.8	− 5 04	181	Globular cluster
6402	17 37.6	− 3 15	181	Globular cluster: M14
6404	17 39.6	− 33 15	183	Cluster
6405	17 40.1	− 32 13	183	Cluster: M6
6416	17 44.3	− 32 21	183	Cluster
6453	17 51.3	− 34 38	183	Globular cluster
6475	17 54.0	− 34 49	183	Cluster: M7
6494	17 56.9	− 19 01	185	Cluster: M23
6514	18 01.9	− 23 02	187	Nebula and cluster: M20, Trifid
6523	18 04.7	− 24 20	187	Nebula and cluster: M8, Lagoon
6530	18 04.8	− 24 20	187	Cluster in M8
6531	18 04.8	− 22 30	187	Cluster: M21
6544	18 07.4	− 25 01	187	Globular cluster
6559	18 09.9	− 24 07	187	Nebula
6603	18 18.4	− 18 26	191	Cluster, in star cloud M24
6611	18 18.8	− 13 47	189	Cluster and nebula: M16
6613	18 19.9	− 17 08	191	Cluster: M18
6618	18 20.9	− 16 11	189	Cluster and nebula: M17, Omega nebula
6626	18 24.6	− 24 52	193	Globular cluster: M28
6629	18 25.7	− 23 12	193	Planetary
6637	18 31.4	− 32 21	195	Globular cluster: M69
6638	18 31.0	− 25 30	193	Globular cluster
6642	18 31.8	− 23 29	193	Globular cluster
6644	18 32.6	− 25 09	193	Planetary
6652	18 35.8	− 33 00	195	Globular cluster
6656	18 36.4	− 23 55	193	Globular cluster: M22
6681	18 43.3	− 32 18	195	Globular cluster: M70
6694	18 45.2	− 9 24	197	Cluster: M26
6705	18 51.1	− 6 16	197	Cluster: M11
6712	18 53.0	− 8 43	197	Globular cluster
6715	18 55.2	− 30 28	201	Globular cluster: M54
6720	18 53.6	+ 33 02	199	Planetary: M57, Ring nebula
6779	19 16.6	+ 30 10	203	Globular cluster: M56
6809	19 40.1	− 30 56	205	Globular cluster: M55
6820	19 42.6	+ 23 05	207	Nebula
6822	19 44.9	− 14 46	209	Galaxy
6823	19 43.2	+ 23 19	207	Cluster
6830	19 51.0	+ 23 06	213	Cluster
6838	19 53.7	+ 18 47	211	Cluster? Globular? M71
6853	19 59.6	+ 22 43	213	Planetary: M27, Dumbbell nebula
6864	20 06.1	− 21 55	215	Globular cluster: M75
6888	20 12.5	+ 38 25	217	Nebula
6910	20 23.1	+ 40 47	217	Cluster
6913	20 24.0	+ 38 31	217	Cluster: M29
6960	20 45.7	+ 30 43	219	SNR: Veil (Cirrus) neb., west part

NGC	R.A. (2000.0)	Dec.	Page	Notes
6979	20 51.0	+ 32 09	219	SNR: Veil (Cirrus) neb., N.W. spot
6981	20 53.4	− 12 33	221	Globular cluster: M72
6992	20 56.4	+ 31 42	219	SNR: Veil (Cirrus) neb., east part
6994	20 59.1	− 12 38	221	Cluster? M73
6995	20 57.1	+ 31 13	219	SNR: Veil (Cirrus) neb., east part
7000	20 59.0	+ 44 20	223	Nebula: North America nebula
7078	21 30.0	+ 12 10	225	Globular cluster: M15

NGC	R.A. (2000.0)	Dec.	Page	Notes
7089	21 33.5	− 0 50	231	Globular cluster: M2
7092	21 32.2	+ 48 26	229	Cluster: M39
7099	21 40.3	− 23 11	233	Globular cluster: M30
7293	22 29.7	− 20 51	235	Planetary: Helix nebula
7510	23 11.3	+ 60 34	237	Cluster
7538	23 13.6	+ 61 30	237	Nebula
7635	23 20.7	+ 61 10	237	Nebula
7654	23 24.2	+ 61 36	237	Cluster: M52
7762	23 49.9	+ 68 01	11	Cluster
7822	0 03.6	+ 68 37	11	Nebula and cluster

IC	R.A. (2000.0)	Dec.	Page	Notes
IC 59	0 56.7	+ 61 04	29	Nebula
IC 63	0 59.5	+ 60 49	29	Nebula
IC 410	5 22.6	+ 33 31	59	Cluster and nebula
IC 426	5 36.9	− 0 14	67	Nebula
IC 431	5 40.3	− 1 27	67	Nebula
IC 432	5 41.0	− 1 30	67	Nebula
IC 434	5 41.1	− 2 25	67	Nebula; contains Horsehead
IC 435	5 43.0	− 2 19	67	Nebula
IC 443	6 16.9	+ 22 47	73	Nebula
IC 444	6 20.5	+ 23 18	73	Nebula
IC 1274/5	18 09.8	− 23 45	187	Nebula
IC 1311	20 10.8	+ 41 11	217	Cluster
IC 1318	20 28.5	+ 39 57	217	Nebulae around Gamma Cygni
IC 1396	21 39.1	+ 57 28	227	Nebula and cluster
IC 1795	2 24.8	+ 61 54	41	Nebula
IC 1805	2 32.0	+ 61 28	41	Nebula
IC 1848	2 51.3	+ 60 42	41	Nebula

IC	R.A. (2000.0)	Dec.	Page	Notes
IC 1995	3 50.3	+ 25 35	51	Nebula
IC 2157	6 04.9	+ 24 02	71	Cluster
IC 2177	7 05.5	− 10 34	83	Nebula
IC 2872	11 28.4	− 62 57	111	Nebula
IC 2944	11 35.8	− 63 01	111	Nebula: Running Chicken neb.
IC 2948	11 38.5	− 63 32	111	Cluster
IC 4603	16 25.1	− 24 28	161	Nebula
IC 4604	16 25.3	− 23 27	161	Nebula near Rho Ophiuchi
IC 4605	16 30.0	− 25 09	163	Nebula
IC 4606	16 29.5	− 26 27	163	Nebula
IC 4628	16 56.8	− 40 23	171	Nebula
IC 4725	18 31.7	− 19 15	191	Cluster: M25
IC 5067/ 70	20 48.7	+ 44 22	223	Nebula: Pelican neb.
IC 5146	21 53.2	+ 47 16	229	Nebula and cluster: Cocoon nebula

Other Name	R.A. (2000.0)	Dec.	Page	Notes
Beehive	8 40.4	+ 19 41	95	Cluster: M44, NGC 2632
Ced 130	16 21.1	− 25 35	161	Nebula (S. Cederblad)
Chi Per	2 22.4	+ 57 07	39	Cluster: NGC 884
Cr 367	18 09.7	− 23 59	187	Cluster (P. Collinder)
Eta Car.	10 45.0	− 59 41	103	Nebula: NGC 3372
Gum neb.	8 30.0	− 44 00	93	Nebula; SNR?
h Persei	2 19.0	+ 57 09	39	Cluster: NGC 869
H7	12 38.8	− 60 36	135	Cluster: Tr 20 (H. Haffner)
H12	16 56.2	− 40 43	171	Cluster and nebula
H16	17 30.8	− 36 51	179	Cluster
H18	7 53.9	− 26 18	89	Cluster
H19	18 17.3	− 13 17	189	Cluster: Tr 32
H20	19 53.1	+ 18 21	211	Cluster
Hyades	4 19.5	+ 15 38	55	Cluster: Mel 25
Kappa Cru	12 53.6	− 60 21	135	Cluster: NGC 4755
LMC	5 23.7	− 69 05	61	Galaxy: Large Magellanic Cloud

Other Name	R.A. (2000.0)	Dec.	Page	Notes
Mel 15	2 33.6	+ 61 28	41	Cluster and neb. (P. J. Melotte)
Mel 25	4 19.5	+ 15 38	55	Cluster: Hyades
Mel 111	12 25.1	+ 26 07	123	Cluster: Coma Berenices
Omega Cen	13 26.8	− 47 29	147	Globular cluster: NGC 5139
Per III	3 27.8	+ 49 54	49	Stellar association
Pleiades	3 46.9	+ 24 07	51	Cluster: M45
Praesepe	8 40.4	+ 19 41	95	Cluster: M44, NGC 2632
SMC	0 52.0	− 72 45	25	Galaxy: Small Magellanic Cloud
Stock 8	5 28.1	+ 34 27	59	Cluster (J. Stock)
Tr 1	1 35.7	+ 61 17	31	Cluster (J. Trumpler)
Tr 20	12 38.8	− 60 36	135	Cluster: H7
Tr 32	18 17.3	− 13 17	189	Cluster: H19
Tr 33	18 24.8	− 19 41	191	Cluster
Virgo Cl.	12 29.5	+ 12 19	116	Cluster of galaxies

Messier Object	Page
M 56	203
M 57	199
M 58	125
M 59	129
M 60	129
M 61	121
M 62	173
M 63	143
M 64	139
M 65	109
M 66	109
M 67	97
M 68	133
M 69	195
M 70	195
M 71	211
M 72	221
M 73	221
M 74	35
M 75	215
M 76	37
M 77	45
M 78	67
M 79	57
M 80	161
M 81	101
M 82	101
M 83	151
M 84	127
M 85	119
M 86	127
M 87	125
M 88	127
M 89	127
M 90	127
M 91	—
M 92	175
M 93	89
M 94	137
M 95	105
M 96	105
M 97	108
M 98	117
M 99	117
M 100	119
M 101	155
M 102	157
M 103	31
M 104	131
M 105	105
M 106	115
M 107	165
M 108	108
M 109	118

LEGEND:
★ GALACTIC STAR CLUSTER
⊛ GLOBULAR CLUSTER
⊙ PLANETARY NEBULA
□ DIFFUSE NEBULA
○ GALAXY

51 MESSIER NUMBER
205 NGC NUMBER
193 BOOK PAGE